Comments on the Book

Dr. Abdul Waheed Khan

Former Assistant Director General for Communication and Information, UNESCO

When I joined the Indira Gandhi National Open University (IGNOU) in 1998 as the Vice-Chancellor, the position of Director, Electronic Media Production Centre (EMPC) was vacant. It was one of the key positions in the University. Earlier I had served IGNOU as the Founder Director of the Communication Division (later renamed as the Electronic Media Production Centre) under the leadership of Professor G. Ram Reddy. The EMPC had a leadership position in the field of educational media in India and was widely recognized as a national resource centre.

Dr. Sreedher was one of the applicants for the position of Director, EMPC. I was familiar with Dr. Sreedher's background and qualifications as I had interviewed him for a position at the National Council for Science and Technology Communication (NCSTC). I was impressed by his innovative work in science communication at All India Radio where I had served as the Director of the Farm and Home programme.

When he joined IGNOU, as the Director, EMPC, I shared with him the concept of Gyan Bharati. Gyan Bharati was a futuristic concept for developing a national knowledge network with three components—Gyan Darshan (knowledge television), Gyan Vani (knowledge radio) and Gyan Vahini (knowledge internet). Dr. Sreedher received the concept with great enthusiasm. IGNOU was ideally placed to translate this concept into reality as it had a state-of-the-art media production infrastructure and skilled human resources. The book describes in great detail how the concept of Gyan Darshan and Gyan Vani was translated into concrete realty.

When I moved to the Commonwealth of Learning in Vancouver, I developed a proposal to set up a Commonwealth Educational Media Centre for Asia (CEMCA). The proposal was based on my experience of developing a Consortium of Educational Media Resources in India. Dr. Sreedher was appointed as Director of CEMCA. Once again Sreedher demonstrated his leadership in developing CEMCA into a vibrant regional centre for promoting the use of electronic media for open and distance learning.

The book presents an interesting story on the use of electronic media in education in India and the Commonwealth Asia. With the phenomenal growth in digital media the book will help the younger generation of educators and media practitioners to enhance their knowledge and skills.

Ashok Ogra

Former Director Doordarshan, Vice-President Discovery Channel South Asia and Advisor, Apeejay Education Society

Everything in Radio: Broadcasting to the Masses is a beautiful journey of a boy born in Tambaram off Chennai in the year of India's independence in an orthodox family who joins All India Radio and gets excited by every new experience that he encounters in discharging his professional duties.

The book is an inspiring story of a pioneering broadcaster who negotiates all sorts of hurdles and challenges.

This book contains the story of Dr. R. Sreedher who has worked in different organizations including a long innings with Doordarshan—joining as a young Science Officer to rise to the position of Controller of Programmes, and has also headed the Kendra as Director—at a time when both reach and viewership of Doordarshan was unmatched; satellite television in India had yet to gain traction.

As the narrative unfolds, the book transforms from being a mere diary of a small town boy and a junior broadcaster to a telescope through which the reader can see and feel the various events and developments that define the journey of broadcasting in India including Community Radio.

What stands out in the book is the single minded devotion with which Dr. Sreedher has worked. His focus has always been to further the cause of public service broadcasting by informing and empowering listeners and viewers. He strongly believes that the public service broadcaster must adhere to the mandate of informing, educating and entertaining its audiences and not be judged either by how popular a programme is or how much it earns by way of advertising.

He views broadcasting in India calmly, in the midst of tensions of all sorts. Whether it is meeting politicians, scientists, policy makers .... Dr. R. Sreedher provides interesting tidbits that keep the interest of a reader alive.

Dr. Sreedher has always worked with distinction across reputed organizations: Director of IGNOU and later as Director of Commonwealth Education Media Centre for Asia, and is currently Professor (Emeritus) with reputed Apeejay Stya University. His passion for promoting Community Radio remains undimmed even at this age.

Beautifully written and narrated by Ms. Kaushalya Rathnam and ably edited by Mr. Biman Basu, this book will interest all those engaged in broadcasting: programme staff, engineers and policy makers. The book helps us understand behind the scenes a little less judgmentally while staying firmly moored to the ideals of true public service broadcasting. It is written with cogency, conviction and perceptiveness, and is studded with fascinating anecdotes and unique experiences. Few broadcasters are insightful, fewer still readable, and none as witty as Dr. Sreedher.

For those who have known and admired Dr. Sreedher—both as a programmer and as an education administrator—this book reminds them why.

Everything in Radio
Broadcasting to the Masses

Kaushalya Rathnam

Edited with a Foreword by
Biman Basu

AAKAR

Everything in Radio: Broadcasting to the Masses

First Published 2019

ISBN 978-93-5002-656-9

Published by
AAKAR BOOKS
28 E Pocket IV, Mayur Vihar Phase I
Delhi 110 091 India
aakarbooks@gmail.com

Laser Typeset at
Arpit Printographers, Delhi

Printed at
Sapra Brothers, Noida

Contents

Foreword

This book is the awe-inspiring story of an individual's life and career spanning four decades in the Indian broadcast media. It narrates the challenges and hurdles that he had to face and how he overcame them with diligence, perseverance and innovative ideas. Often, he even had to bypass normal procedural tangles to get things done in the larger interest. He stood steadfast to put his ideas into action, at times even in the face of stiff opposition, and came out with flying colours, as this narrative brings out brilliantly.

Born in 1947, young Sridharan (Dr. Sreedher's previous name) grew up and did most of his schooling in Tambaram, a sprawling suburb in the city of Madras. An early exposure to writing led him to develop a natural interest in the field of writing and print media, and his uncle further encouraged him to pursue this interest. He advised young Sridharan to come up with his own handwritten Tamil monthly journal as an exercise in writing.

Sridharan started working on his journal that he named *Deepa Chudar* (Flame Lit in a Lamp). He invited the elders and youngsters in the house and in the neighbourhood to contribute to his journal by writing whatever they could. Later he would collect the articles and rewrite the entire 16 pages of his journal in his own handwriting. He would then stitch the bunch of papers together neatly with a thread, as there were no staplers available in those days and his monthly journal was ready. It was then circulated and read by his family members and schoolmates. Apart from helping him develop his writing skills, his journal also made him popular in his school and neighbourhood. It also improved his skill of befriending people as he lost all inhibitions in approaching new people for work.

Sridharan started his professional career as Head Chemist at a chemical factory in Madras. But it did not suit him as the chemical dust in the factory premises caused skin problems and he had to leave. He later joined C.N. Naicker College at Erode as a demonstrator. He moved to Madras in 1972 and started working on a research project for his PhD under the guidance of Professor I.M. Mathai at Madras Christian College.

But the real break came when he got an opportunity to produce a programme for AIR Madras. When it was aired, it received a warm response from the listeners and everyone in the AIR Madras sat up and took notice of the young man's work. Slowly, many such interesting assignments began coming his way and Sridharan found himself immersing more and more in his love for science and passion for radio.

Sridharan got a jolt after he completed his PhD when he was not considered for the post of Transmission Executive in AIR Madras as he was considered "overqualified". But following the new policy of the government to appoint science officers in All India Radio stations, he was appointed Assistant Editor-Science Reporting at AIR Madras. It was the fulfilment of his long desire to be part of the media. He was subsequently appointed as Science Officer at AIR Madras in 1980. His new job would now be a fresh start for him to forge a career path for himself.

In 1985, Dr. Sreedher had an opportunity to visit the US under the Indo-American Sub-Commission on Education and Culture, which allowed Indian radio professionals to visit the radio stations in the US and observe and learn from their functioning and models. He says his first US visit was a most enriching experience and gave him the opportunity of meeting several eminent scientists including the Nobel Laureate S. Chandrasekhar.

In 1987, Dr. Sreedher joined the National Council for Science and Technology Communication (NCSTC) in New

Delhi as Senior Scientific Officer. A major initiative that Dr. Sreedher was involved in while at NCSTC was the *Bharat Jan Vigyan Jatha*—a nationwide initiative to popularize science and encourage people to pursue a scientific attitude.

In 1988, Dr. Sreedher was selected as a Director for AIR and was posted in Delhi, in-charge of educational broadcasts all over the country. After joining AIR as Director, he initiated several innovative science radio serials, including a 143-episode-long serial on "Human Evolution", which were highly popular.

Dr. Sreedher entered the realm of television in 1993 when he was appointed Chief Producer at Doordarshan in New Delhi. At the Doordarshan Headquarters, he took upon himself the task of computerizing every division of DD including Films, News, Sponsored and Commissioned programmes, Parliament questions, visitor entry, etc. He also introduced many procedural changes to streamline selection of movies and commissioning of programmes for telecast over Doordarshan channels, which brought transparency and proved to be of great help in boosting revenue general.

Dr. Sreedher was known as Sridharan till the 1980s when, on the advice of an astrologer, he changed his name to R. Sreedher, purportedly "for better prospects in life". This was among two things that he did, deviating from his usually scientific demeanour. The other was building a big temple around a Ganesha shrine in Madras.

Briefly, the book not only brings out the many facets of a talented person but also makes engrossing reading. The book can be a motivating experience for youngsters, encouraging them to take up challenges and emerge victorious.

January 8, 2019

Biman Basu
Former Editor
Science Reporter

Author's Note

Every life has a story. But it is the immensity of passion and purpose with which we live that sets apart our journey from others. It is my pleasure and a privilege to have you read Dr. Sreedher's life story in my words.

Everything in Radio: Broadcasting to the Masses, is an attempt to share his journey of over four decades in broadcast media. We have also weaved in his personal story in to the narrative, so the reader can appreciate him and his journey better. We have tried to share an honest narrative of the life story of someone whom we may and at the same time, may not know so well.

You may be familiar with Dr. Sreedher as an experienced broadcaster, an academic and a community radio expert. This book will help you live through some of his experiences in these varied roles. A journey through the glorious years of AIR and DD, might inspire you to reminisce the classy content-driven programmes of those times. Also, the tricky and uncomfortable situations he found himself in, during his journey add all the twist and quirk to make this book an interesting read.

Dr. Sreedher is a man who lives in the future. He is always buzzing with ideas and plans for tomorrow. A quick thinker, he is equally quick at action. Once convinced about an idea, he does not wait too long to go ahead and implement it. He also pursues his plans very resourcefully. I hope this book inspires every reader to appreciate these aspects of his life, which are the ones that truly set him apart.

I am grateful to Dr. Sreedher, for giving me this opportunity to know him better and learn from his experiences. I am thankful to writer Mr. Rani Mainthan, who wrote the Tamil biography of Dr. Sreedher, which served as the blueprint for this book. I thank Mr. Biman Basu, for his meticulous editing and inputs. I would also like to thank my father Mr. Rathnam for his valuable advice and guidance. Thank you to Ms. Archana Madhubala for reading through the draft and offering suggestions.

I thank Mr. Natarajan formerly of IGNOU to have gone through the language editing and Mr. Paul Bhaskar and Prof. Ashok Ogra for suggesting the title of the book.

Also, thank you for choosing to read this book.

I have taken a few liberties with the narrative, which I feel is better to apprise the reader beforehand.

Dr. Sreedher was given the name Sridharan, by his family when he was born. He changed it much later to Sreedher, as per the advice of his parents. I have used the name Sridharan in the chapters dealing with his early life—childhood and college years—till he officially changed his name after joining AIR as Science Officer. From then on he is referred to as Dr. Sreedher in the book. Interestingly the name change also demarcates two different phases of his life—as young Sridharan his life was all about exploring interests and finally finding his passion in radio; as Dr. Sreedher, from the moment he joined as Science Officer at AIR Madras, life was all about channelling his creativity, resourcefulness and networking abilities to execute innovative, pathbreaking and successful projects in AIR, Doordarshan, and every other organization he went on to be associated with.

Also, trying to keep with the chronology of events, I have used the older names of Indian cities like Chennai and Kolkata, till we arrive at a point of time when their names were officially changed.

This was done to enhance the experience of the reader, as he/she journeys through the life and times Dr. Sreedher has lived through.

The description of some of the acquaintances of Dr. Sreedher, might not seem very objective when read apart, as they are only presented as seen from Dr. Sreedher's perspective at that point of time.

A Few Words from Dr. R. Sreedher

I was born in the suburban town of Tambaram off Chennai in 1947 in a joint Hindu orthodox family. I studied in a government-aided elementary and high schools and joined a government-aided College. Attended school, walking barefooted a few kilometres, till the age of 14. Got a cycle and a watch after joining college. Knew only second-class train journey and town bus service. Did not have any ambition except to become a teacher in a college in the same town. A pure vegetarian and teetotaller, not interested in sports except watching kabaddi and listening to cricket commentary, my only ambition of becoming a college lecturer got demolished even after completing a PhD. Never knew there was a world beyond Tambaram and Chennai. I got a chance to work with All India Radio—the Public Broadcaster of the country. This was possible due to the kind-heartedness of people in power who never looked at the caste, religion or demanded money for any meaningful jobs.

This opportunity opened the window to the world of today for me. I had to fight from day one the professionals in the industry and earned a name for some innovative work. I have now seen and worked in 20 different countries and travelled the length and breadth of the great country of India several times. I have contacts from America to New Zealand, Germany to South Africa. I have worked in almost all the Indian states including the north-east and Jammu and Kashmir. Stayed in terrorist and militant-infested countries. But I always felt that even after achieving a lot in the broadcasting field, my own state Tamil Nadu has not given me an opportunity to work and share my experience.

I was narrating my experiences a few years ago to Mr. Rani Mainthan, a famous writer, journalist and biographer when he came forward to write a book in Tamil based on my life. The book, titled *Oodaga Theni*, was released on February 11, 2017 in Chennai. Many of my erstwhile colleagues, doyens of broadcasting, past students attended the event. Later, my former student Kaushalya Ratnam, who became a well-known radio jockey and radio broadcaster, expressed an interest to attempt a book in English. The result is this book, which is not a translation but another original work. I spent hours in Rani Mainthan's house, giving voice recordings, which he did on a cassette recorder of the 1990s. For Kaushalya, it was all digital—WhatsApp, iPhone, emails, chats and so on. I have not found a young journalist and writer taking such measures like cross-verifying every statement I made with a secondary proof. The way she Googled or checked the facts is something amazing. She took care of the statistics, the names, the designations; always wanting to be sure.

All the instances that are quoted are based on my memory and perhaps, sometimes I have been quite blunt. We thought of getting such statements vetted by a veteran. I had known Biman Basu, former Editor of *Science Reporter*, a popular science monthly published by CSIR, and engaged in science popularisation for the past three decades. When I approached him, I never thought that he would agree to my request. The way in which he had handled the manuscript and edited it digitally, is something extraordinary. I had doubts about certain incidents and he with his mature journalistic experience asked me to go ahead since what we have stated are facts and not our views. I did consult Mr. Karthikeyan, former Director of CBI on a small incident from the book. He also gave me hopes.

Later, when I shared it with some of the people whom I regard highly and whom I quoted in the book for a brief to appear on the cover page. To my surprise, those whom the media made Icons of bureaucracy, refused to accept the events and even called them fictional. We have decided to remove those passages. The manuscript has been shared with many people who find some good space and the book is being brought out after their consent.

I take complete responsibility for the statements that are attributed to me in this book and if anyone is to be blamed, it must be my memory.

My publisher, Mr. K.K. Saxena of Aakar Books, suggested that I get some views and comments on the book, from some of the reputed media personalities I have worked with. I am thankful to Mr. Kiran Karnik, former Chairperson of NASSCOM and a development communicator, Mr. Ashok Ogra, my long-time colleague and former Vice President South Asia, Discovery Channel, and Dr. Abdul Waheed Khan, former ADG UNESCO for offering their time and kind words that appear on the back cover/panels of the book.

Last but not the least, I would like to thank my wife, daughters and sons-in-law, and grandchildren who offered their suggestions and views. The book is dedicated to my grandparents, parents, especially to my mother and the entire extended family members.

1

The Man in the Making

You don't know a man very well unless you know what he has been through. We as human beings are constantly chiselled and shaped by our experiences in life. The founding years and early life essentially determine the personality and attributes of a person and therein lie answers to many crucial questions.

Those who have worked with Dr. Sreedher would agree that there is never a dull moment working with him. He constantly brims with ideas and plans which he pursues with great zeal and conviction. One might even wonder what makes this man do all that he does, especially in roles where he could get away doing much less. But getting acquainted with his childhood reveals that he has always carried about him a certain resourcefulness and ingenuity that makes him the person he is.

Born on June 6, 1947, in the city of Madras (now Chennai), Sridharan was the eldest among six siblings. His father Ramamurthy worked with the Life Insurance Corporation of India and mother, Pankajam, took care of the family. His maternal grandfather, Gopal Iyer, was a well-known figure in his times. He was the Head of the Tamil Department at the prestigious Madras Christian College (MCC), succeeding eminent Tamil scholars, the likes of Vi K.O. Suryanarayana Sastrigal (popularly known as Parithimar Kalaignar) and Maraimalai Adigal. Sridharan spent a substantial part of his childhood growing up under his grandmother's care. He lived with his two maternal uncles and three aunts, who were a great support to him and his family.

On the paternal side, Sridharan was surrounded by teachers. His grandfather, Rajam Iyer, worked as a teacher in a school in the Pudukkottai district of Tamil Nadu. His paternal uncle worked in the railways and his aunt was the headmistress at the Raja Muthiah Chettiar School, Madras.

Sridharan grew up and did most of his schooling in Tambaram, a sprawling suburb in the city of Madras. The house that he was raised in was a precious part of his growing-up years. The National High School, where he studied, was just a stone's throw away from that house. He remembers, he never drank water from the school taps as he always went home for it and was back in no time.

Academic excellence came naturally to him and he took pride in it. He always stood first in his class till the 6th standard. In the 7th standard he only came second, in spite of having scored the highest marks in his class. Though Sridharan excelled in academics, his inclination or proficiency in other extra curricular activities was less, and that was the reason for not being awarded the first rank, the teacher had said. Sridharan was so offended by this sudden change of criteria in deciding the first rank in class (and that too without prior notice), that he decided not to continue in the same school. He stood firm in his decision and his family then had to enrol him in the Seva Sadan School, which was about 5 kilometres from his home. There, he regained his top rank and continued his studies for three more years, after which he had to move to a different town in Tamil Nadu, to live with his parents.

Sridharan's maternal uncle Jayaraman was a tremendous inspiration to him. He was also his motivator and confidante. Jayaraman, at a very young age, had lost the clarity of his eyesight due to nerve damage caused by typhoid and he also lost one of his legs to gangrene. Though he seemed disadvantaged physically and the family was worried about him, he eventually managed to turn things around for himself with his determination and perseverance. He excelled in academics and went on to do his Masters in English literature.

He later developed an interest in Tamil and started writing stories for a children's magazine entitled *Kannan*. Some of those stories even went on to win prizes and awards.

Owing to his poor eyesight, Uncle Jayaraman used to write his stories in huge block letters and later someone in the family helped him to rewrite them in regular size. Sridharan had seen his mother and aunt helping his uncle with the writing and later he himself started doing it with much interest. Once the stories were neatly written they had to be delivered to the Editor at the magazine's office and Sridharan accompanied his aunt or uncle to the magazine's office to deliver them.

This early exposure to writing led him to develop a natural interest in the field of writing and print media, and his uncle Jayaraman further encouraged him to pursue this interest. He advised young Sridharan to come up with his own handwritten monthly Tamil journal, as an exercise in writing.

Sridharan accepted the challenge and he named his journal *Deepa Chudar* (Flame of the Lamp). He started by acquainting himself with his neighbours by visiting their houses and explaining to them what he was up to. He invited the elders and youngsters in those houses to contribute to his journal by writing whatever they could. Later Sridharan would collect the written articles from the respective houses, sit and compile the content, and rewrite the entire 16 pages of his journal in his own handwriting. He would then tie the bunch of papers together neatly with a thread, as there were no staplers available in those days and behold!... His monthly journal was ready! It was then circulated and read by his family and schoolmates.

He did this meticulously for the next two years and came up with 24 issues of his handwritten journal. Apart from greatly helping him develop his writing skills, his journal also made him popular in his school and neighbourhood. It also improved his skill of befriending people as he lost all inhibition in approaching new people for work.

When Sridharan's uncle Jayaraman got a Fulbright scholarship to study in the US, Sridharan was sent back to his parents who were then living in Paramakudi, Tamil Nadu, as his grandmother could no longer take care of him. This not only involved a change of place and school, but he also had to switch from his English medium education to a Tamil medium school in Paramakudi. He joined the 10th standard in the Government Raja Sethupathi High school in Paramakudi. The transition was difficult for him but there was hope. Sridharan's uncle Jayaraman had made a promise to him before leaving for the US that if he managed to score more than 60 per cent marks in his school finals, he would secure a seat for him in the prestigious Madras Christian College.

He kept his promise and the next year, in 1963 Sridharan enrolled at the Madras Christian College for his Pre-University Course (PUC). Sridharan's mother was very proud that her son was going to a prestigious college in Madras and she promised to support him financially with whatever she could save of his father's salary. Sridharan joined college, determined to make the best use of opportunities that came his way.

After completing the PUC, Sridharan enrolled for the BSc degree in Chemistry in the same college. He was an inquisitive learner and never missed an opportunity to put his ideas to test. So much so that once, in the chemistry lab, in the middle of his experiments, he had an idea to dip his pen with ink stains into an acid solution. When he pulled it out, it came out shining clean. Proud of his clever achievement, he smugly put the pen back into his pocket, only to burn a hole in his shirt. It was a little too late when he realized he had forgotten to wipe the acid off his pen. Incidentally, on that day he was wearing a new shirt that his mother had bought for him and it had to bear the brunt of his experiment.

While still at college, Sridharan got the opportunity to write for the children's magazine that his uncle Jayaraman used to write for. The editor of the children's magazine Mr. R. Venkataraman, popularly known as RV, asked Sridharan to come up with some fresh ideas and articles for the publication. Though Sridharan readily agreed, he could not decide for long what he wanted to write about. He mulled over it for a while and came up with an idea. Back then, there were many students of foreign nationalities studying at the Madras Christian College. He decided to feature their interviews and experiences in the students' section of the Tamil magazine. The editor approved his idea and Sridharan began working on it. When the series was published, it was well received by the readers. The warm and encouraging response to his initiative further inspired him to write more columns that would benefit students. He started writing about colleges and universities and the courses they offered, to help aspiring students make informed choices.

His work was not only appreciated by the readers but also eventually got noticed in the circle of publications. The editor of the children's magazine, Mr. Venkataraman recommended his work to the editorial team of a popular Tamil daily *Swadesamitran* and consequently he was offered an opportunity to write a science column for the newspaper's Sunday edition.

He remembers getting paid Rs. 10 for his articles in the children's magazine and Rs. 20 each for his science columns in *Swadesamitran*. Both his work and the payment, Sridharan felt, were equally rewarding.

Some new and exciting opportunities came his way at college as well. He was chosen to be the Secretary for the Chemical Society, under the Chemistry Department at Madras Christian College. He got into action and busied himself in organizing lectures and seminars, by inviting eminent experts from the industry to interact with the students.

As his new assignments, both inside and outside college, ruled most of his time and mind space, his focus on academics diminished slightly and Sridharan graduated BSc in the second class. Thereafter, he took up postgraduation in the same college.

His paternal uncle V. Venkatachalam, who was well placed with the Tamil Nadu Government at that time, had known about the National Loan Scholarship, which was both a scholarship and a loan. He encouraged Sridharan to apply for it. He received Rs. 720 per year during his undergraduate studies and Rs. 900 per year for PG courses as Loan Scholarship. Sridharan continued writing for magazines during his postgraduation days as well. Two years rolled by quickly and he finished his MSc in the year 1969. 'What next?' was never a question on his mind as he knew that he had to start supporting his family and that it was time to take up a job.

He applied for the role of Head Chemist at a chemical factory named 'Millifine Chemicals' in Thiruvanmiyur, Madras and got through. He was offered a monthly salary of about Rs. 200 and Sridharan was happy that he got a job immediately after college, without much struggle or delay. He was assigned an early morning shift at work.

He would wake up at 3.30 am, and his mother would make him a quick coffee and hand over some packed *tiffin.* He rode on his bicycle till the Tambaram railway station and got on the first train to Madras beach at 4 am. He would then get down at the Saidapet station, walk up to the main road to catch the 5 am bus to Thiruvanmiyur. On some days when he only got a bus till Adyar, he walked the rest of the three kilometres to his factory. The shift began at 6 am and lasted till 2 pm. It was a drill, nonetheless.

As the days passed Sridharan began to realize that the chemical dust in the factory premises did not agree too well with his skin and was causing skin problems. When it could not be ignored any longer, he knew it was time to look for a new job.

He then moved to Gudiyatham town in Vellore district of Tamil Nadu, where he joined as a Demonstrator in the Chemistry Department of the Government Thirumagal Mills College. He worked there for a year and later joined CN Naicker College at Erode as Demonstrator. He was earning about Rs. 450 a month by then, which in those days was a good deal of money. Also, as it was a teaching job, it helped him with his loan repayment. The National Loan Scholarship, which Sridharan had availed for his postgraduation, had a clause that if one worked as a teacher for 10 years, one need not repay the loan; because, for every year of work as a teacher, 10 per cent of the amount of the loan was deemed to have been paid. He was content with what the job had to offer.

Something else that he earned during his stay at this college in Erode was the friendship he had with his roommate at the college campus, who later went on to become the Vice-Chancellor of a prestigious University in Tamil Nadu. Though they were poles apart in their beliefs and ideologies, they developed a friendship that was not affected by their differences. While one was an ardent follower of Periyar[3] and the other was a devotee of Lord Ganesh, with their mutual respect and understanding for each other, they could share a space comfortably.

1. A light South Indian breakfast.

2. A junior level teaching position attached to a College Laboratory.

3. Social activist who started the self-respect movement in Tamil Nadu.

Though everything seemed to be going well for him, Sridharan did not yet feel confident about his chosen career path. He aspired for something more, but was not too clear about it. And it did not help him much when his father compared him with his other cousins and spoke highly of their accomplishments in his presence. On one such occasion, Sridharan's father was raving about his cousins who had performed in a drama on All India Radio. He went on about how good they were and how Sridharan was not doing enough or getting anywhere. Sridharan being a fine young man who took pride in his skills and abilities, on that day, could not stand his father's criticism and all the raving about his cousins.

'Why all this hype about them performing on radio I could do that too!' he thought.

The conversation left him hurt and frustrated. And he wanted to do something to show them what he was capable of. In one desperate moment, he went to his room, picked up a postcard and wrote on it, in big and bold letters in Tamil,

'I am R. Sridharan. I wish to do a programme on All India Radio. Please give me an opportunity,' and posted it.

As with all upheavals of emotion and intensity, this one came down too and a few days later as Sridharan was going about his regular life, having forgotten all about the postcard, he received a reply letter from All India Radio, Madras.

The letter said:

'Received your mail. Do come and visit the All India Radio Station, when you come to Madras'.

Sridharan was thrilled to receive a response. This letter was to be his ticket to a whole new world.

The First Recording

Sridharan was still working in Erode and would often visit Madras to be with his family during weekends and holidays. During one such visit at the time of Diwali, he decided to pay a casual visit to his college Professor I.M. Mathai. His professor had received a grant from the Council of Scientific & Industrial Research (CSIR) for his research and was looking for students to take up the research objective for pursuing their doctorate. Two students, who had taken it up earlier, abandoned it midway and as a third choice, Professor Mathai offered the opportunity to Sridharan. Sridharan liked the idea of living closer with his family and pursuing a Doctorate. He did a quick math in his mind and realised that earning Rs. 300 on a PhD stipend while living in Madras with his family was financially more viable than earning Rs. 400 while living by himself in Erode. He made the decision and accepted the offer. He moved to Madras in 1972 and started working on his research under the guidance of Professor I.M. Mathai. His research objective was to find if acidic natural extracts from the skin of the cashew fruit could replace the use of regular acids in the making of perfumes and ethers. These natural extracts could be less expensive, reusable and much easier to handle than the regular acids.

On the one hand, he had begun his work with acids, but

there was also something else brewing in his mind. In his heart, Sridharan secretly cherished the letter he received from All India Radio. 'Come and visit', the letter had said, and it was beckoning.

Sridharan had grown up listening to AIR during the post-independence times, when the medium was at its peak of glory. Anything that came from the radio set then was like God's own voice, he says. He particularly remembers being encouraged at home to listen to short stories for children, read by Rajaji, the former Chief Minister of Tamil Nadu and independent India's First Governor General, on Sundays. His was one of the privileged homes in the locality to own a valve radio set, and he remembers his neighbours gathering in his house to listen to radio, particularly the cricket commentaries. His paternal uncle was a physicist working with the meteorological department and used to repair radio sets in his spare time. Though as a child Sridharan never aspired to work for AIR, he was nevertheless in awe of the medium and the opportunities it could offer.

Since the moment he received it, Sridharan knew that the letter from AIR meant something more to him. It was a chance for him to prove his worthiness, an opportunity to rise in his father's eyes and it could also be a platform to unleash all his creative potential. His heart was yearning to make a visit to the station and when he could resist no more, on a fine day he found himself at the gates of AIR Madras. He met Mr. Ganesan in the programming department and introduced himself. Mr. Ganesan quizzed him on his education and experience and offered him an opportunity to come up with a variety programme using the facilities at the AIR recording studios. It was a sort of a practical test and Sridharan readily agreed to it.

He did not know much about radio shows and their formats but assumed that a variety programme should cater to different sensibilities with an interesting mix of content and formats. He quickly put his thoughts together and made a plan. He would interview his maternal uncle Jayaraman for the show—a motivational interaction on success and overcoming disabilities; he would get his friends and neighbours who were trained in Carnatic music to perform, and then he would also get a few of his friends to act out a play named 'Kaalaavathi' which was written by one of his colleagues from the past, Mr. N. Gopalakrishnan, who later went on to become a distinguished scientist. All of this put together and presented in a neat flow would be his variety programme, he imagined.

He took all the efforts, made arrangements, put together the team, planned and rehearsed the content and performances, and finally when the day of the recording arrived, Sridharan had taken with himself a team of 25 people to the AIR studio! A popular producer of those times, Ms. Malarkodi Sukumaran was in charge of his recording. Though there were hiccups and breaks, the recording happened successfully and the programme when put together sounded reasonably well. When it was aired, it received a warm response from the listeners and everyone in the AIR Madras sat up and took notice of the young man's work.

Particularly, the Programme Executive Mr. A.R. Krishnamurthy took an interest in Sridharan's work and when he got to know of Sridharan's experience in writing science columns, he suggested that Sridharan do a science programme for AIR Madras. For starters, Mr. Krishnamurthy suggested that he visit a science fair that was happening then at the Anna University campus and come up with a radio report covering it. He also promised an honorarium of Rs. 40 for the assignment. Sridharan geared himself to action and came up with an impressive radio report. His work was once again noticed and appreciated. Next, he got an opportunity to produce a radio documentary on Technical Teachers' Training Institute which for the first time had a colour TV installed in its campus at Madras, at a time when even black-and-white TVs were a rarity. Slowly more such interesting assignments started coming his way and Sridharan found himself immersing more and more in his love for science and passion for radio.

His days were long. He had to report at college at 9 am

and work on his PhD research till 2:30 pm. Then by around 4 pm he would arrive at the AIR station and begin work. After 5 pm, when most of the employees left for home, he could get the editing tables for himself. He would then listen, replay, edit and add music to his programmes till he was completely satisfied with the way it sounded. He would work till 11 pm. A pick-up vehicle was arranged for AIR late shift workers and Sridharan would get into it at night and be dropped at the Guindy railway station. From there he would take a train to Tambaram, and reach home by midnight. This was his daily routine and he thoroughly enjoyed it.

Apart from the regular full-time employees, AIR Madras used to encourage amateurs and enthusiasts to produce good quality content for broadcast. Such members were addressed as casuals. Sridharan was a casual too. Someone who worked as a casual in AIR always had to take a sound recordist from the station along with him whenever he/she wanted to record something outside the studio. This was a hassle as the arrangements would have to be made in advance, sometimes the recordist was busy with other recordings, and the timings had to be suitable for everyone and so on. Sridharan found it a very inconvenient arrangement and when he discussed the issue with Mr. A.R. Krishnamurthy, he suggested that Sridharan buy a new tape recorder for himself. Sridharan was quick to invest Rs. 550 in buying a tape recorder from his colleague Dr. R. Gopala. When he took it to the station to show his colleagues, he learnt that the engineers and recordists did not approve of recorders from outside being used for programme recordings. Nevertheless, Sridharan went to Mr. Krishnamurthy and requested him, that he be given enough assignments so he could recover the money spent on buying the tape recorder. Thus Sridharan became the first casual at AIR Madras to own and use his own tape recorder for his programmes. And he did put it to good use.

Sridharan never refused any opportunity or work that came his way as a casual in AIR Madras. He pursued his role with great passion. Not just his science programmes but he willingly contributed to the other popular shows on AIR Madras as well. Makkal Medai, was a very popular programme on AIR those days. Broadcast every Sunday evening on a state hook-up of all radio stations in Tamil Nadu, the show discussed important events and issues that directly impacted the lives of the people. Sridharan was working on one such episode which discussed a latest development—the lifting of the ban on rice transportation across states from Tamil Nadu. The existing ban was suddenly lifted by the then state government and it was likely to impact rice traders and consumers. Sridharan decided to cover the economic aspect of the recent development and went ahead to record relevant interviews pertaining to it. The tapes were ready by Saturday evening and scheduled for broadcast on Sunday evening. On Saturday night however, the state government decided to reinstate the ban on rice transport once again. It was an unforeseen development and now, Sridharan was worried that the programme he had produced would no longer be relevant. Not only would all his efforts and time go in vain, but he would also miss the Rs. 40 honorarium due for that production. Every rupee he made through AIR was important for him to meet his and his family's expenses. He thought hard and came up with an idea to save his show. He shared his idea with the Programme in Charge Mr. P.S. Rangachar and got his approval. The idea was to redo some of the interviews and try to include the latest developments in his programme. He decided to include the impact and reactions to both the decisions announced by the government—the lifting of the ban and later the re-imposition of the same. This would give an all-round view of the issue and save the content he had already worked on. He immediately set out to work on the newer interviews and edited and put together the final programme again. The programme concluded with a statement that 'withdrawal of the ban and subsequent re-imposition are measures that the government takes from time to time taking into consideration the welfare of the people'. When it was aired the following Sunday, Sridharan was doubly satisfied. One, for having made the little money that he was about to lose and two, for doing his best to cover the issue from both sides.

But that was not all. There was another repercussion he had to deal with pertaining to the show. On Monday when he was at his university, working on his research, he learnt that the Principal's office had received a call from the AIR and that he had been summoned to the AIR Madras office immediately. Worried and anxious, he rushed to the AIR office, to find out what it was all about. Officers from the Subsidiary Intelligence Bureau (SIB) had got in touch with the Station Director Mr. M.S. Gopal and the Programme Executive Mr. A.R. Krishnamurthy, asking for the details of the Special Show broadcast on the rice transport ban and Sridharan had been summoned for the same. When he met the officers they asked him where he did his recording and who his sources were. Sridharan refused to share the details of his sources as it was against journalistic ethics and also the sources had agreed to speak on the condition of anonymity. They further tried to tempt him with a few perks that he could avail of if he agreed to reveal the sources of his recordings but Sridharan declined and stood his ground. It was a sort of a testing situation and it did make him feel uncomfortable. Following that incident, for about three months, Sridharan did not do any programmes for All India Radio. Later, he was called to come back and resume work.

In 1975, there was an unfortunate incident in Madras where hundreds of men were hospitalised due to consumption of illicit liquor. It was a grave issue and when Sridharan read about it in the newspapers, he immediately decided to do a scientific awareness programme on it. He was so moved by the idea that it never occurred to him to get permissions from his seniors at the office before starting his work on it. He got in touch with the then Commissioner of Police Madras, Mr. Senthamarai over a payphone and expressed his interest in doing an awareness programme about the illicit liquor incident. He also explained to him the perspectives and messages the show was likely to carry. The commissioner was willing to help and agreed to provide a police jeep and some constables to support the recording. He put only one condition to Sridharan, that during the interviews he should not ask the patients, uncomfortable questions like—where they had their illicit liquor and how much they had. Sridharan agreed. Then he rushed to the AIR office to share with the Programme Executive Mr. A.R. Krishnamurthy, what he was up to.

"How could you make your own decisions?" Mr. Krishnamurthy asked. "There is a separate producer for health-related shows and he had to be consulted before you decide to do such a programme," he reprimanded.

But not wanting to discourage Sridharan, Mr. Krishnamurthy decided to take him to the then Station Director Mr. M.S. Gopal and discuss the matter. Mr. Gopal was known to be a strict, no-nonsense person and Mr. Krishnamurthy had advised Sridharan to only speak when asked to and keep silent otherwise. Mr. Krishnamurthy then explained to the Station Director that Sridharan was hoping to cover the recent incident involving consumption of illicit liquor with a scientific perspective and solicited his permission for the same.

Mr. Gopal asked Sridharan: "You think you can do a good job of it?"

Sridharan: "Yes Sir."

Mr. Gopal: "You should call the Commissioner of Police and get his help. Request him to provide a jeep for you. Such recordings can be done better with police security only..."

Sridharan: "Yes Sir…I have already spoken to Commissioner Senthamarai Sir and he has agreed to send a few constables and a police jeep...."

"Couldn't you have just said fine sir and left it there?" Mr. Krishnamurthy later reprimanded Sridharan again for being so ebullient. Mr. Gopal, though, did not seem to mind much.

When Sridharan went for the recording, he was accompanied by a sound engineer from AIR and a policeman. It was a gory sight, seeing the bodies of all the victims laid in a row at the

KMC Hospital and the sound engineer Thangamani fainted at the sight of it. As they were in a hospital, they quickly gave him first aid and the recording resumed. They met some of the survivors and started taking their sound bites. In the flow of the conversation, Sridharan ended up asking the forbidden questions—where they had illicit liquor and how much they had. The policeman accompanying him made a note of it and informed the Commissioner. The Commissioner then asked Sridharan to wind up the recording immediately. Sridharan tried apologizing and telling the Commissioner that he would not air those parts of the recording, but the Commissioner would not budge. The News Services Division from the AIR by then had approached the Commissioner to record a message for the public from him. Sridharan tried to put it all together into an interesting show combining the scientific and health aspects of illicit liquor consumption. Later when the show was aired, it received a lot of appreciation. But he had to part with his recordings as they were to be handed over to the then Chief of Health Unit of All India Radio, Mr. R. Mahadevan, to be used in health-related programmes.

On October 2, 1975, the former Chief Minister of Tamil Nadu, K. Kamaraj breathed his last. He was a much loved and respected leader of his time and people were expected to gather in large numbers to pay their last respects to the deceased leader. An elaborate funeral procession had been arranged in the city of Madras and All India Radio was to do a live coverage of the procession as it happened. It was a holiday and the Station Director was not in town. Also, a live coverage of a procession of this scale had never been done by AIR, Madras. Sridharan happened to be in office working on his programmes. He had chosen to work on holidays as the edit desks were freely available and he could take his own time to work. He sat at the edit desk wondering how the funeral procession could be covered, using the technological means available at that time. It occurred to him that a nineteenth century invention—the wireless communication, could be useful in covering a moving procession. He shared this idea with the higher officials at AIR, Madras and also the coverage team. His idea was appreciated and pursued. As Police permission was required for the use of wireless communication, the officials got in touch with the then Inspector General of Police Mr. Stracey and got the necessary permissions.

A temporary wireless tower was installed on the terrace of the AIR building and the Police also provided the coverage team with a wireless van. Key landmarks that the procession would travel through were identified and mapped. There were four such landmark points and two comperes alternatively travelled in the wireless van and successfully covered the entire procession. The live coverage went on to be widely appreciated.

Sridharan realized that he was falling increasingly in love with his work at AIR. He wondered what it would be like to make a career out of it. But for now, he had his research to concentrate on and he also considered the options for higher studies.

In the following year, the then Prime Minister, Indira Gandhi, addressed the public at a political event in Madras. Her speech was to be aired on AIR. Mr. E.V.K. Sampath was doing the spot translation of her speech in Tamil and Sridharan felt as he listened to the speech that Mr. Sampath was not at his best on that day. Time was running out and the speech had to be broadcast soon. Meanwhile the Delhi office was also pressurizing the news services division, with Mr. T.G. Nallamuthu as the Special Correspondent, to send a part of the PM's speech for the nightly newsreel that was broadcast nationwide every evening. And for this purpose, they were recording two copies of the speech at the control room of AIR Madras, one for state-wide hook-up from AIR Madras and the other for the nightly newsreel from Delhi. Sridharan offered to help Mr. Nallamuthu to quickly edit the English portion of Mrs. Gandhi's speech of what she had spoken yet, so that the speech could be sent to Delhi at the earliest. He chose to work in the edit suite that was usually not preferred by the staff, an edit suite made by Bharat electronics. He quickly edited 8 minutes of her speech in time to be sent to Delhi for broadcast in the newsreel. Mr. Nallamuthu quickly put it on the 'hotline' to New Delhi and it went on air all over the country, even before Mrs. Gandhi finished her full speech in Madras. After readying the first 8 minutes, Sridharan sat and edited the rest of the speech as well, which went on for about 90 minutes. Meanwhile the Director of the AIR Madras station, Mr. M.S. Gopal also decided to use only Mrs. Gandhi's speech for the state-wide hook-up at 9:15 pm, excluding the Tamil translation by E.V.K. Sampath. Sridharan sent the edited tapes part by part and the Duty Officer at the door would collect them and put them on air. He had to work very fast as they could not afford a delay in the PM's speech and nor could they play any music intermittently. It was the emergency period and no one wanted to interfere with the PM's speech. Mrs. Gandhi finished her speech announcing Mr. G.K. Moopanar as the chief of the Unified Congress. When about 7 minutes of her speech was still pending to be edited, the duty officer hurried Sridharan up and said a delay or break in the speech could put all the officials in a spot. In the heat of the moment, Sridharan without asking anyone, simply skipped a few minutes of her speech and just included the concluding lines of Mrs. Gandhi appointing Mr. G.K. Moopanar as the chief of the Unified Congress and 'Jai Hind' and handed the tape over to the Duty Officer. Sridharan told no one about having skipped a small part of the speech and no one seemed to have noticed the skip or brought it to attention. It might or might not have been the best thing to do at that time, but, looking back, he feels that sometimes taking a call and acting on it is more important than worrying about the consequences and remaining in a fix.

As an interesting follow-up to the broadcast, Mr. E.V.K. Sampath happened to visit AIR the next day and met the Station Director. He told the Station Director "I heard the Prime Minister's speech on air yesterday. It was aired very well. What about my translation of the speech? Do you intend to edit and air it separately as well?" Sridharan was in college working on his research, when the Principal's office received a call asking him to come to the AIR immediately. When he reached office, he was asked by Mr. A.R. Krishnamurthy to edit the Tamil translation of the PM's speech to be aired separately.

A Dream Goes Up in Smoke

Sridharan was a full-time PhD scholar and later joined as a Demonstrator at the MCC for two years between 1974 and 1976. He fondly remembers his association with his teachers—Prof. S.V. Anantakrishnan, L. Sivasubramanian, Dr. Gopalan, Dr. Gopalakrishnan, Dr. Kalachandra, Mr Ramalingam, Mr. Venkatraman, Dr. P.S. Subramaniam, Dr. N. Venkatasubramanian and Dr. Sundarama of Vivekananda College, Dr. Shanmuganathan of Pachaiyappas College, Dr. Santappa, Dr. Swaminathan of Madras University and others during this time.

Besides, he had also applied for pursuing his higher studies in Australia through the Colombo Plan, which allowed students from India to live and study in Australia. The University of New South Wales in Australia had approved his application. The central government had also given its approval for his higher studies under the Colombo Plan, and conceded that the state government would have to process his documents and forward it to Australia to procure admission. With the help of his uncle V. Venkatachalam, who was then the Deputy Secretary (Home) to the Government of Tamil Nadu, Sridharan could get a meeting arranged with the Chief Secretary of Tamil Nadu at the Secretariat. But Mr. Diraviyam, who was the Chief Secretary then, said he was not in a position to process Sridharan's application. The reason he cited was: "Every year two Indians can go and study abroad through this plan. But if I process your application now, next year I am likely to be flooded with some 2,000 applications for the same. We do not have enough resources to review so many applications. So for now, I am not in a position to help you...," he said.

Sridharan, not wanting to give up, went and met the then

Chief Minister Annadurai's Financial Adviser, Mr. Guhan on the same day. He still remembers the conversation.

"What is your research about?" Mr. Guhan asked Sridharan.

"Transesterification of Methyl Benzoate into Amyl Benzoate using Ion-exchange resins as catalysts and to find out the reaction mechanism...." went on Sridharan. He tried to explain further, "perfumes are in a way esters and ethers were being used for anaesthesia purposes..." and so on.

Mr. Guhan lost patience and cut him short. "So, you are working on alternative methodologies for making perfumes and ethers, right? This will save imported oil and the process is toxin free. Couldn't you have simply put it that way?" he asked.

On that fateful day of his life, though Sridharan was refused the opportunity of doing higher studies in Australia, he remembers having learnt two important lessons of his life. Firstly, he had learnt how senior officials in the government approach an issue and think of broader repercussions. And secondly, he had learnt the importance of being precise in his communications.

Without brooding much, he quickly shifted focus to what he had at hand at that time—his research and his assignments at AIR. Life had different plans for him here, in Madras.

Joining AIR

Between 1974 and 1976, Sridharan was busy sharing his time between his part-time PhD research and assignments at the All India Radio. On the one hand, he wondered if he had taken a difficult research topic for PhD as there seemed to be endless work to do and, on the other hand, the interesting and challenging assignments at AIR took a lot of his time and energy. He got a temporary post of Demonstrator in Chemistry, a post which was somewhat less than a lecturer in Madras Christian College in 1974. He got another year's extension in 1975. He had to take classes/supervise lab work for 14 hours a week and also do his PhD work. As a clever move, Sridharan volunteered to prepare the time-table for the Students' Lab work and allotted himself all the forenoon slots so that in the afternoon he could go and work at AIR.

In 1976, he got to cover the 25th Pugwash Conference that was held in Madras. Earlier in 1974, when the Pokhran I nuclear test was conducted, AIR Madras wanted to do a programme on the positive applications of nuclear energy and the Programme in charge A.R. Krishnamurthy gave Sridharan the responsibility to find an expert to talk about it. Sridharan approached one of his colleagues R. Balakrishnan from the Physics Department at MCC, who agreed to do the programme. He gave a detailed explanation of the process of a nuclear test—what is meant by implosion, how it is different from an explosion—all in layman's terms, along with the possible positive applications of nuclear energy in various fields. It was not an easy task to put the content together for the show, he remembers. With no internet or search engines to assist them, they had to skim through all the existing literature available to find relevant content for the show. They managed to find some meaningful applications of the nuclear energy in power generation, agriculture and medicine, and how a controlled explosion could be used to alter the course of rivers, etc. It made for an interesting show.

Two years later, to reiterate the claims that the 'Smiling Buddha' or Pokhran 1, was all about peace and progress and not for military purposes, Mrs. Indira Gandhi, then PM of India decided to hold a Pugwash Conference in the country. Pugwash is an organization that brings together the scientific community and public figures to work towards reducing armed conflicts and opposes use of nuclear energy for defence purposes. A week-long conference was organized and the who's who of the scientific community was involved in organizing it. Interestingly the responsibility to cover the Pugwash Conference for AIR, landed with Sridharan. It was not just a great opportunity to meet Nobel laureates and the top scientists from India and the world, but he was also provided state-of-the-art technology and supporting staff to do the coverage in the best way possible. He personally interviewed the Pugwash President and Nobel laureate Dorothy Hodgkin, and the interview was aired across the country on AIR and many newspapers took quotes from the interview for their articles.

He also remembers meeting and interacting with the eminent scientist Dr. Yelavarthy Nayudamma, who was then the Director General of CSIR (Council of Scientific and Industrial Research) who lost his life in the Kanishka [AI 182] Bombing Incident in June 1985. He recollects asking him a very sensitive question: 'You were a part of Pokhran I and now you are here at Pugwash talking about peace and avoiding nuclear explosions, doesn't it seem contradictory?' to which the scientist then gave a very sensible reply. He said "Sridharan! That was my official duty to be a part of Pokhran I. As a scientist I am also concerned about the repercussions of usage of nuclear weapons and that is why I advised Mrs. Indira Gandhi, in my capacity, to hold this conference so that the impression the world has about India will change for the better. I participate in this conference in my capacity as a scientist." Sridharan also got acquainted with the diplomat G. Parthasarathy, who served as India's permanent representative at the United Nations.

Through these series of events and incidents, Sridharan was able to present himself as a dependable and smart resource in the AIR Madras Team. But he could not go on working as a casual. He had finished his PhD thesis and now it was time to take up a full-time job and build a career.

He learnt that there were openings for the post of Transmission Executive/Duty Officer with AIR, Madras. He applied for the same and got a call for an interview. 'This would be my big break', he hoped. But the Station Director, Mr. M.S. Gopal thought differently. He was the one interviewing the candidates and during the interview, he told Sridharan, who was now about to be Dr. Sridharan, that he was overqualified to be appointed for the post and it would not be right of him to appoint him for the same.

"Sir, I don't have a job and it is important that I take up one now", Sridharan pressed. But, Mr. Gopal firmly refused.

This left him in a state of despair, but soon he came to know there was another opening that he would be interested in. According to the then Prime Minister Indira Gandhi's new initiative, AIR was to create separate units for programmes pertaining to science and interviews were to be held for the posts of Science Officer, Science Reporter and a Production Assistant for the new Science Cell. Sridharan applied for the post of Science Officer as well as Science Reporter. A written exam was conducted to shortlist suitable candidates and Dr. Sridharan stood first among 76 candidates who appeared for the exam.

It was to be followed up with an interview. He had known and interacted with all the interviewers in separate instances before, having worked as a freelancer in AIR. Prof. A.P. Jambulingam, the Director of Technical Teachers Training Institute, Madras was an expert on the panel. Prof. Raghavan of Pachaiyappa's College was also on the panel.

The interview went well and Sridharan eagerly awaited the results, but he did not receive any communication for a while. When he could wait no longer, he directly went and met Professor Raghavan from the Pachaiyappa's College, at his home and asked him why the results were not out yet. Professor Raghavan told him that he had been selected for the post and things were taking long to be processed as approvals were pending from Delhi.

This was the best news anyone could have given him then and Sridharan could not contain his joy! A government job in his field of interest and that too with a pay of Rs. 550 per month was a dream come true, especially after all that he and his family had been through... .

In 1972, Sridharan's younger sister was married to a well-to-do groom from an illustrious family. But Sridharan's family could manage the expenses of the wedding only through loans. So he and his brothers took up odd jobs to support the family and pay off the debts. One such job Sridharan took up was to help the local residents in Tambaram get a municipal water connection.

Tambaram municipality had just introduced a new scheme called the 'Palar Water Scheme' and the residents were expected to go to the municipality office and enrol themselves for a water connection through the new scheme. Sridharan helped families with elders and women to get the water connection without much hassle. He filled the forms for them, deposited them at the office and followed it up till the connections were installed. When new connections were given, new pipes and taps were also required to be fitted. The families asked Sridharan to help them with that too.

GI metal pipes were popularly fitted for drinking water supply in those days. It required maintenance and there was also the complaint that it was affecting the quality of the drinking water. Sridharan thought of an easy alternative that could save the trouble—installing PVC pipes and taps.

His uncle Mr. Venkatachalam, after his retirement from government service, was in touch with an agency which was marketing 'Wavin' PVC pipes. He was also helping his friends in switching to the use of PVC pipes replacing the age-old concept of galvanized iron or GI pipes. Sridharan got interested and was studying the process. When he realized he could use those pipes for the residents of Tambaram who sought his help, he reached out to his uncle.

He met the customers and told them about the uses of PVC and its economics. The customers were happy with what Sridharan had to offer and were prepared to adopt the change. But the plumbers in and around the locality were unappreciative of Sridharan's initiative. They were skilled at working with metal pipes and taps and as those taps were more expensive than plastic taps, hardware companies even paid a commission to the plumbers for the purchase of those items. As they felt their business was being threatened by Sridharan's initiative to install PVC pipes and taps, they decided to do something to ruin his business overnight. They sneaked into the houses where Sridharan had worked, and in the middle of the night, they tampered with the taps and connections and broke them. All the water would then flow out from these broken pipes and be wasted and the residents would get distressed. The local plumbers would then approach the residents of the house in the morning and try convincing them that the mess happened because of poor quality of work and the PVC pipes.

As more and more customers were complaining, Sridharan was in a fix and he did his best to manage the situation. Anytime he received a complaint, he would immediately rush to the spot on his cycle and mend the damage. Most of the days during his PhD, Sridharan remembers carrying plumbing spare parts with him on his cycle.

The war that the local plumbers waged on him sometimes turned insolent. In one incident, when the local plumbers tried to break a plastic tap connection in a house, they broke the toilet drainage pipe by mistake and all the waste from the toilet started spreading around the house. When the residents of the house noticed it early in the morning, they immediately called Sridharan to fix it. Not knowing what else to do, Sridharan did just that. He fixed the toilet drainage pipe and cleared all the waste by himself. He remembers he did not even have gloves to put on his hands as he was unprepared for such a situation. Though thoroughly upset, Sridharan was sincere enough to do all that his role demanded him to do.

Sridharan's youngest brother Rajagopal also assisted him in his plumbing works. He had inherited the love and passion for Tamil from his grandfather. He used to write poetry, perform stage dramas and he even went ahead and got admission for himself in a college to study for the BA in Tamil. But Sridharan intervened and made him choose economics as his main subject instead. Tamil might get him a good job, but if he took up economics, he could appear for bank exams and get a good job in a bank, he thought. Rajagopal though somewhat disappointed, went ahead to do BA and later an MA in economics. He joined as a clerk in the State Bank of India and went on to become an officer. He later did his MBA in Scotland and now continues to work there in Lloyds Bank. Turning and looking back, it does not look so bad on Sridharan's part to have influenced his brother's decision on what to study. Meanwhile, Sridharan's younger brother Chandrasekaran also, due to the family situation had to abandon his ambition of studying a PG course after his BCom. He started working in small companies and also joined as a part-time instructor in a typewriting institute. He later got a temporary job in the LIC of India, and then moved to the Indian Bank. He grew in his career and went on to be the Acting Chairman of General Insurance Corporation of India, but it is said that he still regrets not having been able to do his PG. Currently he is the Secretary General of the General Insurance Council of India and the government had also nominated him as a Director with the LIC of India. The brothers have proved their mettle and risen in their career, despite the initial setbacks.

Not just with his writing for magazines, or with his work at AIR or his stint with the PVC pipes, Sridharan never hesitated to give his time and mind space to anything worthwhile that came his way. He also never wasted his precious time. During his college days at the MCC, Sridharan developed a close bond with the owner of the East India Book House, a bookshop that was situated right opposite his college. As he lived nearby, Sridharan used to reach college early and help the owner of the book house to open the shop early and get the sales going. He even stayed back in the evenings to assist the owner with sales or other requirements. In return for all the help, the owner provided study material and stationery free of cost to Sridharan.

Sridharan was also close to his family Doctor, Dr. Varghese. He was an avid medical practitioner and was committed to helping the poor. When at a later stage in his life, he was bedridden because of paralysis, he still practised and saw patients from his bed. Sridharan would assist the doctor in preparing medicines for his patients. Those were the days when doctors concocted medicines themselves and would give it to the patients in a bottle. Sridharan being a chemistry student quickly learnt from the doctor the process and science of medicine-making and helped him in his spare time.

By running against all odds and being financially prudent with all that he earned, Sridharan was able to pay off the debt incurred for his sister's marriage even before he got a full-time job with AIR. His new job would now be a fresh start for him to forge a career path for himself.

2

Radio, Science and Innovation

Assistant Editor—Science Reporting (1976-78), AIR Madras

It was a long wait. When finally the job confirmation arrived by mail, Sridharan was delighted. He was to join AIR Madras as Dr. R Sridharan, Assistant Editor–Science Reporting, after four years of courtship with the medium he had begun to love.

No one was chosen for the position of Science Officer that year. Science programming was a newly formed division and there weren't any models or guidelines in place yet. Everything had to be worked on from scratch. The lessons thus learnt would help in forming and refining the guidelines and models for science broadcasts on AIR.

On the day he joined AIR, Mr. A.R. Krishnamurthy, Programme Executive asked him to choose between two senior officials to work with. One was Mr. Mahadevan, who later went on to become the Chief of the Tamil wing of the BBC in London. He was a thorough broadcast professional and his programmes had the highest ratings. He had even won an international award for his programme on various types of 'child's cry', and the reasons behind them. The programme was called 'Vettru Oli Alla Mazhalai Oli' (An infant's cry is not empty/meaningless cry), in Tamil. The other option was to work with Mr. Venugopal Reddy, who had recently joined AIR Madras as a Programme Executive. Sridharan felt working with a youngster like Mr. Reddy would give him a chance to experiment with new ideas for the science cell and a dialogue would be possible between them, rather than working with someone who was already established in his role. So, he made his choice and started working with Mr. Venugopal Reddy. It worked well for him and Mr. Reddy encouraged fresh and innovative ideas for science programming.

They launched a new radio programme, Ariviyal Poonga (Garden of Science) on Madras A channel of AIR. It consisted of a mix of formats and content on science. It covered a wide range of topics on science in the form of interviews, lectures, awareness skits, event coverage, etc. Sometimes the programmes were anchored by popular celebrities including Tamil cinema veterans like Gemini Ganesan and Manorama. Another programme called "Yaen?" (Why?), which answered basic questions in science from listeners, was broadcast on Sunday mornings. It was way before the Google era and people found this as a great opportunity to find answers to questions that piqued their curiosity. Not only did the programme do very well, but also went on to be broadcast on AIR for about eight long years.

A weekly Science Newsreel was introduced which covered all science-related events in the city. Sridharan also went on to start a five-minute daily programme called 'Ariviyal Neram'. He firmly believed that the secret of avoiding procrastination and delay is to get into action in full swing once a plan has been made. Waiting for approvals and for things to fall in place, sometimes ended up killing the initial enthusiasm. Perhaps that is why, Sridharan, was never a man to wait. Many decisions regarding the new science programmes were taken when the Station Director was on tour or on leave. Assistant Station director Mr. Hakim used to approve them using the temporary powers he held in the absence of the Director. That did not make the decision any less valid but the Station Director after his return used to get annoyed at new developments every time in his absence.

The newly launched programmes grew in response and went on to be appreciated by his seniors and listeners alike. Following the success of these programmes, they were adopted by the AIR head office in Delhi, as model shows for science programming across the country. All AIR channels across

India were asked to make science programmes following these Tamil shows as models.

Sridharan tried to include all aspects of science in his programmes—from everyday science to specializations such as neurology. Though he was getting popularly known as a producer of science programmes, he also worked on programmes in other fields whenever possible. He would not only do what he knew best, but also volunteer to work for something new and eventually learn something in the process. He would show as much interest in an event on Tamil literature as he would in atomic energy. When Kamban Vizha, a major Tamil literary event took place in Madras around that time, Sridharan volunteered to cover it for AIR Madras. His coverage was well appreciated by Tamil scholars as well as the audience.

Marriage

It had just been six months since he took up his full-time job at AIR, when Lady Luck came calling. Sridharan's mother felt that it was the right time for him to tie the knot as he was already nearing his thirties. Sridharan had no plans for marriage then but agreed nevertheless. He was to get married to a young and smart lady from Madurai, named after the reigning deity of the city, Meenakshi. She was a double MA holder in English and Economics, and also knew Sanskrit. Sridharan was completely disarmed by her simplicity, and her educational qualifications, when he first met her. Incidentally, Meenakshi was the first and only prospective bride Sridharan ever met. As was destined, he married her on October 24, 1976. After marriage he and his wife continued to live with his parents in Tambaram.

In 1976, for the first time in Madras, FM Radio was introduced on a trial basis and tested for response. But FM technology was not implemented and used properly in India for a very long time. The sets to receive FM were said to be more expensive. And the broadcast on FM was thus considered only for the rich and not poor. Many such excuses were given to put off the technology for a few more years and Sridharan was disappointed at having been denied the opportunity to work with the new technology. While the AIR engineers were commissioning new FM radio transmitters, the programme wing did not appreciate it, he recalls. They saw it as a threat to the existing framework and preferred the status quo instead of progressive technology. Sridharan saw it as a failure to keep up with the times.

In 1977, Mrs. Sridharan was carrying her first child and went to live with her parents for a while. Meanwhile in November that year, a cyclone hit the coast of Nagapattinam district in Tamil Nadu and claimed more than 1,000 lives. Not only did it ruin the coastal districts of Nagapattinam, Thanjavur, Chengalpet and South Arcot (former), but torrential rains also poured in the interior districts of Tiruchirapalli, Puthukottai and Madurai. The whole town of Nagapattinam had submerged and so had the AIR station at Tiruchirappalli. Even before the relief work could be started, there was a threat of another cyclone either hitting the same area or Madras or it could move to Andhra Pradesh, they said. The second cyclone ended up hitting parts of Andhra Pradesh, closer to Madras and wreaked havoc there, claiming several thousand lives, including casualties in a jam-packed parked train in Chirala, Andhra Pradesh. Sridharan's senior colleague Mr. A. Natarajan was given the assignment of covering the impacts of the natural disaster and the relief work that was taking place at Nagapattinam for AIR Madras. He was supposed to leave in an Army helicopter from Madras along with other personnel but somehow, he could not make it. Major Loganathan, the then PRO from the Army rang the Station Director and expressed his unhappiness saying that the helicopter was delayed waiting for the officer from AIR to arrive. Meanwhile Sridharan met the Programme Executive Mr. A.R. Krishnamurthy and volunteered to be a part of the coverage from Nagapattinam. He had studied about the role of radio in disaster management and was keen to get a direct experience of the same. When he got the necessary permission, he travelled along with Mr. Natarajan to the cyclone-affected areas in Thanjavur and Nagapattinam districts. They followed the Thanjavur collector on his visits and were able to see first-hand the loss of lives and livelihood caused by the cyclone, and the pace at which the relief work was being undertaken. They met the state's labour minister Mr. Ragavanandam and the CPM leader and MLA Mr. Umanath in Nagapattinam, where they were stationed and were overseeing the relief work. Mr. Ragavanandam mentioned during an interaction that the media coverage of the relief work had ignored the significant role played by them, by staying with the people and wading/swimming through the flood waters doing actual relief work alongside the people. Sridharan quickly recorded an interview with him and with Mr. Umanath as well. Sridharan and his colleague Natarajan then moved out of the cyclone-hit areas the same night as there was a looming threat of another cyclone. They stopped for the night in the town of Mayiladuthurai, also known as Mayavaram. Even though they reached Mayavaram only by 2 am, they got ready for the onward journey at 6 am. Sridharan's broadcast was due only the following night and he was still reaching Madras. But articles and photographs of the relief work undertaken by the minister were all over the newspapers by the following morning. Those were the days with no email or other digital tools and Sridharan was astonished at the remarkable speed and efficiency with which the then Public Relations officer with the State Government, the late Mr. Natarajan worked. The late Mr Natarajan was the spouse of Ms. Jayalalithaa's close aide, Sasikala.

After coming back Sridharan put together a programme on the aftermath of the cyclone and the relief work and also resumed his other projects in science.

Having dealt with the challenges, his current role had to offer, Sridharan wanted to apply for the post of Science Officer in his Department. No one was chosen for the post in the first year when the Science Cell was newly created. The second time though, Sridharan thought he had a chance, when the applications were solicited, they said those who had applied earlier were not eligible to apply this time. Sridharan tried claiming that he had submitted his PhD thesis and hence had an improved qualification for the role now. But the department still did not approve his application. Interviews were held and a person was appointed for the role. As he was training the new Science Officer when he joined duty, Sridharan learnt of his connections with top politicians and also realized that the new Science Officer might not have much interest in the field of broadcasting.

Sridharan was soon to realize that the new working arrangement did not suit him much and unable to continue working with his new senior for long, Sridharan discussed his issue with Programme Executive Mr. A.R. Krishnamurthy and expressed concern about his daily operations and future. Mr. Krishnamurthy advised him and also suggested that he could apply for the post of *Producer—Spoken Word* at AIR Coimbatore. The post carried a salary of Rs. 650 as basic pay but was equivalent to Class II Gazetted Officer of the Government of India, he said. Sridharan went ahead and applied for the new role.

In the meanwhile, he did his best to keep his work and programmes unaffected by the new influence. He started something called the Graama Vaanoli Ariviyal Arangam (AIR's village science meet). It was an innovative concept, unlike the regular studio-based programmes. Sridharan would take with himself a scientist and visit a village. A small meet was arranged there where the scientist would talk and explain to the villagers about an interesting topic, or a latest development or invention in his field of science. The villagers could then interact with the scientist, ask him doubts about the concepts and its applications. The full interaction, including the reactions of the local villagers—whether they understood the concept or not, the questions they asked, the thoughts they shared—was recorded and presented as a Radio show. The village science meet was an experimental project and Sridharan enjoyed travelling to a new village each time to discuss new science topics, finding the experience to be enriching and revealing. "If the villagers understood how to put science to good use, it could benefit their regular life immensely. Like, in one of the programmes the scientist explained to the villagers how hydraulic mechanism can be used in bullock carts to improve its efficiency. In fact it was a pet idea of the then Prime Minister Mrs. Indira Gandhi, as she wanted the bullock carts in the country to be modernized," he recalls.

For another show in 1977, during Gandhi Jayanti, Sridharan travelled to Tuticorin, to cover a programme where fishermen from a nearby village were being taught about artificial pearl culture by scientists from the Central Marine Fisheries Research Institute. Sridharan recorded a special interaction with the fishermen at the programme and also covered the event as a part of the AIR news bulletin, in which he gave a radio news report over the phone from Tuticorin. The next day when the officials of AIR met for a review at Madras, the Station Director asked the new Science Officer for updates on the Tuticorin event. He expressed his ignorance and said that Sridharan was yet to return from Tuticorin. Then the Station Director had to tell him that Sridharan's report on the event had already been broadcast as a part of the news bulletin on the previous day.

The Station Director of AIR Coimbatore selected Sridharan over the other four local candidates who had applied for the role of Producer—Spoken Word, and Sridharan then moved to Coimbatore with his family, which now had a new addition—his daughter Sripriya.

Apparently, the Science Officer too then left the organization and became an academic.

Coimbatore–1978

Sridharan was told that the Coimbatore AIR station had been operational for the past 18 years. But neither the station nor its programming was in an impressive state when he joined. "The station set up was in a rented house and its kitchen was being used as a studio. The channel aired exclusive content only for half an hour a day and the remaining broadcasts were all relayed from the nearby Trichy AIR station," he recalls. Sridharan couldn't help but wonder at the rationale of running a station in such a condition. He immediately decided to do his best to get the station up and running on its own.

But the local staff was not prepared to accept Sridharan in his new role. Some of his detractors started raising questions and objections. 'Dr. Sridharan has studied chemistry and that too in English medium. What qualifies him to be a Producer for Tamil shows?' he heard one of them say. In response, Sridharan simply took up an MA Tamil literature programme through Distance education.

Within months of his posting to Coimbatore, Mr. K. Kasturi, the then Station Director who had recruited him was transferred to a different location and a new Director, Mr. Premananda, had joined the station. While updating the new Director, of the status of the station, Sridharan also shared his intentions of producing and airing more local content from the Coimbatore station itself.

"Please don't worry about the expenses Sir; I will try to do good programmes with the least expense. I might not stick to traditional norms and might need to bend some rules for the sake of good results. But the shows will be good. You will get a good name and the station will also get a good name. Is that all right?" he remembers asking him.

He was given a go ahead. He initiated two programmes to work on—a youth programme called 'Ilaya Bharatham' and a programme for labourers.

He began by building his network, just the way he did before starting his magazine in his schooldays. He went and met Dr. G.R. Damodaran, a popular and influential entrepreneur and educationist in Coimbatore, who later became the Vice-Chancellor of Madras University. He shared with him the idea of AIR and PSG College of Technology coming together to conduct a cultural fest for youngsters. He also requested his permission to conduct the event in their college auditorium.

Dr. Damodaran readily agreed and Sridharan went ahead and held a grand cultural event in PSG College with music, debate and talent shows for youngsters. The college students performed with full enthusiasm and all the events were recorded to be broadcast on AIR Coimbatore's Ilaya Bharatham programme. The response to the event and its broadcast was phenomenal and owing to its success, Sridharan got to conduct more such events in the PSG premises. As the show gained popularity, students and faculties from other colleges also approached Sridharan to host such events in their colleges. Apart from having developed interesting original content for the Coimbatore AIR station, Sridharan also developed a good network with college faculties and student representatives from various colleges in Coimbatore through this initiative.

It is worthwhile noting that, in all that he did, Sridharan never approached the AIR Headquarters for approvals of his content or ideas. But he always kept his Station Head updated on all initiatives and developments. 'We have built a self-sustaining station from what used to be a relay station and that too at no extra cost. We must be doing something right!' he thought.

When the Station Director from Madras, Mr. M.S. Gopal came to the Coimbatore station for an inspection he told Mr. Premananda that there was no reason to worry while having Sridharan around. 'He has been trained under me and he does things the way I do. Be confident and support him', he had told the Coimbatore Station Director.

Sridharan was encouraged by Mr. Gopal's observations and went ahead to implement all the interesting projects he had in mind for the Coimbatore station including a cultural festival for labourers and a special cultural programme for estate labourers in Coonoor (a neighbouring hill station). He also made the best use of the talents and skills of college students in generating content for radio programmes. He got the local Cheran Orchestra group to produce a radio drama series for AIR Coimbatore. They came up with a radio drama called Avalin Ragangal that continued for 104 weeks on air.

It led to the immense popularity of the Cheran Orchestra in Coimbatore.

Sridharan was often met with the criticism that his programmes were very impromptu. 'A radio programme needs to have scripts and rehearsals and the artists need to be hired on contract basis. How can something as impromptu as this pass for a radio programme?' asked Mr. Kandasamy, popularly known as Thuraivan, who took over as the Station Director of AIR Madras after Mr. M.S. Gopal. He had come to visit the Coimbatore station, and argued with Sridharan on his new unconventional broadcasts. But the response to his shows and the success they enjoyed spoke for Sridharan and his 'impromptu' style of programming.

Sridharan was always grateful for the opportunities and encouragement he received as a youngster in AIR. He felt most grateful to Mr. A.R. Krishnamurthy at AIR Madras, who encouraged him to buy his own tape recorder. It changed his life and helped him earn more. Years later when he was in a similar position, he too encouraged young enthusiasts with his ideas and opportunities. When he met Prasad, a student who was as active and enthusiastic in his projects for radio as himself, Sridharan suggested that he should buy his own tape recorder. The next day he came and met Sridharan with a brand new Panasonic recorder in hand. 'I need to help him to recover the cost', thought Sridharan. Not even a fortnight had passed since the incident when the shocking news came that Prasad had lost his father, who was the sole breadwinner in his family. Sridharan offered Prasad as many opportunities as possible and tried to support him in difficult times. He remembers Prasad as one of the very creative casuals he worked with and remembers him for covering the most high-profile events, even the ones involving the Chief Minister MGR, using his own cassette and recorder only. Interestingly, Prasad also went on to marry another casual from AIR Coimbatore, Lalitha. Prasad now works for an MNC and is well placed, he recalls fondly. Sridharan also supported other students who could do with some financial support, by offering them anchoring opportunities on AIR. He also had a good bond with Devaraj and Prithvi who worked under him in Coimbatore.

When Station Director Premananda retired at the end of his tenure, Mr. G. Selvam took over as the new Station Director. He too was a man of innovation and ideas and Sridharan was able to execute many interesting programmes well with his support. But things did not go smoothly for long and conflicts arose that created a natural distance between the two.

Sridharan still aspired for the role of Science Officer privately. When the post fell vacant for the third time, he applied again and this time, luckily, he got through. A pay of Rs. 700 per month and Class I officer grade awaited him in Madras. Once again in his life, when the interviews were held, he already knew all those who were on the panel. One among them was Dr. Swaminathan, Professor of Organic Chemistry in Madras University. He knew Sridharan as a research scholar. During the interview he offered Sridharan an additional responsibility, to be the Secretary of the Madras Science Association. Sridharan accepted the offer right away as it was a very respectable position and also the best minds in science were a part of the association. Sridharan later took up the additional responsibility at the Madras Science Association after obtaining special permission from the All India Radio headquarters.

Meanwhile he also suggested the idea of starting a Science Literary Society, to popularize science communication in Tamil, to the then Education Minister Aranganayagam, who approved it instantly.

So once again things fell in place for Sridharan and he was all set to move to Madras. However, in Coimbatore, the Station Director was not prepared to relieve him and tried to hold him back until a replacement was found. But Sridharan wrote to Mr. A.R. Krishnamurthy who was now working in Dibrugarh, Assam, asking for advice. He in turn requested intervention from the higher officials in Delhi and instructions were given to relieve Sridharan immediately from his current post.

Science Officer 1980-87

Science Sammelans

When Sridharan joined duty in Madras as Science Officer, Mr. Thuraivan was the Station Director. While discussing ideas for new science projects, Mr. Thuraivan shared an interaction he had had with scientist M.S. Swaminathan while they were in Delhi. Dr. Swaminathan had suggested that, on the lines of the sangeet sammelans (conventions) that were popular in AIR, why not do science sammelans? Mr. Thuraivan thought it was a very interesting suggestion and asked Sridharan to come up with something on those lines. Sridharan agreed and suggested that inputs should be taken from science experts in the city on how and what could be done through a science sammelan. So, a meeting was organized and the science experts in the city, Vice-Chancellors, College Principals and medical experts were all invited to be a part of it. The idea of having a science sammelan was very well received by them as it was first of its kind. The then Vice-Chancellor of Anna University (which was then known as Perarignar Anna University of Technology, PAUT), Mr. P. Sivalingam came forward and offered that the event could be organized in the University campus, free of cost.

The science sammelan was called Ariviyal Per Arangam in Tamil. He planned it as a three-day event during the holiday season in December. He put his thoughts on a piece of paper and took it to the Station Director for discussion. Mr. Thuraivan was a short-tempered man and used to wear thick reading glasses. When he saw Sridharan's note, he sent it back to him, asking him not to come to him with such notes and told him to get it neatly typed with help from his stenographer. When Mr. Thuraivan finally saw Sridharan's plan that included four seminars on the topics of Energy, Safety, Nature, and Health, involving 13 speakers each and with a different Minister being invited to each of the seminars, he was very impressed. He suggested that they invite the Governor of Tamil Nadu to inaugurate the science sammelan and asked Sridharan to accompany him to meet the Governor. At the meeting when the Governor Sadiq Ali asked questions about the event, Mr. Thuraivan pointed to Sridharan and allowed him do all the explanations. Also, the Doordarshan Kendra in Madras showed much interest and wanted to come on-board as a joint organizer for the event.

Sridharan also solicited support from organizations like the Neyveli Lignite Corporation, Madras Refineries, and Tamil Nadu Mineral Corporation in organizing the event. He approached a private company Best and Crompton's to support the event by providing sodium lamps in the campus. This was usually not the way things were done in AIR, but Sridharan went ahead and did all that he could to ensure a successful event. He approached popular songwriter Kannadasan and made him pen two songs for the event, one of which was on the evils of smoking.

Sridharan requested a few private companies to host lunch and snacks for the participants of the Science seminars that were held during the sammelan. Provisions were made for those interested to attend the seminar and others could simply visit an exhibition on the subject in the same campus. All speakers at the seminar were encouraged to make posters on their subject to be displayed at the venue. A compilation of all the talks delivered by the science experts during the event was published by a private publisher in the form of a book and released on the same occasion. Films on wildlife, environment, health, and achievements of science and technology were screened at the venue. In the evening, light music and folk music shows were organized to take science to the masses. With this event, AIR deviated from its usual style of conducting events for the elite through invitations and opened the gates for the common man. It was a real breakthrough.

Station Director Thuraivan who was much impressed with Sridharan's efficiency and initiatives, offered all encouragement and support to help him perform well. Something else that made him swell with pride was his father's reaction to his work. Sridharan had sent a letter requesting his father's Chief at the LIC of India to be a part of the science sammelan. It was opened by Sridharan's father and he was delighted to see a letter from his son in his official capacity.

The event was a huge success and earned Sridharan great respect and appreciation. The Deputy Director General of AIR K.C. Sharma who had come to Madras for the event was also very impressed. A few weeks later when the Director General of AIR, Mr. Baruah visited Madras, the Station Director Thuraivan insisted he give Sridharan a letter of appreciation for his work in organizing the science sammelan. Also, the Director General ordered that all AIR stations across India should replicate and come up with such Science Sammelan Programmes in their respective stations.

Mr. Aranganayagam, who was then the Education Minister of Tamil Nadu, insisted that the next Science Sammelan in Tamil Nadu be held in Coimbatore and Sridharan willingly agreed and started working on the same. The Vice-Chancellor of Tamil Nadu Agricultural University, Mr. Venkataraman came forward to host it in his campus.

The second Science Sammelan in 1981 at Coimbatore was bigger in scale and in surprises. The then Collector of Coimbatore District, Mr. K. Malaichamy IAS, extended his full cooperation in planning the event. The biggest scientific development that the nation witnessed at that time was the launch of APPLE, India's first indigenous, experimental communication satellite. Sridharan decided to keep a model of the APPLE satellite at the Science Sammelan venue so the visitors could see and appreciate it. He had already been in talks with ISRO regarding the coverage of the launch of APPLE satellite for AIR and he additionally requested the Project Director of APPLE Satellite Dr. R.M. Vasagam to share the design of the satellite with him, so he could create a similar model for the exhibition. Sridharan also approached a popular entrepreneur in Coimbatore Mr. G.K. Sundaram of Lakshmi Mills and requested him to help in fabricating the model of the APPLE satellite. He too willingly agreed. Sridharan then approached the Government College of Technology and with their help arranged for an escalator which was designed by their own students. The idea was to place the APPLE satellite model at a suitable height, so it could be viewed from everywhere at the exhibition and people could also go up in the escalator, view it closely and then come down.

Just when everything seemed to be in place for the event to be a grand success, the Chief Guest to the event, minister Aranganayagam pulled out of the event. Some political developments during that time, and difference of perceptions among the state government and central government, led to a situation where the state government had decided not to cooperate with the initiatives of the central government. AIR and Doordarshar. were also on that list and hence minister Aranganayagam was not to attend an event by AIR.

Sridharan discussed this development with the new Station Director Ms. Sathyabhama, who had taken charge following Mr. Thuraivan's exit and requested her to speak to the Chief Minister M.G. Ramachandran (in Malayalam!) reiterating that the purpose of the Science Sammelan was all about popularizing science in Tamil Nadu and showcasing the progress of science in Tamil Nadu and there was nothing political about it. The Chief Minister was convinced with the explanation and approved the Minister Aranganayagam's visit to the Science Sammelan in Coimbatore.

Mr. Aranganayagam was to come by the Nilgiri Blue Mountain Express to Coimbatore when he had cancelled the visit. Sridharan telephoned him at around midnight to inform him of the CM's approval of his visit. The minister promised to come by the early morning flight and asked AIR to inform the Coimbatore collector of his visit. When Sridharan went to the airport in the morning hours to receive the minister, he was surprised to find a sizeable crowd there already, holding banners and felicitating Mr. Aranganayagam for his achievements in establishing universities in Coimbatore, Trichy and Thanjavur. Sridharan thought that he was working fast, but when he saw the felicitation at the airport, he realized that the minister and his followers had beaten him in their speed of action.

And thankfully, everything else fell into place and the event went as planned. The audience response for viewing the APPLE satellite model was huge and people stood in queues for about three kilometres to be at the Science Sammelan. Most of the crowd management was done by the college students of Coimbatore. Cheran Transport had even organized special buses to the venue of the Science Sammelan for people from nearby towns to visit the science exhibition. This time the event also included other attractions such as a fashion show by professionals which was sponsored by the National Textile Corporation, screening of the film *Neerkumizhi* (Water Bubble) and popular artists including singers T.M. Soundararajan and L.R. Eswari performed live at the event.

Once again Sridharan was able to pull off an event of this scale without causing much expense for AIR to bear. Most of the requirements were met through his thoughtful planning, unconventional approach and the network he had built for himself.

But there were other issues that had to be managed with a certain clarity and cleverness.

The Director General of AIR, Mr. M.L. Baruah, after seeing the success of the first Science Sammelan in Madras, had asked Science Officers from various AIR stations in the country to visit the second Science Sammelan at Coimbatore. Mr. HR Krishnamurthy from Bangalore, Dr. Amit Chakraborthy from Calcutta, Mr. Paresh Mankad from Ahmedabad, Mr. Jayant Erande from Bombay, Dr. B. Gopalam from Hyderabad and Mr. G. Jayalal from Thiruvananthapuram were some of the Science Officers who visited the second Science Sammelan at Coimbatore. After sharing the concept and showing them through the exhibition, as most of the programmes were in Tamil and the Science Officers could not understand the language, Sridharan had allowed the Science Officers to take a trip to a neighbouring hill station Ooty for a day. But when the Station Director of AIR Madras, Ms. Satyabhama learnt about their trip she strongly objected to it.

Meanwhile there were also rumours that the students of the PSG College were upset at not being recognized and given an award for their contribution to the Sammelan. Sridharan sensed that some trouble could brew out of it and managed to convince the sponsors of the Sammelan, NTC, to give a special prize to the students of PSG College recognizing their contribution. The Station Director, Ms. Satyabhama objected to this too and questioned the very concept of giving such Awards at an AIR function.

There were also a few other things about the Sammelan that irked Ms. Satyabhama and Sridharan not wanting to add fuel to the fire decided to stay away from the valedictory function citing ill health. But being himself, he decided to sit in the last row of seats at the auditorium and keep a watch on the proceedings in case something went wrong. He was happy to hear the District Collector and the Chief guest Mr. Ramachandran, who was the Deputy Director of ISRO's APPLE project, appreciate his efforts in organizing the Sammelan. During the vote of thanks the then Station Director of AIR Coimbatore, Mr. G. Selvam missed out on thanking the 'UMS Company' that provided CCTV coverage for the event and even provided colour television sets which were very rare in India till much later. The manager of UMS was unhappy at not being acknowledged and Dr. Sreedher had to enter the scene to manage the crisis. He consoled him personally and sent a driver to drive him back home.

The next day when Sridharan met Mr. G.K. Sundaram, the Chairman of Lakshmi Mills, who had sponsored the life size model of Apple satellite, he expressed his happiness about the event and the huge public support. He even asked Sridharan if he could do something to recognize and appreciate the volunteers who had helped in putting together a spectacular show. Sridharan suggested that it would be a good idea to gift them clothing (pant/shirt cloth for the male and saris for the female volunteers), as the festival of Deepavali was drawing near. So the volunteers were asked to assemble for a tea party that was hosted by the famous Annapurna Hotels in Coimbatore. At the event the staff of AIR, along with the many volunteers were presented clothes on behalf of Lakshmi Mills.

The next day when Sridharan was about to leave for Madras, one of his senior officials from AIR asked him to get in touch with Mr. Sundaram of Lakshmi Mills again and get half a dozen more pieces of clothing for his family and some of his guests who were arriving for Diwali. Sridharan flatly refused to do it and left for Madras.

Science Clubs

To make his science programmes more participative and rewarding, Sridharan encouraged listeners to form Radio Science Clubs. Any ten people in a village or a town or an institution could come together and form a science club. They could give their science club a name and could elect their President, Vice President, Secretary and Treasurer. They were then asked to write to AIR, with the details of their newly formed science club. The names of the members and the newly formed clubs were announced on air, just before the morning regional news. People, especially those who lived in far-flung villages, felt very thrilled to hear their names on radio and enthusiastically participated in forming science clubs. The Radio Science Clubs thus formed were given identification numbers and were encouraged to organize events pertaining to science in their localities. The events could be on any scale or simply be as basic as inviting a school teacher to talk on a topic in science. The details of the events were also announced on air and people in the same locality and nearby localities were urged to participate in them. Anyone outside the club participating in such an event could write a report on it and share it with AIR which was broadcast too. This was to encourage people who were not part of these science clubs to visit the science-based events. Thus, not only was an active listenership base created for the science programmes, but the science clubs also helped to create a movement of science awareness in the listener communities.

Sridharan had even invited Scientist A.P.J. Abdul Kalam to be the guest for one of his radio programmes pertaining to science clubs. It was not a formal invitation sent through AIR, but an informal personal request over the phone, to which Dr. Kalam responded positively. Dr. Kalam was then working with the Defence Research Development Organization (DRDO) and was visiting IIT Madras for a programme. He had said that he would drop in at the AIR studios after the event at IIT.

When Sridharan informed the then Station Director of AIR, Madras, Ms. Sathyabhama about Dr. Kalam's impending visit, she was stunned. 'Where is the proposal? I haven't seen anything on my table... Has he signed a contract with us? Show me details of his agreement to attend the programme... without all this I am not even showing up for the programme,' the Station Director said.

Sridharan did not have answers to any of her questions but only ideas to put together a successful programme. He somehow managed to arrange for Dr. Kalam's visit by himself. He asked one of the freelancers, Ganapathy Subramaniam to travel by bus to Adyar, and engage a 'Black and Yellow' taxi to pick up Dr. Kalam from the IIT campus. They had to lie to Dr. Kalam that the office vehicle had a breakdown. Dr. Kalam then visited the AIR office and addressed the listeners very impressively during the programme. The programme however, went on without the Station Director's presence and Sridharan dropped off Dr. Kalam, back at the IIT campus after the event.

The initiative to form science clubs received an enthusiastic response from listeners and around 500 science clubs were formed in various cities and villages of Tamil Nadu. Later, to encourage them, Sridharan also took the initiative to organize quiz contests based on science and invited members of these clubs to the AIR studios to participate, by offering them travel reimbursement and an honorarium.

"A proposal from Sridharan needs to be scrutinized with utmost care", station director Satyabhama used to say. He had this habit of submitting proposals for many different projects and assignments at the same time. This way he could be certain that even if some of them got rejected, the others would get approved. This would save time both for the approving officer and for him, and he could begin work on the approved projects as soon as possible he thought and it worked well for him.

Often, in his career, Sridharan risked neglecting a few formalities, refused to play by the rule book, or landed in issues with his superiors while working for implementing a project successfully. He gave all his energy to see a positive result and the other formalities had to take a backseat. He got used to the fuss and controversies around his method of working by this time and continued to do what he felt was in the programme's best interest.

Association with ISRO

It was the early 1980's and India at that time actively experimented with space projects and satellite launches. ISRO was then working on the launch of an SLV3 vehicle that was putting a Rohini satellite in orbit from the Satish Dhawan Space Centre at Sriharikota. Though the island of Sriharikota is in the state of Andhra Pradesh, the nearest radio station to the satellite launch pad was the Madras AIR.

Sridharan in his capacity as a Science Officer, decided to do a live coverage of the satellite launch from the premises of the Satish Dhawan Space Centre. He approached the ISRO authorities seeking permission to do a live commentary on the satellite launch. Initially the ISRO authorities were somewhat reluctant but eventually agreed to the proposed idea. Doordarshan Madras also approached ISRO and took permissions to do a live coverage of the satellite launch for television.

One thing that the ISRO authorities insisted was that the person doing the live commentary should be from ISRO, as it would require a sound knowledge of space science and an understanding of the processes that take place during a launch. They suggested that Mr. C.R. Sathya, a scientist from

ISRO could do the live radio commentary in English for AIR. Mr. Sathya was then invited to the AIR studios and given basic training for doing the live commentary.

Ms. Sathyabhama, the then station head of AIR Madras, wasn't as enthused about the idea of doing a live running commentary and simply let Sridharan go ahead and pursue his plans. Perhaps she was tired of putting up with Sridharan's non-conforming working style. Sridharan remembers how when he told her that a scientist, Sathya, from the ISRO was to do the live commentary on radio, she retorted by saying "Sathya (truth) or Asathya (untruth)... Do whatever!" Later when it was time for the live coverage from the space centre, Sridharan never wanted to invite her to the venue, as he thought it would not be very encouraging to have her around. He even tried telling her that women were not allowed inside the control room at ISRO. Though she later found out it was untrue, she never insisted on being a part of the event. Sridharan, though was embarrassed about his silly lie.

Sridharan and his team did the live commentary, from a booth inside the control room of ISRO where all the action was taking place and the top scientists and officials were also seated. However, the Doordarshan OB van was stationed at a distance from the control centre and was allowed to take live feed from the ISRO cameras in the launch area. The excitement and the action were contagious in the control room. Everyone was nervous and paid full attention when the countdown began. Suddenly in the middle of the countdown something unexpected took place and someone said 'STOP!' The launch process was halted. What had happened was that the umbilical cable connecting the satellite to the launch tower failed to detach at the appropriate time and thus the lift-off was kept on hold. Sridharan was forced to stop the live commentary at that point, with the anchor connecting back to the studios, where they played some music intermittently. Meanwhile, Doordarshan also had to stop the live feed, as the cameras and lights at the launch venue were switched off. Sridharan learnt that they managed the situation by playing footage of successful shuttle launches in the past.

Mr. T.N. Seshan, who later became the Chief Election Commissioner of India, was then the Additional Secretary to the Department of Space. Sridharan recalls, that he was witnessing the crisis and got furious when he learnt that the Doordarshan channel was broadcasting images from a successful shuttle launch. "Not knowing who the personnel from TV were, he approached me first and I was quick to tell him that I was from AIR and we were only playing music on air. He then went to the Doordarshan team and reprimanded them. "Here in India we are struggling with a rocket launch and you are playing on air the achievements of the US scientists..." he said and asked them to wrap up the live coverage, he recalls.

Meanwhile, just a little later at the control room the launch activities resumed. Though it is not usually allowed, a technician from the team volunteered to approach the launch vehicle and remove the umbilical cable manually, even if it meant risking his life. When he managed to do it, the launch went on to be successful.[4] Sridharan and scientist Sathya resumed their live commentary on AIR and managed to get interviews from top scientists and officials after the successful launch, before they even stepped out to meet the press. Covering the launch event gave Sridharan, an opportunity to know personally and develop a rapport with the top ISRO scientists and officials.

Later, he came back to the AIR studios and put together an edited programme on the satellite launch, trying to include the interviews of all the relevant team members. He chose Ms. Revathi Srinivasan as the anchor to present the show. The show was hooked up for broadcast nationwide and once again Sridharan's work didn't go unnoticed.

Though he did not get much appreciation in his office and his Station Director even criticized him for choosing an unsuitable anchor, three days later he was in for a pleasant surprise when he received a certificate of appreciation from the national Headquarters at New Delhi. His national broadcast was reviewed and rated 'outstanding' by the Directorate General of All India Radio during their weekly Programme Review and Planning (PRP) meeting. (Reference—news articles relating to the incident and news articles relating to the book *A Brief History of Rocketry in ISRO* by P.V. Manoranjan Rao and P. Radhakrishnan, 2012).

The experience of witnessing the satellite launch from the ISRO control room inspired him to take up several initiatives later which would use and showcase progressive technology. He noticed during the launch how several earth stations from different parts of the world were connected to each other through hotlines and how their alertness and response was sought after during a satellite launch. He thought he could use this as a concept for a radio programme and an idea to do a satellite-based radio teleconference programme occurred to him. He saved that for later as something else had come his way now.

It was a tradition that every year on the eve of Independence Day, the speech of the President of India was broadcast on AIR, following which a documentary feature was broadcast across all AIR stations in the country. Usually the documentaries were produced by prominent producers and anchors in AIR like the legendary Melville De Mellow and later Ms. Chitra Narain. This year the opportunity was given to Sridharan following his successful broadcast of the satellite launch that was certified as outstanding. The orders came from New Delhi in May 1981. The broadcast of the feature he was supposed to work on was scheduled for August 14, 1981. The theme assigned to him for the feature was 'Leap into Space'. With slightly more than two months at hand, Sridharan made an elaborate plan for the feature and shared it with the officials in Delhi.

He decided to form a team and along with Mr. Sampathkumar from the engineering wing, he travelled to all the important centres of ISRO in the country. Starting from Thumba in Trivandrum where the first successful rocket was launched from, to the ISRO Satellite Centre in Bangalore where the satellites were designed and fabricated, to the Space Applications Centre in Ahmedabad where the applications of satellite were being planned, and finally to Sriharikota from where the satellites were being launched.

The team planned its travel by train and spent about two months in travel, research and interviews. Mr. Sathya, the liaison officer, who also did the live commentary for the satellite launch earlier, was in charge of helping Sridharan with the necessary research material required for the documentary feature.

When Sridharan was in Bangalore, he remembers that the ISRO Chairman Satish Dhawan refused to give him an interview and said, "It's all team work and you can interview my team if you want". Sridharan got the opportunity to meet the top scientists working at ISRO at that time. He remembers meeting and interviewing Vasant Ranchhod Gowarikar the Indian scientist, who was later the chief of the Indian Space Research Organization and also the Scientific Advisor to the Prime Minister of India in 1991–1993; Udupi Ramachandra Rao, a space scientist who later became the Chairman of the Indian Space Research Organization and also the first Chairman of Prasar Bharati; Professor Yashpal, the great Indian scientist and educationist; and eminent physicist, E.V. Chitnis among many others. He also remembers having interacted with trainee astronauts like Mr. Radhakrishnan.

Sridharan used to be at Sriharikota to cover almost all the launch activities that happened there. Apart from his fascination with science and astronomy, there was something else about ISRO that impressed him. It was the meticulous planning and attention to detail. In the early 1980s when the usage of computers was rare and sharing information was a cumbersome process, Sridharan remembers how the team at ISRO used to be so efficient in planning and looking after the details of an event. Everyone in the hierarchy was rightly informed of the visitors, their access, their purpose of visit and the equipment they could bring along and other details. Not only did it save the visitors the need to explain every time they met someone, but also served for a very smooth experience.

The feature 'Leap into Space' was a half-hour radio programme, where mostly the spoken word would dominate. But still wanting to give it only the best and make it sound as good as possible, Sridharan approached popular violinist, Mr. Kunnakudi Vaidyanathan to lend the background score for the radio feature.

Sridharan's meticulous planning and sincere efforts earned him another certificate for an outstanding radio programme from the Indian government.

Later in 1983, about the time when the INSAT 1B communication satellite was launched, Sridharan wanted to do an audio conference to demonstrate the power of satellite in enhancing communication and how it could be used effectively for purposes like telemedicine, expeditions, education and so on. It was a very ambitious project and Sridharan approached ISRO with a plan to do an audio conference between people from different walks of life, living and working in different zones across the world. A farmer in Gujarat and a scientist from Antarctica could come together in an audio conference through satellite, he suggested. "The idea was appreciated by the ISRO team, but later, the thought emerged that, it was ISRO's responsibility to popularize the role of satellites in communication and the idea of AIR taking the initiative and taking away the credits, made them withdraw support." he recalls.

Not wanting to give up his creative idea, he approached the Telecom Research Centre in Delhi, knowing that the telephone department was using the satellite to test the facility of making long-distance calls through satellite communication. He requested them to share their facility in doing the audio conference. Though in those days the interactions on phone lines were not to be broadcast in the airwaves, the Telecom Research Centre still agreed to support the initiative for the special programme. Sridharan approached the ISRO team again and invited their experts to be the guests for the programme and to interact with the participants during the live audio conference. To this ISRO obliged and the audio conference went on successfully using the INSAT 1B satellite. As a part of the audio conference, children from different parts of the country came together to sing a popular song by the Tamil poet, Subramania Bharathi. An eminent neurosurgeon Dr. S. Kalyanaraman answered a medical question based on diagnosis from a patient in Leh. Through the National Institute of Oceanography in Goa, they were able to connect with Indian scientists on expedition in Antarctica. All this happened on air, LIVE, in one continuous flow. It was planned, structured and coordinated perfectly. What is more important to note is that such an ambitious programming initiative was pulled off practically without any expenditure. All that it cost was the efforts to put together and coordinate it. The team only had to inspire the participants with the idea of innovation and the impact it could have, and everyone came together with goodwill.

M.B. Srinivasan, a music composer who was a veteran with choral singing programmes at AIR, taught children located in different parts of the country to sing a Tamil song together. Anchors from AIR stations were sent to four different parts of the country—the Andamans, Lakshadweep, Shillong and Leh for this particular segment of the audio conference. The anchors in their respective locations gathered young school children around them and Mr. Srinivasan from the Madras AIR studio taught these children to sing 'odi vilayaadu pappa'—a children's song in Tamil by the eminent Tamil poet Bharathiyar. The language and pronunciation were new, but the children cheerfully sang together, the best of whatever they could gather. Mr. Srinivasan politely taught them the song line by line and finally they ended up reciting the song together in one continuous flow. It was very interesting how the children in Leh, who did not speak anything other than their local dialect and had not even been down to the foothills from the 13,000 feet (3,962 m) altitude they lived in, could catch a tune and sing in a language so alien to them. When finally, the children from these four corners of the country sang the Tamil song together, the listeners experienced it like they were all in one place, singing it together for them.

Not only was it an interesting way to take modern technology to the common man while entertaining him, it was also a display of the spirit of India, with children from different regions, speaking different languages coming together to perform a song in a language alien to them. No matter where they are from, children all over are innocent and beautiful. And music being the universal language broke all barriers and made them sing together. The listeners so loved being entertained this way and his efforts also earned Sridharan a National Award.

Meanwhile, during the live audio conference, one of the listeners from Trichy, wanting to test if the audio conference was really happening live, directly called the AIR duty room. He even shared a question for Dr. Kalyanaraman who was on the Studio Panel. The officer from the duty rooms shared the question with Dr. Kalyanaraman who went on to answer it live on AIR. The next day *The Hindu* newspaper came out with a box item on its first page titled 'Telemeet Tested on Phone'.

Other Innovative Formats

On January 28, 1882, the first telephone exchange was inaugurated in Calcutta (now Kolkata), which marked the beginning of telephonic communications in India. In 1982, the Department of Telecommunications decided to celebrate the centenary of telephone services in India and an innovative and promotional radio idea was sought for, to mark the centenary celebrations.

Sridharan once again got a chance to experiment and innovate. Using telephones for broadcast was not allowed in AIR for a very long time, as telephonic interactions were considered private as per the Indian Telegraph Act of 1885. A lot could have been done marrying the two mediums Sridharan felt. Using the special occasion as an opportunity he chose to do something strikingly different that would leave a lasting impression with the listener. A radio play script was written with three main characters, a hero, a heroine, and a villain. He stationed the artistes who voiced these three roles in three different locations across the city. They would play their parts over the phone. Live background music was arranged for from the AIR studio. So, when the hero greeted the listeners with 'hi' from Mount Road in Madras, the heroine would reply with a 'hello' over the phone from Parrys Corner, also in Madras. So the whole play was coordinated to happen remotely, without leaving listeners with even a hint that these characters could be anywhere but in the same place. At the end of the play, it was revealed to the audience that the three characters were playing their parts from three different parts of the city, leaving the audience in awe. It was an exemplary radio idea which served its purpose brilliantly, showcasing the advantage of telecommunication and the seamlessness with which it integrates into our lives.

Again in 1983, on World Telecom Day, Sridharan took another initiative and produced a show that earned him his next National Award. As usage of telephones for radio programmes, was still not in practice and with no special permissions with him this time, he had to think of another way around to showcase the latest advancements in communication. He envisaged a show, where four anchors, each, commuting in a different mode of transport, namely a bus, a train, a plane and a ship, would get to report live on a radio show and interview a panel of guests who were at the studio. So special permissions were obtained for the anchors to travel and report from these modes of conveyance and permissions were also sought from the Tamil Nadu Police, Indian Airlines, Indian Railways and Chennai Port to use their wireless service for broadcast. A few press reporters, police personnel and supporting staff travelled along with the anchors for the show. Anchors, who were well-known personalities, were chosen to host the show. Ms. Rekha Shetty, reported live from the ship, while Ms. Jennifer Arul was travelling on a train from Egmore station and Ms. Malini Sheshadri was travelling in a plane from Trichy to Bangalore, and another anchor reported from a moving bus. It was rehearsed well in advance, to ensure perfect planning and coordination.

When the show was aired, it was greatly appreciated by the listeners, the local Press and also by the Delhi Office. On the other hand, in Madras issues cropped up on using the secure wireless frequencies of the police and Indian Airlines, for public broadcast.

By now, Sridharan had come to terms with it. Anytime he tried something new, there were some issues or the other that came up later. He had learnt to explain and navigate his way through them, never having created any real trouble, but he never let these issues deter him from taking new initiatives.

Another interesting programme that was received very well by the audience in Madras was on sky watching. It was a borrowed idea, as a Science Officer in Ahmedabad was already doing such a show on new moon nights, when the stars were more clearly visible. It was called Akash Darshan. Sridharan attempted something similar in Tamil and named the show Vinmeen Arimugam (An Introduction to the Stars).

On the day of broadcast there were constant reminders on radio through the day asking listeners to go up the terrace of their homes with their transistors at a specific time at night. During the programme an expert stationed at the AIR terrace would help the listeners locate the stars and constellations in the sky and know them better. As they heard the programme the listeners could learn more about the night sky as they were watching it.

Listeners were also given friendly reminders to lock the front and back doors of their homes before going to the terrace, as anybody could enter their houses while they were busy watching the stars. Listeners loved these reminders and were hooked on to their radio sets with rapture.

Next, Sridharan took upon himself to a do a special programme on HAM or amateur radio users in the city. He intended to have a moderated HAM discussion on radio. However interesting it could be, there were also dangers that someone could interrupt and say something during the live discussion that might not meet the broadcast standards. Even the LTTE were known to be using HAM network in those days. Sridharan had his own fears but he decided to go ahead and do the show nevertheless. With some clever thinking he approached, Mr. Deodhar, who was then the Wireless Adviser to the Government of India and invited him to moderate the discussion on the show. When he agreed, Sridharan shared with him his fears and doubts that something might go wrong during such a live programme. Mr. Deodhar was more confident and said there should not be much trouble.

Sridharan had one more desire. He wanted the then Prime Minister Mr. Rajiv Gandhi to speak and give a message to the listeners on the show, as he was also an avid user of HAM radio. Sridharan considered all possible ways to approach the Prime Minister for his recorded message on HAM Radio. Approaching through his seniors, crossing many levels of approval and explanations could have taken endless time. Instead, he got in touch with the secretary of the Madras amateur radio operators, Mr. Mahalingam and requested him to ensure that the communication reached the Prime Minister at the earliest and requested for a voice message from him, for the special show on HAM network.

The day of broadcast arrived, but Sridharan had not received any message from the Prime Minister's office. So the live show went on without the Prime Minister's message. Though the show went well, Sridharan still wondered about the lack of response from the PM's office. Only the previous evening the Delhi AIR office had received an envelope from the PM's office. But unaware of its urgency, the duty officer had left it unopened until the Delhi AIR review meeting the next day. So, just a few hours after his live broadcast, Sridharan learnt that the Prime Minister's office had responded to his request. The envelope had a neatly typed message from the Prime Minister on HAM Radio. There was also a note included that the Prime Minister could not send a voice message owing to his busy schedule.

Though he got to know of it somewhat late, Sridharan was glad to receive a response from the PM's office. He included the Prime Minister's message as a part of the edited version of the same programme, broadcast on the national hook up the same night. Many newspapers highlighted the PM's message in the show in their articles the following day.

In 1986, Sridharan was producing a national programme on 'Light House' to be broadcast in Hindi by AIR Delhi. He visited many lighthouses in India including the one at Point Calimere (Kodiakkarai) in Tamil Nadu for the project. During his travel in and around Vedaranyam and Nagapattinam areas of Tamil Nadu, he saw many members of groups who were fighting for the cause of Eelam. He also had a chance meeting with LTTE supremo Prabhakaran and another leader Sabaratnam of the same group while having lunch at a wayside restaurant.

Halley's Comet 1986

Sridharan also used science programmes to dispel myths and superstitions. When Halley's Comet approached close to the earth in 1986, there were rumours that watching it would bring bad luck or damage the eyes. There was also a belief that a comet appearing in the sky is not a good sign and particularly dangerous for the king or the ruler of a nation.

Sridharan visited the Astronomical Observatory in Kavalur in Vellore district and watched the comet live through a telescope. He also covered his personal experience of watching the comet for the special show on Halley's Comet on AIR. Sridharan had also written a Tamil book on the Halley's Comet. It had a foreword written by Dr. V.C. Kulandaiswamy and the introduction written by the famous astronomer Sivaraman of the Indian Institute of Astrophysics, Bangalore.

It was during this time that the Prime Minister Rajiv Gandhi was inaugurating Asia's largest telescope in Kavalur Observatory in North Arcot District of Tamil Nadu and Sridharan was deputed to do the coverage for AIR. He remembers that Mr. Rajiv Gandhi attended the event with his in-laws from Italy and Mr. Mani Shankar Iyer who was the Joint Secretary to the PM, and Prof. M.G.K. Menon accompanied him.

At the inaugural function, the Prime Minister spoke very briefly. There was nothing interesting in it for broadcast, Sridharan felt. During a conversation, Prof. M.G.K. Menon mentioned to Sridharan that the PM was planning to have a look through the telescope later and that Sridharan could also come but without any recording equipment. Sridharan was glad to join them and he also informed the cameraman from Doordarshan about the PM's impending visit.

This is how he recollects what happened next.

"The security guards at the Observatory did not know about the PM's visit and many of them were resting under the telescope building. Suddenly they were asked to clear the place, and Mr. Rajiv Gandhi walked in with his brother in-law. And I also went behind Prof. M.G.K. Menon. Rajiv being a pilot, went up the ladder very fast and had a look at the sky through the telescope. He then was coming down on the ladder and the cameraman, whose name I forget now—switched on the lights and asked him three questions. The main one was about the PM's feeling of watching the sky through a telescope. Though Mr. Rajiv Gandhi started to answer him casually, Prof. Menon and Mr. Mani Shankar Iyer felt that the interview inappropriate as it was not on the agenda and asked the DD cameraman to switch off. The cameraman was happy that he had exclusive recordings of the PM and rushed to Madras with it. The next morning it was telecast as an exclusive interview on DD."

"Later when Mr. Rajiv Gandhi was flying back to New Delhi, he was accompanied by Mr. Cho Ramaswamy, the famous political commentator and editor of the *Tamil magazine Thuglak*. The Prime Minister was giving him an exclusive interview when Mr. Cho asked the PM why he gave such amateurish answers to DD and why did DD telecast the same? All these were in the papers the next day. And the DD staff member later found himself a better job in Delhi", he recounts.

Sridharan also thought of doing a 'live' Akash Darshan (Vinmeen Arimugam) programme from the Kavalur Observatory in the early hours of the day (around 4 am) and wanted the listeners to come out of their homes with their radio sets and watch the comet. This would help change the superstitions associated with it, he thought. "The Director of AIR Madras then, Mr. Subrahmanyan being a traditional Hindu, did not like the idea. but he did not stop me from pursuing it", he recalls. So, as planned Sridharan went to the Observatory with a team a day before the broadcast. The Posts & Telegraph Department made special efforts to provide AIR with leased lines for the broadcast. But as soon as the AIR team alighted from their vehicle and removed their equipment, the hand brakes of the vehicle failed, and the new AIR van simply rolled down the road. Whether it was a coincidence or an accident, no one knew, but it did seem unfortunate. Sridharan was worried about the cost of repair for the vehicle and what the Director would say. The next day the programme was broadcast live as planned and AIR asked listeners three simple questions on the comet. If they answered them right, it was announced that 12 among them could get an opportunity to watch the comet through the telescope at Kavalur. Within the next three days, AIR Madras saw sack loads of letters from listeners. The Director was very impressed and the cost of the vehicle repair was no longer a concern. They wondered how to select 12 people from the thousands of letters received. Sridharan suggested that the Director could pick 12 letters from the lot in the presence of a TV camera. Though it was an unscientific method, it was the quickest way to decide on the 12 candidates and plan their visit to the observatory before the comet vanished. Overall Sridharan felt fortunate that the comet gave him scope for his many programming initiatives.

Science Sammelan at Thanjavur

Another myth Sridharan wanted to dispel was during the

the third Science Sammelan at Thanjavur in 1983. Unlike the other two science sammelans, this one did not go as planned. Sridharan intended to conduct the science exhibition in the huge and historic Palace Grounds, in Thanjavur. But many local people advised him against it.

'Whenever we organize a programme there, there is always some fire accident that happens. It seems unavoidable, they said. So sentimentally, they were not in favour of going with Sridharan's choice of venue. But Sridharan did not want to buy their explanations and chose to be practical. He could not see why fire accidents should be linked with the venue or event and decided to go ahead with his plans anyway, but with the necessary precautions. He approached the Director Fire Service, Tamil Nadu Government, Mr. Bhaskara and arranged for two fire engines to be stationed at the venue, to be prepared to handle any unexpected emergency. The main fire station in the city was also located right opposite the palace grounds.

Initially, there was an issue pertaining to the invitations printed for the event. The invitations were in three languages—Tamil, English and Hindi and questions were raised on why Hindi should be included at all. The event was jointly organized by the Tamil University and the Founder Vice-Chancellor Prof. V.I. Subramaniam was a man of vision. When the syndicate members raised the issue, the VC tackled it smartly by saying that the Tamil University's goal was to develop Tamil, but not oppose any other language. The invitations were printed by AIR and the Tamil content appeared in front. By having the invite in three languages, the other universities in India could also get to know about the happenings at Tamil University, he explained.

Everything else seemed to flow smoothly and the event got off to a good start. On the third day, however, when a special poetry session on science was going on in the arena, unexpectedly two stalls at a distance caught fire. People started running and there was panic. The fire engines stationed in the campus had a starting problem and people had to push them to get them started. The fire was then extinguished in less than five minutes and though no lives were lost and no one was injured, the two stalls which belonged to BHEL and the Directorate of Health got completely burnt. The district collector arrived at the venue and preliminary enquiries were ordered. But once the fire and the initial panic was settled, within an hour the poetry session at the arena resumed.

Many fingers were pointed at Sridharan and he was questioned for his choice of venue. There were also rumours that he was about to lose his job. But he let none of them dissuade him and decided to continue the Science Sammelan for seven full days as planned. The Vice-Chancellor of Tamil University also intended to continue the exhibition and ensured that the exhibits were back in place just the next day. Sridharan had shared the news of the fire accident with the AIR news team, and once it was broadcast, many visitors thronged the site to see the place of fire accident and the damage caused.

The local press, though it did not bother to give much coverage to the Science Sammelan event, gave great importance to the fire accident. *The Hindu* came out with a news article highlighting that there was about two crores loss at the AIR exhibition. When Sridharan realized that the response of local media was not too warm, he decided to promote the event on the national media. He had a quick idea and contacted Mr. T.G. Nallamuthu, of Press Information Bureau and asked him to organize a National Press Team visit to the Sammelan. He talked to Mr. V.R. Deenadayalu, Chairman of Madras Refineries and requested him to sponsor the press tour. Madras Refineries had put up a futuristic stall in the exhibition, wanting to promote themselves as an energy company rather than a petroleum company. They had set up a 'model village' in the exhibition that used only non-conventional sources of energy like solar and wind power for its energy requirements. They even harnessed energy from the human waste that was generated during the Sammelan. It was a very progressive attempt at that time and they also agreed to sponsor the national press team's visit. Consequently, the event received adequate press coverage across the national media.

Sridharan had invited Dr. A.P.J. Abdul Kalam to preside over the valedictory session at the Science Sammelan, but he could not attend due to prior commitments. Sridharan had also invited Dr. V.C. Kulandaiswamy, the Vice-Chancellor of Anna University to be the chief guest of the event. Sridharan had come to Madras on a Saturday night to attend his cousins' wedding and was at the airport to take a plane back to Trichy and then travel to Thanjavur by road. His plan was to accompany Dr. Kulandaiswamy in the same plane to Trichy. At Madras Airport they both ran into Dr. A.P.J. Abdul Kalam, who was waiting to board a flight to Bombay. On seeing Sridharan, Dr. Kalam enquired about the damage caused by the fire accident and asked if it was a total wreck, as reported in the papers. Before even Sridharan could respond, Dr. Kulandaiswamy replied to Dr. Kalam, and said that 'if it had been a total wreck, Sridharan would not be taking me with him to Thanjavur right now. The press has overplayed the damage...'

Three months after the event, the Director of Health Services, Tamil Nadu Government, whose stall had burned down at the Sammelan, filed a case against AIR claiming damages for the loss suffered by his department due to the fire accident. Sridharan met Vice-Chancellor V.I. Subramaniam of Tamil University who happened to be in Madras on that day. "The VC lifted the phone and talked to the then CM, Mr. M.G. Ramachandran and suggested that whoever is authorized should write off the costs. The matter got settled with that one phone call," he recalls.

Sridharan went on to organize two more Science Sammelans in the capacity of Science Officer AIR. The fourth Science Sammelan was held at the IIT Vanavani School in Madras in 1984. And the fifth one was at Tirunelveli in 1986 in association with the Science Centre. This time the highlight of the event was a lecture by eminent violinist, Kunnakudi Vaidyanathan, who scientifically interpreted and explained the sounds of a violin. The lecture was greatly appreciated and so was the Science Sammelan. In 1987, Sridharan joined the Department of Science and Technology, New Delhi and in his new capacity, financially supported the sixth Science Sammelan that was held in the Madurai Kamaraj University in Madurai. The last edition of Science Sammelan was held in 1988 at Madras Refineries Limited.

3

Courting Science, Spirituality and Controversies

Sridharan prided himself on being a man of science. But he was a man of faith too. Being born in an orthodox Hindu family, Sridharan was initiated to hymns and prayers at an early age. As an adult, he never displayed much devotion and did not make much of the rituals. But, he always kept images of Lord Balaji with him, for good fortune. Two things that Sridharan did during the early 1980s deviated from his usually scientific demeanour. One, he built a temple for Lord Ganesha and the other was changing his name.

In 1981, when Sridharan was quite stable in his career and family life, his mother advised him to build a home for himself, to settle in. He bought a piece of land from his cousin, Raghuraman, who grew up with him in his early school days. Raghuraman parted with his piece of land and gave it to Sridharan's father to build the new house, without even demanding the market rates.

There was a small shrine of Lord Ganesha (which according to the residents was an abandoned piece/idol) right opposite to the house. The shrine was quite popular, but there was some bias. Though the shrine was located in a common area plot, a certain group of people, who mainly worshipped Lord Rama, had taken ownership of the land and used to organize Ram Navami and other music festivals there. The festival of Ram Navami was celebrated with much fanfare and saw eminent artistes perform. Many prominent Carnatic music artistes like M.P.N. Sethuraman and M.P.N. Ponnuswamy (Nadaswaram),

Sulamangalam Sisters, Sikkil Sisters' flute, Mandolin Srinivas, and vocalist Madurai Somasundram participated in the festival and performed. The celebrations lasted for 45 days, during which the front gates of the Ganesha shrine were kept covered with a black cloth or simply shut off for outsiders. Though the shrine was famous, a small section of ardent Ganesha worshippers in the community were a wounded group, as the shrine was out of their control and access.

Sridharan was a staunch believer of social and religious harmony and he did not appreciate the fact that, only festivals belonging to a particular sect were celebrated in the shrine and not others. 'Let them do their Ram Navami, I will do my Ganesh Chaturthi celebrations there', he decided.

And as an offering to the deity, who was also his neighbour, as the shrine was right opposite his house, Sridharan decided to organize a huge celebration for Ganesh Chaturthi. He began to make arrangements. On a personal note, he invited Mr. P. Murari IAS, who was then the Chairman of the Tamil Nadu Electricity Board and later became the Secretary to the President of India, to preside over the Ganesh Chaturthi celebrations. And as a positive fallout, when the local employees of the electricity board learnt that the Chairman was attending the event, they put their best efforts to restore the electrical connections in the area. The famous performer of folk music, Villupattu, Mr. Subbu Arumugam performed during the celebrations. In fact the whole function was organized with just about Rs. 400, out of which Rs. 200 was spent to arrange for the artistes. Everyone from the neighbourhood contributed by lending a bench, or a tube light and everyone including the Chairman and the artistes sat on these benches. When Mr. Subbu Arumugam addressed the gathering at the celebrations, he expressed his desire that, the head of Kanchi Mutt—Shankaracharya, more popularly known as the Kanchi Periyava, should visit the shrine and give it a name.

Later, Sridharan took it upon himself, the task of building a bigger temple around the shrine and he got into talks with a temple architect from Thanjavur, who promised to complete the construction in 18 weeks at a cost of Rs.18,000 as his fees. Meanwhile he got busy in his coverage of the Asian Games held in Delhi and the construction work had to wait for him to be back.

In the meanwhile, when Sridharan was away covering the Asian Games, the head of Kanchi Mutt- Shankaracharya, the late Jayendra Saraswati visited the Ganesha shrine and gave it a name—the shrine of 'Ashta Siddhi Vinayakar'. Sridharan never got to know who invited him to the temple. He only knew that the temple was located on Shankaracharya's way to Kanchipuram from Madras. The mutt leader had been on a padayatra, or a journey on foot for a very long time and was returning to Kanchipuram via Madras. Recollecting the incident, he interestingly notes how the religious leaders in the country shifted to helicopter travel from pada yatra within a decade's time.

When he came back from Delhi, Sridharan decided to do all he could to raise funds for the construction of the temple. He was advised by some members of the other group who maintained the temple, to organize a ritual called Koti-Archana that would help him raise a crore of rupees. It was a trap Sridharan fell into. He performed the ritual and found that organizing the ritual cost more money than it generated. The donations were meagre. He now had to think of his own ways to raise donations. He went ahead and requested the Health Minister of Tamil Nadu, Dr. H.V. Hande and the Speaker of the Tamil Nadu Assembly, Mr. Munu Adhi, to arrange for a free medical camp near the temple area, as it would serve a good cause and increase the visibility of the temple, thus helping to raise donations. A free medical camp was organized by Dr. Arumugam, the Dean. Professors and students of Madras Medical College participated in it and around 5,000 people were benefited through it.

Sridharan finally got to meet the head of Kanchi Mutt-Shankaracharya when he was in Madras for a programme. He spoke to him personally and informed him about the lack of funds to build the temple. The Shankaracharya interrupted him midway and told him to schedule the temple consecration or the Kumbabishekam ceremony on 18th August. Sridharan was intrigued with the response. On one hand he was not getting any money to build the temple and on the other hand, the pontiff head even fixed a date for the Kumbabishekam. Every Friday evening, Sridharan's team used to go out collecting donations from people in various markets and colonies. The collection did not amount to much. Many businessmen used to take empty receipts from the team and gave them Rs. 5 or Rs. 10 for donation. No one knows what amounts they filled up in those receipts for their tax saving purposes. Meanwhile the cost to construct the temple also escalated. Rs. 18,000 was just the fee for the architect, and the material and other labour cost much more. He was left with no choice but to borrow money and take up the costs by himself, if he wished to get the temple ready for consecration by the date given by the Shankaracharya. He went ahead and did just that. He borrowed money from a few affluent contacts at an interest rate of 12 per cent and went ahead with the construction plan. Some of them were generous to convert some amount of that loan into donations.

The Kumbabishekam was a grand ceremony, conducted by an eminent priest from the famous Kalikambal temple in Madras. The ceremony was covered live by a popular anchor, Koothapiran, for broadcast on AIR. On the same day Sridharan decided to hand over the temple to the Tamil Nadu Government's Hindu Religious and Charitable Endowments (HR CE) Department for operations and maintenance. He got the petition signed by about 80 residents in the area and submitted it to the department and the request was accepted. The Commissioner HRCE Department had told him that they did not take control of temples unless the public money involved was of the order of a few crores of rupees. But still, with his AIR background, Sridharan could convince him. On the Kumbabishekam day the Deputy Commissioner, HRCE Department, was deputed to officially take over the temple.

Using his contacts with the General Manager of Madras

Telephones, Sridharan installed a pay phone booth in the temple premises, at a time when telephones were a rarity. The General Manager of Madras Telephones was kind enough to personally inaugurate the same. The telephone booth served the people of that locality for about 10 years and also brought some revenue to the temple. It took Sridharan two years to pay back all the loans he took to construct the temple.

The temple was later expanded with the installation of Navagrahas (a shrine for the nine planets), and the donation for it came mainly from a fisherman from Ponneri. Later to serve the North Indian population in the locality, especially the families of those working in the nearby Indian Air Force campus and the Madras Christian College, Sridharan convinced the temple committee to install a Radha-Krishna idol made of sandstone in the premises, "a poor replica of the Birla Mandir idol, if one could call it so. Here the devotees could go near the idol, touch the feet and do aarti themselves, just like in the North Indian temples. In fact Ikram Rajasthani, a Muslim working with AIR Jaipur had helped us to source the Radha-Krishna idol," he reminisces.

The temple, to this day, draws several visitors and devotees from all sections of the society. But the groupism still continues, he says. "The other group had later built a Ram temple in the premises and wanted to bifurcate the land. One fine morning they created a separate entrance for the Ram temple. The government got annoyed and went to the High Court which asked them to close the gate stating that there could be only one entrance to the temple," he recollects.

He was successfully able to fulfil his mother's wish of building a temple premise at the Ganesha shrine. That gave him much satisfaction. Also another blessing that marked the year 1983 for him was the birth of his second child, another daughter, Gayathri.

Change in Name, Change in Fortune?

It had been about six years since he joined AIR and things were going well for him. It was around this time that Sridharan's parents had visited a popular astrologer Bala Josier, who in those days was featured in a popular Tamil weekly. He had suggested that Sridharan change his name to Sreedher for better prospects in life. Though Sridharan was a headstrong man, he was not exactly a rebel. He did not think, analyse or question much, and simply agreed to go ahead with the name change. He changed his name formally in the documents, placed ads in newspapers, and paid the fee to Tamil Nadu Gazette and Indian Gazette to publish his new name. He was now Dr. R. Sreedher. Whether due to the name change or not, but better prospects did await him in the years to come. Most of his colleagues and acquaintances, whom he met after he moved to New Delhi for work, know him and relate to him by this name. Hence, from here on in this narrative, we will refer to him as Dr. Sreedher, the name he is popularly known by.

The First Trip Abroad (US 1985)

A new National Council for Science and Technology Communication had been created in Delhi and they were organizing a workshop on science communication that Dr. Sreedher intended to attend. But AIR was not sending any participants to the programme, so he tried applying in the capacity of Secretary, Madras Science Association and got through. Only 25 members from across India were chosen to be part of the workshop. Dr. Narender Sehgal, who headed the team, was a well experienced man, who later went on to win the UNESCO's Kalinga Award for popularization of science. Dr. Gauhar Raza, a famous science communicator was also one of the trainees along with Dr. Sreedher.

When as a part of the workshop, they discussed the various possibilities of science programming in the country, Dr. Narender Sehgal was surprised to hear about the many science initiatives taken at AIR by Dr. Sreedher. 'With all your experience and skills, you should be one of the trainers in this workshop, not a participant ', he told Dr. Sreedher. He also advised Dr. Sreedher to apply for the post of Principal Science Officer in his team at NCSTC. There was also another opportunity, under the Indo-American Sub-Commission on Education and Culture, which allowed Indian radio professionals to visit the radio stations in the US and observe and learn from their functioning and models. Dr. Sreedher was chosen for that too.

Suddenly, there was so much to do and look forward to and in the middle of it all, he developed a few complications with his health and was advised to undergo surgery. He planned his time such that he did not have to miss any of his opportunities or his surgery.

When he reached the US in September 1985, he was received at the Washington airport by Jeff Rosenberg an American from the National Public Radio and a member of the Indo-US Sub-Commission. Jeff Rosenberg took Dr. Sreedher to the hotel accommodation arranged for him. When Dr. Sreedher saw the very small, cramped room that was allotted to him, he declined to stay there and insisted on being taken to a better room and a better hotel. 'Indian visitors usually stay here,' Jeff Rosenberg tried telling him. He later took Dr. Sreedher to his home instead, saying he could stay there for a night and some other arrangement could be made the next day. At home, he introduced Dr. Sreedher to his wife Mrs. Alison Rosenberg (who was working in the State Department of the Government of USA) as an Indian and a vegetarian. The next day Dr. Sreedher went to the Indian Embassy, where he was received warmly and was also handed money and approval to stay at a star hotel.

His first US visit was a very enriching experience. His stay was supposed to be for three weeks, which was later extended to four weeks officially. He visited many interesting places like Washington DC, New York, Florida, Chicago, Los Angeles, San Francisco, San Diego, Pittsburgh, and more. He even got to see and experience, a space shuttle launch for the very first time at NASA. He also got an opportunity to meet and interview the otherwise media shy, Nobel laureate scientist Dr. Chandrashekar. It took a lot of convincing, to make him agree for an interview, says Dr. Sreedher. He still considers his interaction with Dr. Chandrasekhar to be one of the best radio interviews of his career. He also met and interviewed other established names in the field of science and technology like Mr. Sam Pitroda, during his stay in the US.

His visit to the National Public Radio was an eye opener in itself. It is truly something the nation can to be proud of, reckons Dr. Sreedher. The way, the stations approached people for funds, by promising content that would appeal and be relevant to them and people coming forward to contribute to the stations' establishment and operational costs, the endless possibilities of radio and the faith that people had in the medium, inspired Dr. Sreedher. He also found Mr. Jeff Rosenberg to be a committed radio professional and continues his association with him till today.

Another important experience during his stay in the US was his tryst with computers. Though this was the first time he was being exposed to working with computers, he picked up the skills almost instantly. Those 28 days of exposure to computers gave him an additional expertise that later helped him in leading the computerization initiatives in AIR and DD offices.

During his last few days of stay at the US, he got a call from the Director General of AIR. He was given the assignment to cover the 'Festival of Indian Films' held as part of Festival of India that was then taking place in New York. The then Prime Minister Rajiv Gandhi was also in New York to take part in the festival. Veteran Bollywood actor Raj Kapoor was also present. Dr. Sreedher was delighted at the opportunity and did an impressive coverage of the festival. While covering the festival, he had the opportunity of staying in Tata Lexington, a hotel which then belonged to the TATAs along with other eminent guests like Raj Kapoor. Prime Minister Rajiv Gandhi stayed in Hotel Astoria, right opposite to their hotel, he remembers.

Dr. Sreedher had to go to Delhi for debriefing before finally returning to Madras after his US visit. He was to take a train from New Delhi to Madras. He called his mother from

New Delhi to learn that in his absence, his brother had gone to Arunachal Pradesh in the capacity of an officer with SBI, on a rural mission. After reaching he had sent a telegram home, which read 'Sick in Pasighat'. His mother got worried and shared this with Dr. Sreedher. There was no direct telephone to reach his brother. Dr. Sreedher took a flight and hurried home. From Madras, he got in touch with Major Loganathan, PRO of the Ministry of Defence and explained the situation. He in turn contacted the Army officials at Jorhat and they had asked for 24 hours' time to get an update on his brother. After talking to the collector, they called back to report that his brother was safe. The problem was that the telegram, instead of saying 'Back in Pasighat' got delivered as 'Sick in Pasighat' and hence all the confusion.

While he was away in the USA, his regular programmes with the AIR Madras were taken care of by other freelancers who were called casuals in those days. Dr. Sreedher remembers that he was really impressed with the work put together by the team—Indumathy, Rukmani, Lakshmi, Hema, Gurumurthy, Govindaraju, Selva Raj, Athiyaman, Jeyashree, Karunanidhi, and Sangeetha in his absence.

It was customary that after his return, he should submit a report to his seniors at AIR, sharing his experiences and learnings during his visit to the USA. There were two key points he mentioned in his report. One was the computerization of data in media organizations, which helped them work faster and more efficiently and that it would be great to have computers at the AIR as well. Secondly, he also mentioned the way FM radio channels were being used in the best possible way. He expressed his concern that the technology of FM though available in India was barely being put to use and a number of stale reasons were being offered for the same. He noted how more localized content and utilities could be shared effectively through the medium and how it was ideal for broadcasting creative and musical programmes with good sound quality.

Response to Natural Disasters

While in the US, Dr. Sreedher also got an opportunity to experience how the American people and media responded to natural phenomena like cyclones, for example. One day, he heard Mr. Jeff Rosenberg (who was taking care of him while he was in the US) saying, "she is coming...she is coming..."

Dr. Sreedher: "Who is coming?"

Mr. Jeff: "Gloria!"

Dr. Sreedher: "Gloria who?"

Mr. Jeff: "A cyclone. Looks like it will hit us pretty soon. We need to get you an umbrella! "

He took Dr. Sreedher to a shop selling umbrellas.

It was interesting to note that the umbrellas which were usually priced at 5 dollars were being sold for 3 dollars only. Owing to the great demand for umbrellas during rains and cyclones, the shopkeeper had reduced the price.

Dr. Sreedher adds how Madras was also hit by a cyclone the very next year and he tried to apply the techniques he learnt at the NPR at AIR Madras. He also recalls a incident , where his friend went to buy candles from a shop in Mylapore to be prepared for the power cuts during the cyclone. The candles that were usually sold for Rs. 5 were now being sold for Rs. 10. "Sir!. Haven't you heard the radio? Cyclone is coming… This is the time I can do some business," the shopkeeper had told the friend. His friend was Mannar Mannan, son of the famous poet Bharathidasan.

Dr. Sreedher could not help noticing the difference in attitude and approach of the people and the way media and businesses were run. There was a lot to learn and unlearn about the way we do things, he thought.

Another important lesson Dr. Sreedher learnt during his tenure as Science Officer in Madras was dealing with criticism and critics. Critics can be very annoying, especially at times when their point rings of truth. Dr. Sreedher recalls an incident in the 1980s, when a cyclone had hit Madras badly and as a result the AIR transmissions were interrupted. Essential news and information like weather reports and emergency announcements could not be aired. The next morning, in an article in *The Hindu* daily, neurologist Mr. B. Ramamurthy, criticized AIR for its non-performance during the critical situation. He remarked in the article that, even if AIR did not have the twentieth century equipment, at least it was expected to have used nineteenth century technology to tackle such situations.

The bitter truth in the criticism stung Dr. Sreedher badly and he ensured this was not repeated. He always ensured that whenever heavy rainfalls or cyclones were predicted in the city, a standby police wireless tower was installed in the premises with permissions, to ensure uninterrupted broadcast.

Dr. Sreedher was later involved in organizing the Indo-US Workshop on Science Broadcasting, wherein experts from the USA and all Science Officers from AIR stations across India were to meet and discuss Science Broadcasting. Dr. Sreedher was given the responsibility to make all the arrangements for their stay and training in India. Mr. Jeff Rosenberg, who had hosted Dr. Sreedher in the US, was to head the team of American professionals visiting India and he expressed his wish to stay and get trained from Bangalore rather than Madras. He wanted the stay to be arranged with the Taj Group of hotels. So when Dr. Sreedher met the Director General of AIR, to discuss the arrangements, he requested him that if the foreign delegates who come for the training stay at a Star hotel in Bangalore, he wanted the same for the Indian officials too. The Director General told him that government officials were not allowed to stay in five star hotels. He did not want officers from India to be treated any differently from the Americans, Dr. Sreedher explained. The Director General then advised him to use his discretion and proceed with his plans, but within the limitations of the rules and approved budget. Dr. Sreedher got talking with the management of the Taj West End in Bangalore and got a deal with no extra expenses incurred for the stay of his team members from various parts of India. He ensured that the science officers and other officials from

AIR also stayed at the same five star hotel, only that they had to share rooms and could not claim any allowance thereafter.

All the twelve science officers Dr. Amit Chakraborthy from Kolkata, Mr. H.R. Krishnamurthy from Bangalore, Mr. Paresh Mankad from Ahmedabad, Mr. Jayant Erande from Mumbai, Dr. Gopalam from Hyderabad, Mr. Jayalal from Thriuvanathapuram, Mr. H.K. Pani from Cuttack, Ms. Aparna Vaish from Jaipur, Ms. Deepa Chandra from Bhopal and others dealing with Science programmes at AIR Delhi and Lucknow, namely Ms. Neelima Harjal and Dr. Satish Grover attended the workshop. Even though it was the forte of AIR Bangalore, it was left to Dr. Sreedher to coordinate the event. He did it exceedingly well with the support of AIR Bangalore.

Dr. Sreedher also invited neurologist Dr. B. Ramamurthy, as a special guest to the event, to share his thoughts on the topic 'science communication for the common man'. The Director General of AIR then was an IAS officer and a professional radio person was the Additional Director General. "The ADG Mr. Amrit Rao Shinde, who was not happy with the DG assigning the responsibility to handle the event to me, chose to write on his file that 'Dr. Sreedher does not reveal everything that happens between him and the American counterparts. It was customary in those days to blame everyone as agents of foreign intelligence agencies," says Dr. Sreedher. But due to exigencies when the DG, AIR could not attend the valedictory session of the training, Mr. Shinde met the delegates and gave away their certificates. This time he was very impressed with the way the delegates' visit was organized and his opinion on how the workshop was conducted changed.

Once he was back in Madras, as per the advice of Dr. Narender Sehgal, Dr. Sreedher applied for the post of Principal Science Officer with his team at NCSTC. He also applied for the post of Senior Scientific Officer Grade 1 in the same team, just in case the former did not click. But the latter clicked first and Dr. Sreedher joined as a Senior Scientific Officer with the National Council for Science and Technology Communication.

Before joining he ensured that the science programmes that

he had nurtured at AIR Madras were transferred to good and capable hands. Dr. Sreedher suggested Mr. Chandramurthy, who was handling educational broadcasts with AIR Madras, to take over the responsibility of the science programmes as well. Even though Mr. Chandramurthy was appointed specifically for Education, Dr. Sreedher's request was accepted by the Station Director in the interest of the station.

On February 11, 1987, Dr. Sreedher took up his new responsibility in Delhi. Dr. Narender Sehgal had by that time joined as Director, Department of Science and Technology. When Dr. Sreedher met him in Delhi,he advised Dr. Sreedher to always think big and reminded him that any project that he designed must have national footprints. Soon after his joining, the team at NCSTC had begun work on a plan to celebrate 'National Science Day' every year for the promotion of 'science popularization' initiatives in the country.

Concerning institution of the National Science Day, Dr. Narender Sehgal recalls, "It started with a postcard from a citizen, which was received even before the first meeting of the NCST Council took place some time in February 1984. In the postcard, it was suggested that, just like Teachers' Day, Childrens' Day, etc, a day should be instituted for scientists. At the time, I had a Senior Scientific Officer grade-I and one Scientific Assistant on my staff, in addition to a PA. It was only after the first meeting of the NCSTC, that we started thinking in terms of actualizing some programmes. In due course, some time in 1985 or early 1986, I moved a proposal to institute November 7 as the National Science Day. (It was C.V. Raman's birthday).This was rejected by PM, Rajiv Gandhi, because, according to him, there already were several days in November marked for celebrations, like Children's Day on 14th November, Indira Gandhi's birthday on 19th November, Child Rights Day on 20th November, and so on. So, after some research, 28th February was proposed for institution as the National Science Day, coinciding with Sir C.V. Raman's discovery of the 'Raman Effect' in 1928. This proposal was accepted and the rest, as they say, is history."

The team at NCSTC had then to plan the event and publicity in great haste as the event was now just a few days away. The then government took very innovative and encouraging initiatives to promote science awareness in the country, recalls Dr. Sreedher. "Five awards in different categories pertaining to science popularization were to be announced on National Science Day. Another initiative that was very well received was the announcement that, the central government would reimburse 50 per cent of the expenses incurred for any initiative or celebration marking the National Science Day in the country," he adds.

The response to these announcements was huge. The main event for National Science Day was organized at the India International Centre in New Delhi, with the then HRD Minister Mr. P.V. Narasimha Rao as the chief guest. This was Dr. Sreedher's first assignment at NCSTC.

When the then Vice-Chancellor of Madurai Kamaraj University, Prof. S. Krishnaswamy, approached Dr. Sreedher for ideas on initiatives pertaining to the celebration of National Science Day, Dr. Sreedher advised him to start a new BSc course in Science Communication in his University and that the central government would support the initiative. The Vice-Chancellor liked the idea and he set up a team under Dr. Shantha Arunachalam, to work on the proposal for the new course. Meanwhile, in the middle of it all, the Vice-Chancellor suddenly died. The university however submitted a detailed proposal, without the signature of the Vice-Chancellor. Dr. Sreedher then took the unsigned proposal on file and the project was processed for funding. The new course was then successfully started at Madurai Kamaraj University. Prof. Shantha Arunachalam from the University took up the responsibility of shaping and managing the BSc Science Communication Course and carried it on for many years.

Dr. Narender Sehgal took notice of how eager and enthusiastic Dr. Sreedher was with his work and asked him what he would like to work with next. Dr. Sreedher was quick to express his interest in working with computers. 'When other countries are getting the benefit of technology, why should we stay behind?' Dr. Sreedher had suggested. Dr. Sehgal agreed and ordered a word processor for the team and advised Dr. Sreedher to learn to operate it by himself.

Another major initiative that Dr. Sreedher was involved in, while at NCSTC was Bharat Jan Vigyan Jatha –a nationwide initiative to popularize science and encourage people to pursue a scientific attitude. Five buses from five different parts of the country—Srinagar, Aizawl, Calcutta, Sholapur and Madras—started their journey across the length and breadth of the country, touching various people and villages, spreading science awareness messages. Science teachers on these vans would interact with the people, make presentations, screen films along with some traditional art forms all along the journey. The journey began on October 2, in 1987, marking Gandhi Jayanti and all the convoys were to converge at Bhopal on November 7, 1987, which marked the birthday of Sir C.V. Raman.

"Though the project was interesting and done on a massive scale, I felt uneasy when some political messages were also being spread on the pretext of science. Later I also ended up with the responsibility to generate a report on the event, and I remember having to do nothing short of a sting operation, to find out the details from the on-ground events, as no details were shared with the NCSTC team," he says recalling the experience of working on the project. He could sense his discomfort working in such a situation and considered that moving back to his hometown would be a good idea, for both personal and professional reasons.

In December 1987, the whole of Tamil Nadu was in a state of frenzy, after the death of the State's Chief Minister M.G. Ramachandran. Dr. Sreedher was also in a sort of crisis as his mother had taken ill and was admitted to St. Isabel Hospital in Madras for a surgery. After the surgery, her stitches were removed on 25th December, the day the Chief Minister was to be buried. It was also a Christmas holiday. Unexpectedly his mother suffered a sudden complication that evening leading to a heart attack. She was taken to the emergency ward. To make things worse, there was no oxygen cylinder available at the hospital. Due to the crisis in the city, essential supplies like oxygen did not reach the hospital for two continuous days. They managed by manually pumping oxygen for the whole night and finally on the next day they managed to get the oxygen cylinders and the situation was brought under control. But those two days were nothing less than a nightmare for Dr. Sreedher, he recollects.

Once his mother was better, it was time for him to resume work. When he got back to Delhi, he learnt that there was going to be Direct Recruitments—lateral entry, for the post of Directors in 22 AIR and Doordarshan Stations across India. Dr. Sreedher applied for it. He awaited the call for interview, but it never came. He was sure he was an eligible candidate with the necessary skills and experience. In those days, UPSC (Union Public Service Commission) used to recruit officers for AIR and for the Department of Science and Technology. So, he approached Mr. Suresh Mathur, the Secretary of UPSC, who was earlier the Director General of All India Radio, and shared his disappointment at not being called for interview despite his eligibility for the post. He was later called for the interview which he cleared and stood second in rank among the 22 candidates selected for the post of Director. This gained him seniority over about 88 other Station Directors in AIR. Dr. Sreedher was ready to join AIR again by August 1988.

In 1988, while he was still at NCSTC, a Committee was constituted by NCSTC to suggest new communication initiatives for science popularization. An action plan was drawn up by this committee to make use of all kinds of electronic and non-electronic media, including radio, television and the print media. Dr. Sehgal in a communication to Dr. Sreedher recalled his earlier attempts of engaging AIR in joint initiatives—"Incidentally, I remember mentioning it to you (Sreedher) that, even before I came to know you, we had discussed the possibility of joint programmes with AIR. Our initial attempts were unsuccessful, as the person AIR had sent to represent them at our meetings had responded very negatively to the idea of joint programmes with NCSTC, at the time."

But this time following the plan drawn up by the committee, NCSTC decided to explore radio again and Dr. Sreedher was asked to write to the Director General of AIR, Mr. Amrit Rao Shinde from NCSTC on their offer for joint productions in science. This time things worked out positively and when a few days later Dr. Sreedher joined AIR, he was handed the same letter by Mr. Shinde and asked to write a reply on behalf of AIR. The first interactive multilingual science series with a captive audience, known as Vigyan Vidhi or Method of Science was born this way. The late Mr. Rangachar from AIR, though he had initially reacted negatively to joint programmes with NCSTC, later became a leading member of the Method of Science team and was a part of it till his unfortunate death in a road accident in 1992, recalls Dr. Sreedher.

Director, AIR 1988-1993

When he was selected as a Director for AIR, Dr. Sreedher had requested to be given a posting in Tamil Nadu. But the Director General of AIR insisted that his services were much needed in Delhi and made Dr. Sreedher the in-charge for educational broadcasts all over the country. When Dr. Sreedher tried telling him that he was more interested in science programming, he was offered the responsibility for both science and educational broadcasts. Incidentally, Dr. Sreedher was now working under the same Director General, who earlier as ADG had written a report on the workshop with US professionals, citing that 'Dr. Sreedher might have foreign connections'. A while after Dr. Sreedher joined AIR in Delhi, the Director General gave him the task of organizing an international workshop with media professionals from the US on 'weather forecasts on radio'. Dr. Sreedher did not hesitate to show him the old file and pointed out to the Director General, the negative comment he had made about him earlier during the international workshop with US delegates.

Nevertheless, this time the Director General expressed his faith in Dr. Sreedher and asked him to go ahead and plan the workshop. Dr. Sreedher later found the Director General to be very supportive and encouraging of his initiatives. He later enjoyed an excellent rapport with Mr. Shinde and remained in touch with him till his death.

Just the day before the international workshop on weather forecast, there was a daylight burglary at Dr. Sreedher's residence and many essential and precious items were stolen. He was then living in a government quarter in the Sarojini Nagar area. As police were searching the site and mapping evidence, the family had to wait outside in the cold Delhi winter, before the police let them back inside the house. Though it was a testing situation, Dr. Sreedher managed it and successfully planned the event for the next day in spite of the crisis at home.

Vigyan Vidhi

Dr. Sreedher knew that the role he had been assigned was a very significant one and approached it with complete dedication. In 1987, Dr. Sehgal launched a series called the Vigyan Vidhi or 'Method of Science' to impart the methods of science through radio to student listeners across the country in an easy entertaining manner. In this programme, scientific messages and concepts were conveyed in simple language through radio drama format. The programme was produced in all Indian languages separately while retaining the same scientific theme. This was done to ensure more effective communication and reach, so that the situations and language were appropriate to the local audience. The highlight of this initiative was that, at the beginning of the series the students were asked to write to the nearest AIR station expressing their interest in the science programme. Several letters came in and these students became registered listeners for the show. One month before the launch of the programme a colourful wall chart was prepared in all Indian languages and sent by post to these students who received them in their own mother tongue. It gave a preview of all the 13 episodes of the Vigyan Vidhi series. They were also sent another 'do-it-yourself' kit. All these correspondences went in covers containing the Government of India logo and the postman delivered them as mail to the students. The students were thrilled to receive the material and looked forward to the broadcasts. And thus, great listenership, participation and response were ensured for the programme even before it went on air.

The series went on to be a success story on air. "About 146,000 students from all over the country were registered for the broadcast in 14 languages. Tamil had the highest number of students with about 27,000 of them registered. Following the success of the programme, AIR created a new unit named CEPU (Central Educational Planning Unit) and it was decided to carry forward the project with different themes and different audiences", adds Dr. Sreedher recollecting the success of the series.

Radio DATE

Once, while Dr. Sreedher was travelling from Singapore to India with the AIR Director General, Mr. Amrit Rao Shinde, both saw two ladies who were a part of the Airline cabin crew, smoking at a distance. Mr. Amrit Rao shared his thoughts with Dr. Sreedher about starting a mass Anti-Smoking Drive on AIR. Mr. Shinde had been a chain smoker before he quit smoking. Dr. Sreedher got interested in the idea and he quickly came up with a proposal for Radio DATE (Drug, Alcohol, Tobacco Education), a real-time initiative on radio started jointly with the Indian Council for Medical Research. The famous medical scientist, Dr. A.S. Paintal was the chief of ICMR then.

At the beginning of the series, listeners were invited to share information about their smoking habits and what they thought of it, through postcards. Dr. Sreedher thought mostly smokers would not take part in such an initiative by writing to a radio station about their habit. But to everyone's surprise, many postcards did arrive, carrying stories of somebody smoking in the family or neighbourhood. More than one lakh responses were received from all over the country. Then a series of 26 programmes that were both entertaining and educating about the ill effects of alcohol and tobacco were broadcast on radio over a period of 26 weeks. There was not one direct message in any of these episodes asking listeners to quit smoking, but all messages were subtly and sometimes not so subtly incorporated in the script. The programmes had a good listenership and towards the end of the series, the listeners were asked if any of them really quit smoking after listening to the programmes. "3,600 postcards came answering in affirmative. Some 75 people wrote that they tried but couldn't," says Dr. Sreedher. The Indian Council for Medical Research sent their teams to the homes of these listeners in Bangalore and Calcutta to check if the listener response was true. Their research found most of it to be true. The data from the postcards sent by listeners was very revealing of the effectiveness of the radio as a medium in addressing social and health issues. The findings were shared at the WHO Conference in Geneva by the scientists of ICMR. Also, the DAVP (Directorate of Advertising and Visual Publicity) came out with a colourful publication of pictures (sketches) drawn by listeners depicting the difficulties faced by them because of smoking, drinking and drugs.

While organizing the press meet for Radio DATE, Dr. Sreedher met Mr. Biman Basu, the Editor of *Science Reporter* magazine. He was very critical of the project and expressed his views openly to Dr. Sreedher. Dr. Sreedher took his criticism in a positive sense. Through him he met Dr. Bal Phondke (G.P. Phondke), the former editor of *Science Today,* who later became the Director of the Publication Information Directorate of the CSIR (Council of Scientific and Industrial Relations). Dr. Sreedher felt the need to do a national series on Popular Science and wished to work in association with Dr. Phondke and Mr. Basu.

Dr. Narender Sehgal who visualized and funded the Vigyan Vidhi Serial wanted Dr. Sreedher to come up with a plan for mega-serials on science for children. Since it was to be funded 50-50 by AIR and DST, Dr. Sehgal was confident of managing the costs relating to creation of contents. Mr. Shinde who was about to retire soon, also wanted to do a major and worthwhile project in AIR, recalls Dr. Sreedher. So, when Dr. Sreedher pointed out that it might cost over Rs. 2 crores to produce and broadcast 144 episodes of a serial in 18 different languages, the answer from Mr. Shinde was "so what?" In those days the power of the Director General was only up to Rs. one lakh. But Dr. Sreedher came up with the idea of pre-informing the AIR stations to include the costs in their annual budgets, so that it could be approved easily. Also, the programme was spread over a period of three financial years and hence getting the approvals was not too difficult. A national level advisory committee was formed and Dr. Phondke and Mr. Basu were also made a part of it. Together they came up with what was the world's largest radio science serial for children—'Human Evolution'.

The Advisory Committee was headed by the Jnanpith Award winner and former Director of the Indian Institute of Advanced Study, Shimla, Dr. S.C. Dubey. It had neurologists, space scientists, environmental activists, biologists, geologists, mathematicians, physicists, chemists, archaeologists and anthropologists as members. Mr. Sujatha, the famous science fiction writer and Dr. Narendran, a neurologist from Madras were its notable members from the south. The members of the committee held meetings with the script writers and producers in different parts of the country, including Udaipur, New Delhi, Bombay, Pune, Shimla, Mahabalipuram, and Mirik near Darjeeling in West Bengal.

The Human Evolution (Maanudam Venrathu in Tamil) science series went on to capture the imagination of audiences countrywide. "It went on to be the longest running science radio serial for children in the world with 143 episodes of 20 minutes duration, broadcast simultaneously in 18 languages from all stations of AIR with 1,76,000 children registered as captive listeners. The serial was divided into eight segments of 13 episodes each. It was Mr. Biman Basu who, after many unsuccessful attempts by the advisory committee at a meeting in Pune, came up with segments and episode titles that were acceptable to all the members. Every line of the script for the serial was vetted for its accuracy by Dr. Phondke and Mr. Basu. The programme was recreated in each language and broadcast by AIR on Sunday mornings, just before the broadcast of the Ramayana and Mahabharata in Doordarshan. Though the series was a huge success story, most of the credit to it went to the regional producers of the series, who never bothered to acknowledge it as an adaptation of a national serial," says Dr. Sreedher.

Later in 1991, Dr. Sreedher and Dr. Phondke shared the NCSTC National Award for Science Popularization through media. Recalling how he earned that award, Dr. Sreedher says, "I was not a candidate for selection for the awards. In fact I had applied on behalf of my organization, AIR for the National Award. The committee which was then headed by Mr. Kiran Karnik is understood to have taken a decision that instead of awarding a government institution, it would be better to award the individual. So Mr. Kiran Karnik proposed my name for the award. When I came to know of the award in my name, I was afraid of talking about it to the Director General. But thanks to Mr. Karnik, as he himself spoke to Mr. Shinde and explained the rationale behind the award."

Later, Dr. Sreedher was also made a member of the prestigious Research Council of PID (Publications Information Directorate). Dr. Phondke tried to expand the scope of the institution and renamed it National Institute for Science Communication (NISCOM). Today the institution has merged with NISTADS (National Institute of Science, Technology and Development Studies, and is called NISCAIR (National Institute of Science Communication and Information Resources). "Dr. Phondke was very innovative in his thoughts and expected precision, perfection and punctuality in his endeavours... He had to overcome several challenges at work," recollects Dr. Sreedher. Mr. Biman Basu still remains a good friend of Dr. Sreedher's and in their association spanning three decades they have jointly worked on several national projects on science popularization and communication. During this time, Dr. Sreedher was also once again associated with Mr. Rangachar from AIR Madras, who had now come to head the Central Educational Planning Unit (CEPU).

Doordarshan (1993-1998)

In 1992, the Indian government announced an all-India service called the IB (P) S—Indian Broadcasting Programme Service with four sub-categories—radio management, radio production, television management, and television production. All the existing employees of broadcast media were asked to opt for any one of the streams, and Dr. Sreedher opted for television production. In about a year or so after that, he was assigned to television.

In the meanwhile, he had taken up a teaching role at the Staff Training Institute of AIR as it offered a 30 per cent hike in salary. But it did not take him too long to realize that he was not challenged enough in his new role. Teaching and training seemed to be a slowdown compared to being at the helm of action and getting things done in the media. Also for some reason the salary was reduced by 15 per cent. Dr. Sreedher then decided to move back to mainstream broadcast again and was posted for a while as Deputy Director Sports and Director, Farm and Home programmes respectively.

In about six months' time, the appointment order from Doordarshan arrived and he was posted as the Chief Producer at Doordarshan in 1993. He was hoping to get a posting in Tamil Nadu, but was posted instead at Mandi House, New Delhi and was given the responsibility of computerization of Doordarshan stations across the country. "People coming from AIR to Doordarshan were looked down upon and were not given any responsibility in the mainstream TV departments", says Dr. Sreedher.

At the Doordarshan Headquarters, he took upon himself the task of computerizing every division of DD including Films, News, Sponsored and Commissioned programmes,

Parliament questions, visitor entry, etc. He submitted a proposal to have a word processing network at Doordarshan named MANDINET (Management of Doordarshan Network) as the place where Doordarshan HQ was located was known as Mandi House.

In those days if any officer from a government organization wanted to purchase a PC, it had to be referred to the National Informatics Centre. They used to depute an official who first got convinced about the need for a computer at the office and then used to process the purchase. The reason being, officers sometimes demanded a PC simply because along with it came the luxury of air conditioners in their rooms. Hence, the deputed official was also given the responsibility to suggest a suitable place in the office, to set up the computer. This was a long-drawn process and Dr. Sreedher while working in DST found a simpler way to deal with it. It was suggested to him by a scientist in his department. He suggested to use the term 'word processor' in his proposals instead of 'computers', as then it would only be considered as an extension of the electronic typewriter or just another office equipment and it would not have to go through the extensive formalities of buying a computer through the NIC. Anyway, most of the PCs in the country till today are only used as a substitute to typewriters and no computing is ever being done through them, says Dr. Sreedher. Mr. Ratikant Basu in his capacity as DG had approved Dr. Sreedher's proposal for computerization and wanted the engineering wing to go in for purchases.

"Mr. V. Krishnamurthy from Infotel Software gave the least quotation and got the contract for developing custom-made software and DCM got the contract for hardware. Mr. Krishnamurthy employed some youngsters in his team and started interacting with the staff of Mandi House to develop software. He was also able to digitize all parliament questions and a system was developed in such a way that the questions were all answered digitally and reached the Ministry by electronic fax. The computerization of the film section, which I was given the responsibility to manage, was one of the most successful ones. Other sections did not cooperate well for obvious reasons. But Mr. Krishnamurthy also developed software for the vigilance section of DD. Through these efforts, I could get an overall view of the working of the entire DD network," says Dr. Sreedher.

A few months later, Dr. Sreedher was given the additional responsibility of Controller Feature Films and Sponsored Programmes. He neither knew Hindi nor had any interest in Hindi films. He hesitated when he was offered the role. "I am a science person, are you asking me to watch movies, Sir?" he asked.

But the Director General insisted that his services were required in the Movies Department as there were reports of corruption and other problems that needed to be attended to. Dr. Sreedher then agreed to take up the new role and requested that he be allowed to handle it independently, without much pressure from seniors or the Ministry. The Director General assured him of the same.

The day he assumed his new responsibility, Dr. Sreedher remembers, his mother fell ill and he had to make arrangements to travel to Madras. He had just booked his train tickets, when someone he had just met at his job, asked him, "why train? I have a flight ticket, why don't you take it?"

'Maybe this is how they lure you into corruption in this department,' thought Dr. Sreedher and replied, "No, Thank You!".

He used his authority to close the 'Adult only' films shown by DD during late hours on Fridays and Saturdays and the old classics telecast on Wednesday nights. In those days Doordarshan used to pay for the movies that were telecast on it. A substantial sum was paid to the producers or distributors who owned the rights of the movie, for telecasting it on Doordarshan. So naturally, there were many forces trying to influence the choice of movies for broadcast and there was corruption at many levels. After having bought the film at a huge cost, there was also the additional burden on the Doordarshan team to find sponsors to earn back that money.

Dr. Sreedher decided to no longer pay for the movies to be broadcast on Doordarshan. Rather he encouraged the private agencies to market the films with a minimum guarantee. Those who wished to telecast their movie could bring in their own sponsors as per the new norms. This way a lot of money was saved and the pressure for getting ad revenue was reduced on Doordarshan. For all these efforts he had the solid backing of his Director General Mr. Ratikant Basu, who later went on to be the first CEO of the Star TV network.

"Once in the media pulse column of *The Hindu*, in 1993, Ms. Sevanti Ninan, a media columnist, referred to him as the part-time DG of Doordarshan. Later Mr. Basu and even I used to work in the office till 9 or 10 pm every day trying to increase the revenue of DD", recalls Dr. Sreedher.

Dr. Sreedher also went ahead and gave press ads to invite the attention of those who wanted to broadcast their movies on Doordarshan, asking them to apply for broadcast along with the certificate of copyright. Thousands of entries arrived and Dr. Sreedher needed only 52 films, to be telecast on 52 weekends in a year. A team of six members was constituted to select 52 movies from the list of entries received. Of course, this time too, there was a lot of pressure from all sides and above, on what movies should make it to the final list, but Dr. Sreedher ensured that none of this interference bothered the selection team. He deviated from having face-to-face discussions and got a computer program ready. He circulated the details in sealed covers to the experts and asked them to list 52 +10 films as their choices to be telecast on Doordarshan. They were analysed by computer and the first 52 movies which had maximum preferences were identified. When the list of 52 movies was ready, the team undersigned a clause stating that these movies were selected by them fairly, following official procedures. He also tried to bring more transparency by computerizing the records in the Films Division. All the movies, along with their scheduled broadcast dates and details were fed into a computer and formally shared. Mr. Krishnamurthy was given the responsibility of digitization and he was assisted by Mr. Tholkappian. Dr. Sreedher firmly believed that creating transparent documents in the system would reduce anxiety and corruption. "It made things convenient for the film producers, rights holders, marketing agencies and viewers as everyone had the data with them, that too well in advance. This helped in films to be marketed to their full potential and the revenues soared," he adds.

Once the list of the 52 films chosen for telecast was ready and Dr. Sreedher took it to the DG, Mr. Basu and appraised him that he had got the signature of all but one expert who had shortlisted the movies as he was not in Delhi and that he had asked his Asst. Controller of Programmes to get the signature of that one last person, in the evening by meeting him personally. After appraising Mr. Basu, Dr. Sreedher went to Madras and the DG himself travelled to Bombay. After the weekend, when they both met in New Delhi at the office, Mr. Basu asked Dr. Sreedher what happened to his clause of secrecy, as the list of 52 films minus the signature of that one expert was already available among the distributors of films in Bombay the next day, he said. It was to be kept confidential until officially revealed. Clearly someone from the office leaked the information. Dr. Sreedher found out who the black sheep was and took the necessary action to get him removed. "It's really sad that how sometimes people are prepared to sell data for paltry sums without realizing their value and importance," he says.

After streamlining the telecast of films, now it was time to review the TV serials. By the time Dr. Sreedher joined Doordarshan, the epic *Ramayana* and *Mahabharata* serials were already over and off-air. This was the time when soaps like *Shanti* and *Chandrakanta* were set to rule the audiences. Dr. Sreedher remembers that his predecessor had left a note regarding the selection of sponsored serials, as per which *Shanti* was scheduled as the first afternoon serial. Ronnie Screwvala, the then proprietor of UTV met Dr. Sreedher to collect the letter approving the afternoon time slot for *Shanti*. Dr. Sreedher remembers asking him to wait and collect the letter from his office later in the afternoon, and he also remembers signing a half page letter on an A4 sheet, approving the afternoon time slot for *Shanti*. He had no idea whatsoever that this serial was going to be a huge sensation that would turn the afternoon slot on TV into prime time, nevertheless.

One thing that irked Dr. Sreedher from the beginning was that the production teams of the serials, especially the more popular ones, took much advantage and did not comply with the official rulebook. The tapes would arrive late, sometimes just a few hours before broadcast and there was not enough time for viewing and approving the content before it went on air. As these serials raked in immense revenue and viewership, the previous controllers never bothered to take it up as an issue. Sometimes, the producers of these serials were close to seniors in the Ministry and played it to their advantage. But Dr. Sreedher, wanting to streamline the process, insisted that the tapes arrive at his table 48 hours before broadcast.

So once, when even after strict enforcement of procedures and repeated reminders, the tapes for the TV Serial *Chandrakanta* continued to arrive late, Dr. Sreedher decided to take action. He took a call saying, that weekend, the broadcast of the serial would be withheld and the live coverage of the Puri Jagannath Temple festival that was to be aired after the serial would now be advanced by an hour instead. When he went ahead with his plan, the producers of *Chandrakanta* were infuriated and decided to take the matter to court. Though the Delhi High Court ruled in favour of Doordarshan, they later lost the case in the Supreme Court. But by then it was too late for the producers to resume the telecast of the serial on DD.

While computerizing all DD's records, Dr. Sreedher chanced upon the first vigilance case against a production company engaged in the production of a famous weekly programme on Doordarshan. The case was about having used DD's betacam tape and submitting the same as their tape. It was the first case to be computerized in Doordarshan, he remembers. Later in 1994 one of the same company's proposals landed on his table, regarding the special coverage of the assembly election results of that year. "The proposal was to hire computers for about 45 days and the cost of hiring went well beyond the cost of acquiring. Even the food allowance was claimed exorbitantly. I studied the proposal and pointed out the anomalies to the Director Finance. Then the costs were reduced before the contract was issued," says Dr. Sreedher.

Offering Slots to Private Producers

During his Doordarshan days, Dr. Sreedher earned both friends and foes, merits and controversies for the work he did and the way he did it. But nevertheless, he continued with his duties relentlessly. *Rangoli* was a popular programme on national television that was outsourced by the then Director General Mr. Basu and given to an external agency to manage. "Mr. Basu had only given it to them on an experimental basis. But the satellite channels, which were just entering the market, wanted to scuttle the effort. In those days DD used to broadcast songs which were older and never from a film that was about to be released. It had its own rule book. But the private producers could now bring in the new songs easily. The other private TV channels wanted this to be stopped. They went to the Bombay High Court through a third party and got a stay on outsourcing *Rangoli* on a minimum guarantee basis", says Dr. Sreedher, who was then given the responsibility to get the stay vacated. The Supreme Court was approached with a special leave petition. The Additional Solicitor General of GoI, Mr. Altaf Ahmed was to argue for Doordarshan. An advertisement agency, which had filed the petition, on the strength of a private satellite channel, engaged renowned lawyer Mr. Soli Sorabjee and the firm to which the programme was sanctioned engaged Mr. Ashok Desai. "When the Supreme Court judges were hearing the special leave petition, they were erroneously told that the day, on which the Bombay High Court gave the stay, there was a Bandh in the city. I prompted the ASG to counter it. But the apex court did not want to waste time in hearing a petition involving song and dance sequences. But when the ASG told the court that by staying DD's decision, revenue of

Rs. 2 crores would be lost in a quarter, their lordships then observed that they were concerned if there was a loss to the public exchequer and ordered that the Bombay High Court should decide the case within 30 days and the petitioner should give a bank guarantee of about Rs. 2 crores to the Registrar of the Bombay High Court. The producers panicked at this and when the Bombay High Court again heard the petition, they were unable to produce a bank guarantee. The case was dismissed. But Doordarshan was asked to come out with a transparent scheme for privatization of the programme within seven weeks," recalls Dr. Sreedher. The scheme was then worked out and advertised in the papers. Dr. Sreedher also took the opportunity to offer another programme *Chitrahaar*—the popular Friday evening programme featuring movie songs to private producers,and also desired to implement the same model at regional levels.

How the Decisions Impacted Doordarshan's Revenue:

The measures to privatize certain programming slots served well in ensuring a firm revenue base for Doordarshan which was now competing with Satellite channels like Star and Zee, for revenue. An article in *India Today* dated March 1995, states that Doordarshan's earnings between 1993-94 was Rs. 370 crores and the private producers made about Rs. 90 crores by marketing the slots given to them. Between 1994 and 1995, Doordarshan's earnings was Rs. 400 crores and an additional revenue of Rs. 200 crores per annum was made by the private producers. Programmes like *Rangoli, Chitrahaar* and *Oliyum Oliyum* (the Tamil version of *Chitrahaar*) now had a minimum guarantee of Rs. 18 Crore, Rs. 20 crores and Rs. 13 crores respectively. Serials like *Junoon* and *Chandrakanta* had a minimum guarantee of Rs. 23 lakhs per week. "The movie slots on Friday and Saturday were also sold for huge minimum guarantees. Overall, approximately one-third of DD's revenue came from the film and TV serials section handled by me", says Dr. Sreedher.

"Also, a huge part of Doordarshan's revenue came in

the form of sponsorship and ad revenue from one of the prominent FMCG group of companies. So, representatives of this multinational company used to dictate terms in the market and lobbied for the advertisement rates. When DD decided to have a minimum guarantee amount for each film, and quoted the rates the producers who were marketing the films were up in arms. Also, the said FMCG Company refused to pay more money to these producers who had been selected to exhibit their films on Doordarshan. Major newspapers then started criticizing the actions of the Mandi House Mandarins. I also categorically told the advertisement and marketing agencies that no one needs to fix the advertisement rates for Doordarshan," he adds.

The producers marketing the film were given slots and some free commercial time for every 30 minutes of a film shown. Once, there was an instance of a superhit film being shown on Doordarshan where the original film was about 2 hours 55 minutes or so. The person who was marketing the film got the duration extended by another 8 minutes by repeating the song sequences at several places. So, he got seven half-hour slots and he could get advertisements for a longer duration. Dr. Sreedher found out that something was fishy and contacted an official from Doordarshan Kendra, Bombay and requested her to collect the original certificate of the film from the Censor Board. The movie duration was found to have been extended and the man was exposed. There were many supporters inside and outside Doordarshan for him and the marketing firm. They even threatened Dr. Sreedher that they would complain about him for blocking additional revenue to DD. Dr. Sreedher never paid attention to all that and ensured that nothing wrong was happening right under his nose.

"In all these attempts to streamline revenue generation, I had worked closely with the marketing wing and particularly with Mr. Ashok Ogra, who was the controller of sales at that time," says Dr. Sreedher. Incidentally Mr. Ashok Ogra was also from the same batch of officers selected by direct recruitment, as Station Directors in 1988. Later he became the

Founder Vice President of Discovery Channel Asia, which was based in India. He is now an advisor and the head of the Apeejay Institute of Mass Communication and continues to be a good friend of Dr. Sreedher's.

DD Movie Club

When Dr. Sreedher was dealing with films for Doordarshan national network, he remembers that DD and Zee TV always had legal battles pertaining to telecast rights of films. "It was around this time that the news that the Zee network was to start a 24-hour movie channel, was out. Mr. Ratikant Basu, the then DG of Doordarshan asked me to launch a DD Movie channel before Zee launched theirs. This happened in the last week of March in 1995. Mr. Basu was also doubling as Chairman and MD of National Film Development Corporation, a public sector undertaking under the same Ministry. He suggested that the entire sourcing of films for the new channel be done from NFDC. But NFDC was based in Bombay and Doordarshan did not have any telecast facilities there, so it was decided that capsules would be canned and sent to DD towers at Pitampura in New Delhi and the movie channel called DD Movie Club could operate from there. Ms. Deepa Chandra was the Deputy Controller of films then. The launch of the new channel was planned for the first week of April 1995. NFDC also signed up with the Amitabh Bachchan Corporation Limited to get exclusive blockbusters of the star every month. A prominent TV marketing agency from the house of a leading English newspaper group approached Doordarshan and offered exclusive marketing for one year. I remember that, Doordarshan wanting to maintain its standards of home viewing had to do some editing in the sequences of the first film itself. With not many digital facilities available then, they took risks to manually block captions and replace them with some other caption," recalls Dr. Sreedher.

Dr. Sreedher handled the channel for just about a month after its launch, as later he was transferred. Recalling what happened with the channel later, he adds, "The marketing agency was not able to market the channel for reasons best known to them and slowly the number of advertisements came down to one per day. Wanting to retain their exclusive marketing rights, they were buying time. Finally, after long discussions between the DG and the top boss of the agency, the marketing rights were cancelled. The channel was on air for another 5 years or so and today DD does not have a movie channel of its own".

The Returned Gifts

Dr. Sreedher remembers covering events like the Superhit Muqabla Nite, Miss India, SCREEN Awards, and RAPA Awards for advertising, while he was working at Doordarshan headquarters at Delhi. Dr. Sreedher's take home pay at Doordarshan was about Rs. 3,800 per month. Offers of daily car lifts, dinner in five star hotels, etc., were plenty, he remembers. Deepavali gifts were delivered to the house—huge in value and numbers. There used to be all sorts of gifts like shirts, pants, saris, computers, watches, gold chains, liquor bottles, etc. But Dr. Sreedher had taken a resolution that he would return all the gifts and only keep the sweets packets. He had told everyone to take their gifts back. Dr. Sreedher's Personal Secretaries and office staff at AIR, DD, and later IGNOU and CEMCA helped him to return those gifts, retaining only the sweets or dry fruit packs which were consumed by everyone in the office.

Dr. Sreedher also undertook the task of outsourcing the 'Oliyum Oliyum' show (Tamil version of *Chitrahaar*) on Madras Doordarshan. He went to Madras, met the contenders and finally awarded the show to a private producer Ms. Kutty Padmini who promised a much higher revenue than what was being made. Though he tried to be as fair as possible in his approach, the powers that be in Madras Doordarshan killed the project, he says.

Another assignment that he led for Doordarshan Madras was when applications were sought for producing Tamil TV serials for Doordarshan. There was a huge response with around 5,000 applications and each application had a demand draft of Rs. 3,000 attached to it. It was all piled up in the office, with no necessary means to process them. Dr. Sreedher assigned Mr. Krishnamurthy, a computer expert working with Doordarshan Delhi, the task of digitizing the applications and processing the Demand Drafts in Madras. It was carried out successfully. "Dr. N.C. Rajamani, was the in charge at DDK Madras for the processing of applications and he later went to Malaysia and now holds a very senior position at Astro, a Malaysian satellite channel company," adds Dr. Sreedher.

Dr. Sreedher was hoping to get his next posting as a Director in DDK Madras. It was very likely and people were already talking about it. Once during his Madras visit, Dr. Sreedher was at the Doordarshan office talking to the then Director of Madras Doordarshan Kendra, Mr. A. Natarajan, who he had earlier worked with in AIR Madras. A journalist was also present in the room. While introducing Dr. Sreedher to his friend from the press, Mr. Natarajan casually mentioned that he was to be the next Director of Madras Doordarshan Kendra. They exchanged pleasantries and the conversation moved on to other topics. While leaving, the press reporter requested Dr. Sreedher to give him a photograph. Dr. Sreedher unsuspectingly, shared one that he had carried with him in his wallet. He least expected an article in the paper the next morning with headlines that read, 'Meet Madras TV Station's New Director' with an accompanying photo and article. It was too late when, Dr. Sreedher realized his mistake in sharing his photograph with the reporter. He was criticized for being overweening for sharing with the press, something that was still only at the talks stage. Not only did the article get him some negative publicity, it also destroyed his chances of becoming the Director of Doordarshan Madras. "The article had caught the attention of some prominent politicians in Madras who were then powerful and they insisted that the Current Director of Doordarshan Madras be retained," recalls Dr. Sreedher. Later when Dr. Sreedher did receive an appointment order as a Director for a TV station, it was not for Madras, but for Calcutta.

4

The Unexpected Ordeal

Director, Doordarshan Kendra, Calcutta (May 1995 – March 1996)

Life throws many challenges at us, at times when we least expect them. Sometimes it packs the intensity of a lifetime, in just a matter of a few months. Dr. Sreedher did not know that he was in for a roller coaster ride when he received his transfer orders to join Doordarshan Calcutta as their new Director.

It came as a jolt to Dr. Sreedher and he was totally unprepared. He had for long, nurtured the dream of going back and working in Tamil Nadu, so he could give back to the place which gave him a head start in his career. But that did not happen, and he was handed the transfer order to go to Calcutta instead.

Though somewhat disappointed, Dr. Sreedher decided to explore the opportunity that had come his way and moved to Calcutta alone, leaving behind his family in Delhi. But what awaited him at Calcutta, was more than unwelcoming.

The staff at Doordarshan Calcutta went on a strike, as they were opposed to the idea of a non-Bengali Director taking over the Doordarshan Kendra in Calcutta. They protested, shouting slogans and had even blocked the passages to the Director's Office, determined not to let the new Director assume duty. The news of it had already reached Dr. Sreedher, as he was preparing to join duty. But he still decided to face what lay ahead as he did not have much choice.

"The head of the Programmer Staff Association of AIR and DD was then a Bengali, Dr. Amit Chakraborty, who operated from Delhi. He had a good rapport with me, having earlier worked in the capacity of Science Officer at AIR Calcutta. When I discussed the issue with him, he assured me that his association would never approve of the protests in DD Calcutta. But that did not seem to help the situation much and the protests continued," he remembers.

When Dr. Sreedher entered the Doordarshan Calcutta office on the day he joined, he was confronted by the staff and not let into his office. Not wanting to leave defeated he simply chose to stand amidst the protestors and wait it out, all the while wondering what his next course of action should be.

Here's how Dr. Sreedher recalls the incident. "I went to the office of Dr. Hembram, the Deputy Director General Eastern Region, which was situated in the campus of Doordarshan Calcutta and signed the joining report. He was my direct boss. Then I went and stood with the protestors who were not letting me into my office. But after a while, a staff member… Subash Sanyal, very generously came to me and offered to open the doors to the Director's office. "Please sir" he said, "you can go to the room and sit on the sofa....it's not nice to see you standing like this. We'll take you around Calcutta for sightseeing today if you want... And you could take a flight back home tonight."

"They did not want me to stay. Amidst all the tension around, all I felt like was to laugh at their offer", says Dr. Sreedher.

Dr. Sreedher was then led into the Director's office and he sat there for a while contemplating the situation. A little later he received a call from the Delhi head office to confirm that he had reported to the office and had taken charge. Merely reporting to the office was not enough and he would have to at least sign one file on his table to officially assume duty, he was told. Dr. Sreedher skimmed through the table and found a casual leave application of the previous Director. As Dr. Sreedher was not authorized to relieve him, he simply wrote—'forwarded for competent authority's action', signed it and faxed the application across to the Delhi office. Now his joining was official. Having nothing more to do, he simply sat on the sofa in the room for some time. It was already lunch time by then. After lunch, he decided to have an honest talk with the protesting staff members and see what he could do.

Here is what Dr. Sreedher remembers telling them: "See... I understand that you are not happy in me taking charge as your new Director. In fact, I must admit even I am not too happy doing this. I wanted to go to Madras and I don't know why I have been posted here. I have respect for your sentiments that only a person knowing the regional language should have been posted here as the Director. I agree with you... And will even support your cause. But please understand that as of now...I have already taken charge and assumed duty as Director of DD Calcutta. You can keep shouting slogans, but that is not going to bother me.... Whether you like it or not... You have to accept the fact that this second, this day...I am your Director."

Listening to him speak, the staff seemed to calm down and began opening up about their issues. The then Deputy Director of DD Calcutta, who was a Bengali, had just been transferred and the staff were unhappy about it. They wanted Dr. Sreedher to not relieve but retain him. Dr. Sreedher agreed to keep the Deputy Director's transfer orders pending for a while. This gave the staff some satisfaction. They also complained that there was no uniform policy on official transfers and that it was essential for the team. Dr. Sreedher agreed with that too and said that he would work with them to put things in place.

When the protestors found support for their cause and concerns, they softened in their approach to him. Slowly, by taking small appeasing steps each day, Dr. Sreedher undertook his responsibilities as the Director of the Doordarshan Kendra, Calcutta.

Reviving DD 7 (Now Known as DD Bangla)

Dr. Sreedher noticed that even in 1995, black-and-white television sets still had a stronghold in West Bengal. DD 7, a Bengali satellite channel operating in colour, was not taking off well and was being operated in namesake from the Doordarshan Kendra. Dr. Sreedher discussed the operations of the channel with Mr. Abhijit Dasgupta, a pioneer in television sports and live coverages in India, who was then working with Doordarshan Calcutta. He took Dr. Sreedher to the control room and showed him a playback machine on which an engineer was playing some tapes of old programmes that he had been given.

His heart ached at the way the channel was being run and giving shape and boosting the popularity of DD 7 naturally fell into Dr. Sreedher's agenda.

Most of the staff members at Doordarshan Calcutta at that time seemed to believe that cable TV and satellite transmission were for the rich and the common man would watch only the terrestrial black-and-white TV.

Dr. Sreedher could not ask much of his staff in his early days at Calcutta. So, he simply requested them to provide him a list of all the best programmes available with them on tapes. He took the help of a Bengali staff member in assessing and rating the content on these shows. He chose the best among them and with the help of a production assistant started airing them on DD 7 channel. As the content was good, within no time DD 7 started receiving a better response from the audience.

Just within 15 days of having started working on DD 7, Doordarshan Calcutta received a letter from the Indian High Commissioner in Dhaka, appreciating the programmes and mentioning their popularity in Bangladesh. They had written asking for the list of programmes and their broadcast timings on DD 7, so that they could publish it in their local dailies in Dhaka. When Dr. Sreedher shared this letter with his team, it was all the inspiration they needed to change their perspective and start anew. "If there is such a huge response, we could even consider creating fresh content for the channel, why air the old ones?" they said. That's exactly what Dr. Sreedher would have wanted them to do. Thanks to the letter from the High Commissioner, the programming team volunteered to create fresh content for DD 7 without even being asked to. In fact, they did that without any additional payments or equipment. Thus began the early morning live transmission for DD 7, which was started by just providing some basic transport facilities and dormitory accommodation to the staff. The efficiency and the quality of the work they put in soon started showing in the increased ratings of DD 7 channel.

Working with Veteran Producer Abhijit Dasgupta

Dr. Sreedher first met Mr. Abhijit Dasgupta, a veteran producer at Doordarshan Calcutta, on the day he assumed duty. By then, the producer had already submitted his resignation and was serving his mandatory notice period. But Doordarshan was never in a mood to let go of him as he was an asset to the programming team. "An absolute professional, he was a role model to the other staff in the way he functioned. He was one of the few tech-savvy members in the Doordarshan Calcutta team and seemed to be indispensable at that time," says Dr. Sreedher. He also confesses to have learnt a lot from the veteran producer during his initial days at Doordarshan Calcutta. Later when Abhijit Dasgupta started his own production company called Sukruti Productions, Dr. Sreedher offered him a slot in Doordarshan to do a Bengali sports magazine programme.

Respect for his talent and professionalism earned Dr. Sreedher a lifelong friend in him.

Janani, the Super Hit Television Soap

Ashok Surana, of Channel Eight productions was also a well-known film distributor. But he did not seem very popular with the staff of Doordarshan Calcutta. He had filed a couple of cases in the court against Doordarshan regarding some payment dues and royalty issues. When Dr. Sreedher took over as the Director of DD Calcutta, with the intent of improving viewership for DD 7 and DD Bangla channels, he offered Ashok Surana, a prime-time slot in DD 7 and an afternoon slot in DD Bangla to start a family-based television serial. The serial was to be produced for DD 7 and the repeat broadcast was to be aired in DD Bangla in the afternoon.

Afternoon slots were not too popular in those days. But having seen success with the popular soap *Shanti*, which was produced by UTV featuring Mandira Bedi, in the DD national network, Dr. Sreedher wanted to try something similar in Bangla. Mr. Ashok Surana took up the challenge and produced the serial *Janani* (Mother) where actress Padmashree Suchitra Sen played the role of a mother. The serial took off well right from the very first week.

"Initially we had signed an order for 13 weeks. But as the TRP started soaring, we decided to increase the sponsorship rates every 13 weeks and Channel Eight Productions willingly paid for it. The TV serial *Janani* had a response comparable to the *Ramayana* and *Mahabharata* serials on Doordarshan and Calcutta's life almost came to a standstill during the afternoon telecasts. The soap went on to be the longest running TV serial in any regional language in Asia. Mr. Ashok Surana, after seeing vast profits from the serial withdrew all cases against DD and the serial continued to be on air for a few more years," says Dr. Sreedher.

NDTV

Dr. Sreedher also wanted to provide a slot for private current affairs programme in Bengali, like the 'World This Week', 'Newstrack' and a few other shows like the Karan Thapar show on the national network. "I considered giving it to NDTV and asked Mr. Prannoy Roy for a pilot show. Mr. Prannoy Roy asked me if it was fair of me to ask for a pilot from such a reputed and experienced organization. But I told him that I wanted to follow the rules and get the programme approved by the committee for sponsored programmes at DD Calcutta. But later the project never took off as there was much opposition to my initiatives calling it the privatization of DD," recalls Dr. Sreedher.

Increasing Sponsorship Rates

"Mr. Ratikant Basu, the then Director General of Doordarshan had complete faith in me and my abilities. He encouraged me to take up my experimentation with the satellite channels, including the fixing of sponsorship rates. But the only thing I was told was not to meddle with the primary terrestrial channel, which I didn't," says Dr. Sreedher.

When Dr. Sreedher saw the soaring TRPs for some of the shows like *Janani* and the Horlicks Jalsaghar Quiz on DD 7, he decided to review and increase the sponsorship rates for these slots every 13 weeks. Considering the high TRPs and Doordarshan's monopoly then, the producers willingly paid the price. Otherwise, there were others waiting to take the slot for the same price.

Dr. Sreedher recalls "at a time when the other regional Kendras in the country had the sponsorship rates fixed for prime time at Rs. 10,000 per hour and non-prime time at Rs. 5,000 per hour, the rates at DD 7 went up to Rs. 65,000 per episode during prime time." This was the highest it peaked to, says Dr. Sreedher, after which complaints began to arise. Eventually a press meet was arranged by the Calcutta Press Club to condemn the newly imposed high rates of sponsorship and Dr. Sreedher's autocratic behaviour in implementing the same.

Owing to the pressure from the press, Dr. Sreedher tried to contact the Doordarshan headquarters in Delhi and get their formal approval for the new sponsorship rates that he had fixed, as many advertisers were prepared to pay that price.

"Mr. Ashok Ogra was then the Controller of Sales of Doordarshan", remembers Dr. Sreedher. "An approval letter from him came just ahead of the press meet, which fixed the maximum price for a prime-time slot at Rs. 50,000. I quickly went ahead and announced it and promised a refund of the excess amount or adjustment of the same in future bills of the agency".

A stitch in time saves nine. An approval that came from Delhi on time saved him from a major controversy for having increased the sponsorship rates without prior official approval.

21st Birth Anniversary of DDK Calcutta

August 9, 1995 happened to be the 21st anniversary of Doordarshan Calcutta. Dr. Sreedher had made plans to celebrate it in a big way at the Nazrul Mancha indoor stadium in Calcutta. He built a creative idea around the number '21'. He wanted 21 children who were celebrating their birthdays on that day to light the lamp along with the Director during invocation. He had arranged for 21 people, who were born on the same day as DD Calcutta was launched, to host the show on the special day for 21 hours. He had even invited 21 Bengali poets to be a part of the special programme, the then Vice-Chancellor of Shantiniketan being one of them. The celebration had a mix of programmes ranging from Ananda Shankar's ballet to Bappi Lahiri's light music. They even premiered a Bengali film on the occasion. The Calcutta police came riding 21 horses for the show and left riding 21 motorcycles in modern uniforms. There were also programmes for agriculture, women and industrial workers that were all performed in front of the audience while being covered for Doordarshan Calcutta. The event was a huge success and was talked about everywhere.

Organizing and putting together an event of this scale was not easy. Bringing in the funds was a challenge too. Dr. Sreedher admits that he considered commissioning a private firm to take care of the auditorium, hotel accommodation for the artists, and their travel and hospitality. But better sense prevailed and he later came up with an idea to offer the event as a joint venture between the National Film Development Corporation (NFDC), a public sector undertaking under the Ministry of Information and Broadcasting and DD Calcutta.

"All performers were paid as per the then norms followed by Doordarshan and the NFDC took advertisements and donations to meet its share of expenditure. Rs. 1 lakh was donated for the special event by Ashok Surana of Channel Eight Productions, out of goodwill. There were also other sponsors like Monginis Cookies and Coca Cola, who had their banners inside the stadium," he recalls.

After the success of the grand event, Dr. Sreedher had to go on a 13-day-long leave to his hometown as his father had died. But in the middle of his leave he was asked to rush back to office for another important event that had come up. The Parliamentary Panel on Official Languages was visiting the central government establishments in Calcutta and Doordarshan Kendra was one of the prime organizers of this visit. Dr. Sreedher was asked to be in the office to ensure that all arrangements were in order, but when he came back and resumed duty, he was in for an unpleasant surprise.

He recalls, "Someone in the organization had recorded the Doordarshan Anniversary Celebration on a VHS tape and given/sent it to a premier investigating agency in the country for an enquiry, alleging that over Rs. 2 crore of money was made through the event, out of which one crore had been given to a political party. Following the allegations, the offices of NFDC and Channel Eight were raided during my absence. Though it did create a climate of tension in the organizations, no evidence was found to support the allegations that had been made. Later an official from the investigating agency told me that they had found nothing incriminatory and even if there were violation of any norms, it ought to be enquired by the concerned department only."

Averting Controversies in Political Recordings

In 2017, the 71st Independence Day celebration in Tripura churned out a huge controversy when the then Chief Minister Manik Sarkar alleged that the Doordarshan and AIR did not broadcast his Independence Day speech in spite of having recorded it. The Prasar Bharati had wanted the Chief Minister to reshape the content of his speech which the Chief Minister refused to do. Hence, the recording was not aired.

Dr. Sreedher recounts having averted a similar controversy in Doordarshan Calcutta in 1995, during the recording of the Independence Day speech by the then Chief Minister Jyoti Basu. "Mr Jyoti Basu, had never given a special address for Independence Day through AIR and DD before and he decided to do it for the first time in 1995. Prasar Bharati, as an autonomous body was yet to be formed back then. The Congress government was holding fort at the centre and to avoid any controversies or issues cropping up later with the contents of the speech, I requested to see the script for the Chief Minister's address in advance. The Chief Minister's Office though, refused to oblige.

So, when the recording was fixed, two days ahead of 15th August, Dr. Sreedher took along with him a veteran television anchor from DD Calcutta, Mr. Pankaj Saha. He was known for his programme 'Letters from the Audience', which he hosted for over two decades.

The Chief Minister's recording was fixed at 12 noon at the Writers Building in Calcutta and at 11:55 am, the secretary to the CM gave them a copy of the speech. Mr. Pankaj Saha skimmed through it hastily and seemed satisfied with most of the content, but for a few lines towards the end of the speech. He discussed that with Dr. Sreedher, who advised him to talk to the CM and suggest suitable modifications in the script and handle the situation with poise and diplomacy.

Mr. Pankaj Saha managed to do just the same and convinced the Chief Minister to modify the last few lines of his speech, without offending him in any way. No one got to know about it and a possible controversy was averted.

But there was another problem. Earlier, while planning the recording, the engineering staff, who were still to warm up to Dr. Sreedher, did not allow him to take an experienced cameraman with him for the recording. They insisted that only the person on regular duty would do the CM's recording. The technician assigned did not have much experience with Beta Cams. So, when the CM's recording was over, and he wanted to play back slightly to ensure proper recording, he rewound it and by mistake got the last portion erased. By then the Chief Minister had already returned to his chambers. Here Mr. Pankaj Saha's skills were tested once again, and he managed to convince the Chief Minister to repeat the last part of the speech once again and this time it was recorded in the Chief Minister's chambers.

"There was no non-linear or digital editing in those days. So, the problem of continuity in the video did crop up but was managed," recollects Dr. Sreedher.

Diligence and diplomacy are the two keys to handle such situations and Dr. Sreedher opines that the Tripura controversy could also have been averted if the situation had been handled differently.

Civic Polls in Calcutta: The DD Coverage

A year ahead of the General Elections in 1996, Calcutta went for civic polls in the year 1995.

"A few days ahead of the polls, the then I&B Minister had called asking me to meet another prominent leader who was the party's in-charge for the 1995 civic elections. I went and met him at the Taj Bengal. As we got talking, the leader mentioned that 'there were 120 and odd polling booths in the city and they were afraid that some violence or booth capturing might happen.' He went ahead to enquire about how many cameras DD had and expressed his desire to be able to record the proceedings from all the polling booths to ensure smooth proceedings. In those days, CCTV cameras were a rarity and also expensive. So Doordarshan used to do the recordings of the polling process using its cameras and share them with the Election Commission. DD Calcutta had half-a-dozen professional cameras and so I told the leader that a booth-by-booth coverage could be done by borrowing cameras from neighbouring DD stations and from freelancers.

The leader then asked if I could share with him all the video recordings from the poll booths. I politely told him that the recordings were to be given to the Election Commission only. The leader was upset and he asked me how I intended to manage the expenses incurred for the coverage. I replied saying, 'you leave it to me sir!'. In those days Doordarshan was a government body and all such expenses were normally reimbursed. The leader then asked me to take a look into the adjacent room. I went and found huge bundles of currency notes kept in that room. I was told I could take as much as I wanted, but the coverage had to be done. I told the Minister that I did not need any money but DD would still be able to do a booth-by-booth coverage for the Election Commission. Then I left the place," he recounts.

"As anticipated, there were instances of poll-related violence during the elections and a Doordarshan camera was broken by the mob." he recalls.

Though he had found himself in an awkward situation at the Taj Bengal on that day, it seemed like nothing compared to a few other distressing situations he had to face during his tenure at Calcutta.

Gherao and the PSO

One such instance was having to re-arrange the News team at DD Calcutta. One fine day, Dr. Sreedher received an order over the telephone from his bosses at Delhi . "They wanted me to transfer certain members of the News Production team, who were known to have a political leaning towards the left, to some other sections and replace their positions in the news team with other members," says Dr. Sreedher.

"Two producers and a production assistant were chosen to be transferred. There were allegations that these left leaning members of the team had a tendency to give more visual coverage to the left government and would not cooperate with the others who were allied differently. Even though the news editor edited the news, the visuals were mostly controlled by this team," he adds.

So when the order to do an internal transfer of the three members of the news team came, Dr. Sreedher insisted he would take such a step only when his senior officers were in the city, as it could put him in a very uncomfortable spot with the team he was just starting to build a rapport with. He tried talking to the members individually before that. He tried luring one of the producers to undertake responsibility for the coverage of upcoming World Cup Cricket matches and attend training in sports coverage in London for the same. He tried convincing the other to take up a current affairs programme instead of the main news slot. But his persuasion did not seem to be working much with them.

One of his senior officials from Delhi was coming to Calcutta. Dr. Sreedher issued an order transferring the three members of the News team just before he left his office to receive the official at the airport. By the time Dr. Sreedher reached the airport, he received a letter from one of the transferred employees, which was written in blood. As they discussed the issues, it was decided that it was essential to get security for the Director and the Kendra under the present circumstances. They rang up the Chief Secretary of the West Bengal Government, and asked him to make arrangements to provide security to the Doordarshan Kendra and the Director.

This is how Dr. Sreedher recalls what happened after he reached the office:

"As soon as I entered my room at the office...both my Deputy Directors, came rushing to me saying that the staff was unhappy about the internal transfer order. Before I could blink my eyes...a group of staff members came shouting and screaming into my room, removed all the phone, fax connections and surrounded me. I could not even go to the bathroom. The gherao continued for about four hours. I was unable to contact anyone. Then at around 3:30 pm, when I could think of nothing else to do, I called both my Deputy Directors and asked them to give me a joint note citing the unhappiness of the staff and suggest that the order be kept in abeyance. In fact, I dictated the note to my Personal Assistant and they just signed it. Hence the order was put in abeyance and my phone connections were restored after a while. The staff was now kind to me and even offered me some cool drinks and snacks. They also invited me to their homes for dinner. Then at 5:30 pm, when things were settling down, the official rang me up and I told him what happened. He asked me not to yield to the situation and simply do what was needed. With no choice left, I called all the three employees to be transferred and explained to them my position and requested them to compromise a little. I got another producer, who was also in their own association All India Joint Action Council (AIJAC), but of a South Indian origin to take charge of news on alternate days.

Meanwhile the official went back to Delhi and updated the government on the happenings in Calcutta. The Government of India wrote to the Chief Secretary of West Bengal to provide protection to the Director and the Doordarshan Kendra at Calcutta. The matter was then supposed to have been discussed by the Leftist Government's Cabinet. Later, one fine evening a police officer came to me and said that they would provide personal security to me from then onwards. I requested the officer to provide the security to my Bengali counterpart in the engineering wing Mr. Sen as well. I also asked officers to come in plain clothes, with their revolver hidden. So, I had a personal security guard at my service till I left Calcutta in the middle of March 1996. But somehow, whenever there were agitations in the Doordarshan Kendra, the personal security officers seemed to be away dealing with their personal issues, and providing a substitute always took time", remembers Dr. Sreedher.

Total Solar Eclipse 1995

India witnessed a Total Solar Eclipse on October 24, 1995, which also marked the important festival of Diwali. It being a rare event and a visual spectacle, Doordarshan had made elaborate arrangements to telecast the solar eclipse live from three different locations in the country—Neem Ka Thana in Rajasthan, Diamond Harbour in Calcutta and another location in Allahabad. Dr. Sreedher even went to Delhi to attend the coordination meeting that was conducted to plan the coverage.

Scientist Prof. Yashpal was to anchor the event along with Ms. Aparna Vaish, who had earlier worked with Dr. Sreedher at the Directorate of AIR, New Delhi. Prof. Jayant Narlikar was anchoring from Allahabad. Dr. Sreedher had arranged for (scientist) Partho Ghose of the Birla Planetarium to anchor the show from Calcutta. The plan was to carry the live telecast on DD 7 satellite channel, so that the Delhi station could download and relay the signals on the National Terrestrial Network. As all arrangements were falling in place, suddenly, there was pressure that the live commentary for the solar eclipse should be available in Bengali for the West Bengal audience. So now a change of plans was in order and Dr. Sreedher had to arrange for another transponder to send signals to Delhi. Subash Sanyal from Doordarshan Calcutta was handling the event coverage as the Producer.

Bata Shoe Company was the main sponsor for the special telecast and they had given instructions that their advertisement should be aired during the totality of the solar eclipse. This was similar to the trend of advertising during a boundary, sixes or a fall of wickets during cricket matches. So, when the total solar eclipse happened in Rajasthan and Allahabad, the producers on the panel in Delhi cut the live telecast and rolled in the advertisements. The idea of interrupting the peaking curiosity of viewers with a commercial break did not go down well with Dr. Sreedher and he did not want to lose the programme aesthetics. There were no cell phones at that time to coordinate at the back end and make a sudden change in plans. So Dr. Sreedher requested the anchor Partha Ghose to make an appeal to the Doordarshan producer at Delhi through the live telecast not to roll out the Bata advertisement till the team from Calcutta gave clearance. The appeal was made on air during the live telecast. As a result, they were able to beautifully capture and telecast the diamond ring and the following totality during the total solar eclipse.

Witnessing a total solar eclipse is not a vague experience. It is deeply etched in the minds of the viewers as rarely does one get to watch such a grand display of splendour in the skies. Fondly recalling the memories of the coverage, Dr. Sreedher says, "the last time the country witnessed a total solar eclipse in the 1980s, Doordarshan had telecast a blockbuster movie starring Amitabh Bachchan, so that people stayed indoors and did not venture out during the eclipse. We had come a long way since then ...In Calcutta, we were eating laddus during the eclipse to demonstrate that we did not believe in superstitions like we should not eat during a solar eclipse. May be due to sheer coincidence or I don't know what...I had to go to Delhi for an event the next day and I was running a very high temperature. The Ministers were inaugurating the Broadcast Expo at Pragati Maidan organized by the Broadcast Engineering Society of which I was a fellow. When I met the Minister of State for Broadcasting who was from Lakshadweep, he praised our coverage of the solar eclipse and all the while I was wondering what had caused my high fever."

The Governor's Flag Day Recording (December 7, 1995)

The governor of a state usually gives a message to the people urging them to donate liberally to the armed forces on Flag Day. The message was usually recorded at the Raj Bhavan and the custom was that, first the Doordarshan camera team would go and set up the camera and recorders in place and later just before the recording began, the Director of the Doordarshan Kendra would join in the process.

Dr. Sreedher recalls his first meeting with the Governor very fondly. "When I reached Raj Bhawan, I saw my recording team asking someone about the 2-pin and 3-pin plugs in the room to connect their equipment. I was surprised to learn later that they were discussing this with the Governor himself. "

After the customary greetings when the recording was about to begin, an ADC (aide-de-camp) to the Governor came and stood near him, so close that his belly was showing in the frame. And if a longer shot was taken then he was seen towering over the Governor which did not look good either. So Dr. Sreedher requested him to kindly move out of the frame. But he refused and the Secretary to the Governor told Dr. Sreedher that in Raj Bhawan things will happen the way they wanted it. So Dr. Sreedher had no choice but to request the Governor himself to get the ADC out of the frame. He remembers explaining to them that "every leader including dictators while appearing on TV to give a message, is seen alone in the frame. There are no bullets in the camera".

After the ADC moved out of the frame, the recording went on just fine. But there was a noticeable difference in the way he and his staff were treated at Raj Bhavan that day after the recording, says Dr. Sreedher. Usually after the recording the staff from Doordarshan got to enjoy the hospitality of the Governor's office. But this time Dr. Sreedher says, "Nothing was offered, not even water".

"When I was returning to the car, the Secretary to the Governor came and told me that he would see to it that by evening I was transferred out of Calcutta. I thanked him for his help and told him that I too wasn't having a great time and wanted to move out of Calcutta".

Later, on Independence Day in August 1995, Dr. Sreedher as the Director of Doordarshan got an official invitation for a reception hosted by the Governor at Raj Bhavan. "I went to the reception and was standing in the queue to greet the Governor in person. The ADC to the Governor spotted me in the queue and told me that it was not necessary for me at all to meet the Governor in person. But the new OSD (Officer on Special Duty) to the then Information and Broadcasting Minister, who was also in the queue with me insisted and took me to meet the Governor," he recalls.

Making Peace with the Protestors

The CPM party members used to often organize small protests in front of the gates of Doordarshan Kendra in Calcutta, remembers Dr. Sreedher. "Time and again they would have something to oppose or something to demand from the Doordarshan broadcasters. Like, on the eve of Ishwar Chandra Vidyasagar's birthday, they wanted Doordarshan to broadcast more programmes on literacy," he recalls.

"Usually they organized a day-long agitation in front of the gates and their speakers/horns used to be pointed towards the window of the Director's chambers. The whole day the Director had no choice but to listen to the speeches and songs being played by them. At the end of the day it was usual for them to submit a memorandum to the Director on the issue they were raising. The news services division never gave these protests much importance to cover them as news. Once, one such protest was being held outside the Doordarshan gate when I chose to react differently. This time the protest was opposing the telecast of the afternoon serials on Doordarshan—*Shanti* and *Swabhiman,* as they alleged that they were not in tune with the moral standards of society. On that day instead of letting the protests go on unattended as usual, I decided to give it some attention. I asked the cameramen to record the protests in front of the gate and cover them in a 5-minute special slot just before the evening news at 7 pm. The Programme staff also interviewed Mr. Biman Bose, a CPM Polit Bureau member as a part of the special broadcast. Mr. Bose later came to the Director's office to submit the memorandum as usual and had tea with me. Because of the interactions that day, some goodwill developed between Doordarshan and the CPM," says Dr. Sreedher.

This event was an example of sorts. While covering the events in a city, even if the news services failed to give adequate coverage to certain events due to some perceived political reasons, if the Director considered it to be important, he could find other ways to telecast them. Of course, he was answerable to the superiors if questioned. But Dr. Sreedher willingly took the risk on this one, as the worst that could happen to him was an official transfer. And any place—Calcutta or Kashi, away from the family would still mean the same to him.

Dealing with Bad Press Articles

During his initial days at the Doordarshan Kendra, Calcutta, Dr. Sreedher landed in a few controversies and ended up receiving some bad press for the same. He recalls one such incident like this: "I was sitting in my chamber late one evening in DDK Calcutta and going through some files. It was around 6:30 pm. A lady came to my room and said that the AC in the studio was not working and that it would be difficult for her to present the news at 7 pm. I told her she had to complain to the engineers as I was not an AC technician. As I wasn't familiar with her, I asked her about who she was. She said that it was a pity that I did not recognise her. Later I learnt that she was a famous newsreader back then and was reading the news for the past 20 years. I had told her that if she found it difficult to read news without AC, I could make some other arrangements and someone else could read the news that day. I also told her that it was all the more necessary for me to find some new faces and encourage new talent in Doordarshan. She became furious and left. The next day I found that there was a news item in a prominent English daily that the Director, Doordarshan Calcutta had insulted a lady newsreader. Later I got to know that she was also the wife of a senior journalist from a prominent newspaper group based out of Calcutta."

In another incident, a few days after joining DD Calcutta, Dr. Sreedher remembers to have called a meeting of the announcers and casual presenters working with the station. It was on a Saturday as the team used to work six days a week. When the discussion came up about costumes for the shows, Dr. Sreedher advised the presenters to wear costumes befitting the occasion and nature of programmes. When a casual announcer asked him if she could appear wearing a salwar kameez on her show, not knowing about the history of campaigns against salwar kameez in Calcutta during the early 90s, he said she could do so. He did not know what repercussions his advice could have till the next day. A member who was present at the meeting had reported this to a journalist and the next day a daily called *Aajkal* carried an article on how 'A non-Bengali Director at Doordarshan was killing the Bengali culture'. The article was brought to Dr. Sreedher's attention by an officer he had met at a dinner party on Sunday at Fort William, Calcutta. Meanwhile, the Head of the Press Information Bureau Calcutta had sent a note on this press article to the Minister himself. On Monday morning, Dr.

Sreedher got a call from the then I&B Minister, K.P. Singh Deo. He asked Dr. Sreedher for the script of his conversation with the team of announcers. When Dr. Sreedher told him that it was an unscripted internal discussion, he was reprimanded. The Minister categorically told him that "Bengalis will wear dhotis and saris and you have no business to interfere in it".

In another incident that happened much later, Dr. Sreedher remembers a press article that appeared while he was away in Delhi to attend a meeting. The news item said that the Director, Doordarshan Calcutta was summoned by Delhi, regarding the deterioration of the quality of programmes in DD Calcutta. This was not true and when Dr. Sreedher returned to Calcutta in the evening along with the then I&B minister Mr. P.A. Sangma, the reporters asked the Minister, 'when they could expect a new Director for Doordarshan Calcutta?'. The Minister turned towards Dr. Sreedher for an explanation and Dr. Sreedher took the liberty to tell the press that as of then, he was still continuing as the Director of Doordarshan Calcutta.

Noticing that every now and then there were articles appearing about him in the *Aajkal* newspaper, Dr. Sreedher enquired and found out who was writing it. It was a youngster in his twenties. When Dr. Sreedher asked him why he came up with some distorted news item about him each time, he simply said he was assigned the Doordarshan Beat and his news items were a result of his interactions with the staff members in the corridors. Dr. Sreedher told him, that every day he himself had many more interesting files and allegations that came up to his table. Even if he gave him two stories out of them every day, they would sound more authentic than the gossip he picked up from the corridor, he told the journalist. The journalist agreed and started meeting Dr. Sreedher every day to collect stories for his newspaper. When those stories started getting published, the staff at Doordarshan Kendra got annoyed. When they confronted Dr. Sreedher about it, he simply told them,"all this while you were leaking information about me and now I did this against you. Now you will understand my feeling!"

One day during a casual conversation, Dr. Sreedher asked the young journalist from *Aajkal* how much he earned with his stint as a journalist. About Rs. 3,000 per month he said. Dr. Sreedher told him that he was a good journalist and he could consider doing some talk shows on television, on the lines of the Karan Thapar show. If he got sponsors for his show, he could get paid double or triple the salary for each episode, Dr. Sreedher suggested. The journalist was smitten by the idea and decided to pursue it. "Those days DD was the only platform available and there were advertisers who were willing to advertise on certain time bands irrespective of the quality of the programme. So, finding a sponsor would not be difficult either. So, a prime-time slot on a weekday, 7:30 pm was offered to him and he went ahead and produced a talk show named 'Katha'" he recalls.

Back then only a handful of local accredited advertising agencies were eligible to book slots on DD and were required to pay for the same within 90 days period. One such firm came forward to sponsor his talk show. The programming staff of Doordarshan Calcutta objected to this idea of selling out a slot and called it 'privatizing' of Doordarshan. Dr. Sreedher had an idea. He decided to offer his staff at the Doordarshan Kendra the same time slot on a different weekday and asked them to come up with another talk show. Both these shows could compete for eye balls and revenues, and prove who did better, he said. The staff agreed.

After 6 weeks, Ms. Amita Malik, a very well-known media critic of those times visited DD Calcutta. She was called by *Time* magazine as the First Lady of Indian Media and the public broadcasters commonly used to await her opinions on their shows with their fingers crossed. So when she paid a visit to the station, Dr. Sreedher played some of the best programmes to her. She was very impressed with the talk shows and praised them highly in her column. She also praised Dr. Sreedher in her column for his efforts in reviving the monthly programme magazine that was renamed as *Doordarshan Bichitra,* while the earlier one was called *Betar Jagat*.

All seemed to go well till about 8 weeks later, one night around 9 pm Dr. Sreedher got a call while he was at home. At the other side was this young man who hosted the talk show *Katha*. He sounded too low and depressed. Dr. Sreedher got worried. He tried sending his personal guard to the journalist's house, but he would not go. So, he sent his driver to the journalist's place and asked him to bring the young man to his home.

When the journalist was brought home, he opened up after a while and told Dr. Sreedher that he had lost all his money in the production of his TV show. The advertisement agency had not paid him a single penny yet.

The next morning Dr. Sreedher took him to the office and discussed the matter with the Commercial Programme Executive, and his staff. They summoned the Ad agency and made them settle the accounts with this young man. They even warned the Ad agency against losing their accreditation. The Ad agency in turn shared their difficulty in getting the money from the clients. However, they paid up 50 per cent of the money they owed the young man at the earliest. This cheered the young man and Dr. Sreedher was glad to help.

Not all press coverage he received was bad. Some media persons, like Ms. Amita Malik did notice and appreciate the good work Dr. Sreedher was up to during his Calcutta posting.

Owing to the great response to the Bengali programmes on the terrestrial and satellite channels of Doordarshan network, and the interesting and innovative strategies adopted by Dr. Sreedher, Zee's Bengali broadcasts could not compete too strongly for viewership and business. In fact, some of the producers and artistes of Zee's Bengali programmes chose to shift and work for DD 7. Zee's Bengali broadcasts had to eventually shut down in January 1996. *The Statesman* newspaper then came out with a 6-column news article titled 'Zee at Sea' where they praised Dr. Sreedher for his strategies and work. To mark the success of the Doordarshan team over Zee, Dr. Sreedher got a promo made and telecast on January 14, 1996 calling DD 7 'The only Bengali channel in the world'.

A Smoke Free Doordarshan Kendra

There was a canteen within the premises of Doordarshan Kendra Calcutta which also used to sell tobacco products. The canteen used to supply tea, refreshments and sometimes even lunch and dinner for the events at the Doordarshan Kendra. It was facing issues of delayed payments from the Doordarshan Kendra for a long time. The annual hospitality funds allocated for a Director then was Rs. 10,000 and the amount that Doordarshan Calcutta owed to this contractor was over a lakh. It needed 10 years to wipe out the debt. Dr. Sreedher made arrangements and cleared 50 per cent of their dues. In return he made them promise not to sell tobacco products in the canteen. Tobacco, at the Doordarshan Calcutta office was not just a health issue but a hygiene issue as well.

The staff used to smoke or chew tobacco and spit it all over the place in the campus, even in the studios. Dr. Sreedher issued an order not to smoke or chew tobacco in the office premises and got the office walls painted anew. As a part of his daily morning walk at 6 am, Dr. Sreedher checked in and inspected the studios and if he found some tobacco stains on the wall, he would identify the members in that shift and ask them to clean it up.

Once when the Minister of I&B, Mr. P.A. Sangma visited the Calcutta Doordarshan Kendra, he started to smoke in Dr. Sreedher's office. Dr. Sreedher politely showed him a notice on the wall that said, 'No smoking' and he obliged by never again smoking in the Doordarshan premises. Dr. Sreedher admits that he could tell him so, on account of the cordial relations he already had with him and it may not have gone down well with any other minister in his place.

Dr. Sreedher considers it no less than an achievement that till the day he was relieved from office, the Calcutta Doordarshan Kendra was a smoke-free zone and there were significantly fewer stains from spitting on the walls.

Relations with P.A. Sangma

Dr. Sreedher had a very cordial relationship with the I&B minister, P.A. Sangma. Mr. Sangma was kind and approachable and Dr. Sreedher cherishes the good moments he shared with him.

His personal favourite is once they were joined at the breakfast table by Tutu Bose, the then chief of the Mohun Bagan Football team. On being introduced to Dr. Sreedher, Mr. Bose bluntly asked the Minister why a non-Bengali should be heading Doordarshan Calcutta. Mr. Sangma wittily remarked that if he had appointed a Bengali, he would have either been a Mohun Bagan supporter or an East Bengal supporter and that he wanted someone neutral. Later, it was the same Minister who approved Dr. Sreedher's transfer order to Madras in March 1996.

Computerization of DDK Calcutta and Vigilance Enquiry

Dr. Sreedher was never a man to hold back his ideas and thoughts. He never hesitated to go ahead and do something that he thought worked in the interests of the government and the people. Often in his career he operated not fearing the consequences, sometimes even refused to play by the rule book, when he was sure about his intentions and their outcomes. His detractors have often used this against him to tarnish his reputation or get him into trouble. But eventually Dr. Sreedher came out clear in any enquiries that would follow, as he never indulged in any malpractice himself and made sure no one in his team got away with any.

One such initiative that landed Dr. Sreedher into trouble was the decision to buy computers for Doordarshan Calcutta and train his staff in using the same. Having had prior experience in computerization of AIR and Doordarshan Network at Delhi, Dr. Sreedher decided to computerize certain processes in programming and administration in DD Calcutta, as he saw that there was a genuine need to do so.

Initially when he proposed it, most of the staff were against it and seemed to think that it would lead to unemployment. But Dr. Sreedher could see beyond that. "The Doordarshan Kendra in Calcutta made about Rs. 25 crore annually and Rs.2 crore or so a month through advertisements at that time. The bills had to be computerized and sent to the agencies for payment. The usual process was that every six months, a staff member from Doordarshan Calcutta Kendra would travel to Delhi to get the bills computerized and then the bills would be sent to the respective agencies. Some simple mental calculations could reveal that for every Rs. 2 crore pending to Doordarshan, it was losing about Rs. 2 lakh per month as interest. In those days the interest rates on fixed deposits was around 12 per cent," recalls Dr. Sreedher. Just the delay in sending the bills caused a great revenue loss to the government and Dr. Sreedher thought that by buying a Personal Computer and being able to generate invoices every month, the revenue to the Kendra could be significantly improved.

When Dr. Sreedher decided to buy a PC for Doordarshan Calcutta, he realized that he did not have much funds at his disposal for administrative expenses. But he had enough in the funds allocated for set design and properties which could be used for buying sofas, tables or any such kind of requirement while shooting a serial. So Dr. Sreedher thought of making a 26-episode television series on computers and assigned the project to Producer Subash Sanyal at Doordarshan Calcutta. As computers were required to produce the series, Doordarshan had to either buy them or rent them. "Those days the hiring cost for a personal computer came to around Rs. 500 a day. So, hiring a computer for 78 days of shooting would have cost around Rs. 39,000, but buying one would cost only Rs. 33,000. The Director's power of purchase in those days was Rs. 1 lakh. So, I ordered three computers to be purchased at the cost of around Rs. 99,000", recalls Dr. Sreedher. The purchase procedure was initiated and ET&T, a government firm provided the computers at the lowest price. Dr. Sreedher's idea was to save money on computer rentals, while making computers available at the disposal of Doordarshan

Calcutta for programming as well as administrative purposes.

Dr. Sreedher also made efforts to train his teams—both administrative and production—in using computers. "Computer Maintenance Corporation, a public sector company was approached to train the staff members in computer usage. An amount of Rs. 1 lakh was agreed to be paid to CMC for training 100 Doordarshan Calcutta staff members in computers, a couple of hours every day for a fortnight, at a five-star hotel," he recalls.

Dr. Sreedher remembered to get a signed approval for the same from the Director General, while the latter was on a tour. But what he did not remember to follow up was to get the approval ratified by the Director General's office. That was the procedure to be followed if the Director General approved something while he was on tour and Dr. Sreedher did not remember to follow that through. So, though the training went on successfully, the approval for it was not yet fully ratified even until Dr. Sreedher was transferred to Madras on March 11, 1996.

This was noticed by some of his detractors who were unhappy with the computerization and Dr. Sreedher was accused of having committed a grave financial impropriety by diverting the funds meant for quality programming to administrative matters. A preliminary enquiry was ordered on the issue, but they could not find any malafide intention on Dr. Sreedher's part. Nevertheless, Dr. Sreedher remembers being taunted over the computerization issue by his detractors and some senior officers, for the next three years in his career.

Lok Adalat

Dr. Sreedher also had the opportunity to be a part of the Lok Adalat sessions in Calcutta. "The then Chief Justice of India Mr. Ahmadi had suggested to the Chief Justice of Calcutta High Court to include me and more such people playing key roles in the society to be 'People's judges' in the Lok Adalat programmes in the Calcutta High Court. Thus I had the privilege of sitting on a Judge's seat in a High Court. Having experienced the Lok Adalat session first hand, I expressed my wish to do a live telecast of a Lok Adalat session on Doordarshan, to the Chief Justice of India. As doing a live broadcast from the court premises could be disturbing to the court proceedings and would also cost a lot, I asked if such a session could be done from the studios of Doordarshan. The Chief Justice of India asked the Chief Justice of the Calcutta High Court Justice Agarwal to consider the proposal and the possibilities of temporarily shifting a bench of the High Court to the Calcutta Doordarshan studios," reminisces Dr. Sreedher.

The programme team worked on collecting the cases in advance and plans were made to do a pre-recording of the history of the cases. Dr. Sreedher wanted the live telecast to be on a Sunday, replacing the telecast of a sponsored feature film, as he had plans to market the Lok Adalat show as well. The first telecast was fixed for the last Sunday of March 1996.

But things turned out differently as Dr. Sreedher got transferred out of Calcutta well before that. And his successor simply cancelled the programme, citing that it would cause financial loss to Doordarshan. Dr. Sreedher notes that till today there are no live or recorded telecasts of court proceedings in India.

Cricket World Cup 1996

Dr. Sreedher's last few days at Calcutta Doordarshan were packed with action and drama and the number of crisis situations to be handled seemed to be endless. Amidst all the drama and feeling of being kicked around by situations at work, there was an additional challenge of covering the Cricket World Cup Opening Ceremony at Calcutta.

The matches were to be played in India, Sri Lanka and Pakistan, and a grand Opening Ceremony was to be held at the Eden Gardens, Calcutta. Doordarshan Calcutta was in charge of the coverage and had to ensure all technology was in place to share the coverage with the national network and also some international broadcasters. But there was an issue with the coverage. "There was a case regarding the telecast rights of the World Cup, which was still pending judgement in the Supreme Court, even on the eve of the Opening Ceremony. The then BCCI President Mr. Jagmohan Dalmiya, was not willing to allow the Doordarshan team into the stadiums even a day prior to the Opening Ceremony to finalize camera and crew positions as the judgement was still pending in court. The Supreme Court order allowing Doordarshan's coverage of the World Cup came late in the evening and I was left with a huge challenge to set up the team for a live coverage the very next day," recalls Dr. Sreedher. He had done everything he could to be as ready as possible. All the necessary equipment and OB van were already moved and kept ready at the AIR Calcutta campus, which was located close to Eden Gardens. Now all that was required was the permission to enter the premises and set up the equipment and staff positions.

"As soon as the judgement arrived, I made efforts to meet the BCCI President, to request him to provide space and permissions for the Doordarshan coverage team. I finally got through to the BCCI President post-midnight, but I was simply told that the Doordarshan cameras and commentators could cover the ceremony from the galleries, along with the rest of the audience, with no extra furniture or facilities allocated for them," he recalls. As he could not do much to help the situation, he moved on with the other arrangements he had to take care of.

Doordarshan was also supposed to share its coverage of the World Cup with some foreign broadcasters in a digital format. An encoder imported for that purpose was on its way from Delhi to Calcutta and Dr. Sreedher had the additional responsibility of ensuring that it reached the Dehra Dun Satellite Earth Station by the night. In the middle of all this, there was also a last-minute order from Delhi to arrange a Hindi commentary for the event and Dr. Sreedher had to accommodate a Hindi commentator at the stadium. Somehow, he managed that too.

To manage the live coverage for the next day, there was no

time to arrange for phone lines or hotlines to coordinate with the team in Delhi. Cell phones were relatively new, rare and expensive. The handsets were heavy and the incoming calls were charged for too. Dr. Sreedher having seen some private serial producers using the same got in touch with them and requested to borrow two handsets for a day, promising to pay them for all the calls made. They agreed to lend their cell phones and Dr. Sreedher informed the Director General about his plans to use cell phones to coordinate the live coverage. It was agreed upon as there was no better alternative, but when the cell phone bills came much later after the broadcast, it was for a substantial amount running into six digits, remembers Dr. Sreedher.

By the time, the World Cup semi-final match was played at the same venue, Dr. Sreedher had already been transferred to Madras. He remembers watching the live coverage from the comforts of his home. Disappointed at the game, the crowd got into a frenzy and started throwing bottles into the field and even lit fire in the stands.

In Madras, Dr. Sreedher was glad just to be back home. But getting his transfer order was not easy and the events that led to it were trying and taxing.

Here is how he recalls it:

Transfer of a Union Leader and the Repercussions

"When Mr. Ratikant Basu left Doordarshan, Mr. K.S. Sarma took over as the new Director General. The chain of events started when an engineering assistant who was also a leader of the ARTEE (Association of Radio and Television Engineering Employees) Union, had lost the union election after two decades. There was pressure from Delhi to execute his impending transfer to Arunachal Pradesh. The engineering assistant had agreed to move to Arunachal Pradesh, as he would still be able to retain his government quarters in Calcutta where his family would continue to live. Meanwhile, there was an issue around a misunderstanding between a lady production assistant and himself. There were visible fights between two factions (engineering and production) and the team of producers wanted the engineering assistant to be suspended."

Dr. Sreedher had just come back from the launch of a new transmitter at Sheikhpura in Bihar. The trip to Sheikhpura had been an ordeal in itself as he and the Deputy Director General for the Eastern Region had to travel all the way to Dhanbad by road, which took all day and then take an overcrowded night time passenger train to reach Sheikhpura. The train was taken as it was advised that driving down to Sheikhpura at night was dangerous and avoidable. The next day the local MP was inaugurating a low-power transmitter in the village of Sheikhpura. Though there was no live coverage to be done, Dr. Sreedher did arrange to put a scroll on the national television welcoming the viewers of Sheikhpura, with a picture of the local MP, exactly at the time of the launch. After the event, Dr. Sreedher had to travel all the way back to Patna by road and take a flight to Calcutta to attend to the crisis that had come up at the office. He saw a Doordarshan vehicle right behind his car, on his way to Patna. He was surprised to find that it was carrying the low power transmitter and an antenna after being dismantled from Sheikhpura. The engineers on that vehicle told him that they were being taken to another location and were brought to Sheikhpura only for the sake of the inauguration function. Dr. Sreedher could not conceal hide his disbelief. Also, they said that there was no guarantee for the safety of the transmitter if placed at Sheikhpura.

'Oh whatever!' thought Dr. Sreedher.

As soon as Dr. Sreedher returned to the Calcutta office, he ordered a preliminary enquiry into the case involving the engineering assistant and a report to be submitted based on the prima facie of the enquiry. He also requested the other members of the staff to wait patiently for the enquiry report without creating any disturbance to work.

Meanwhile, Minister P.A. Sangma was in Calcutta to inaugurate the new Doordarshan studios at Shantiniketan. Dr. Sreedher was supposed to send a coverage team to

Shantiniketan and was to accompany the Minister to Shantiniketan in a helicopter. Dr. Sreedher pulled himself out of the engagement due to the tense situation at the Calcutta office. He requested the members of the coverage team to cooperate and sent them off to Shantiniketan by road.

On the very same evening, Doordarshan Calcutta had organized a large-scale event—a classical music night called 'DD Music Club'. It was planned as a whole night live concert with the likes of Pandit Shiv Kumar Sharma, Hariprasad Chaurasia, V.G. Jog and Pandit Jasraj performing. Dr. Sreedher had also invited the Minister for I&B, Mr. P.A. Sangma, who was in town, to attend the event. Also, other prominent personalities from Calcutta were invited to grace the event. The event was to be covered live on the DD 3 National Network. This was also the first live concert being covered on DD 3. The Calcutta AIR FM channel was to relay the live audio from the event through the night. Everything was planned and in place, but only until the programming team gave Dr. Sreedher a shocker that evening.

The preliminary enquiry report found the engineering assistant to be at fault and the programming staff went on a flash strike insisting that the engineering assistant be suspended immediately. Originally the programme staff had promised that that they would not disturb the live telecast of the concert. But later they backed out and even persuaded the other casual announcers and camera persons not to cooperate till action was taken.

There was a crisis, but somehow the live show had to go on.

As a first, Dr. Sreedher requested the Deputy Director General R.N. Chakraborty to meet the I&B Minister at the guest house and keep him engaged in watching the live show from there only and not bring him to the venue. Dr. Sreedher did not want the Minister to show up in the middle of the crisis.

Secondly, Dr. Sreedher sought the help of the engineers and told them to at least keep the cameras fixed in the absence of camera persons.

The receptionist from the Doordarshan Office promised to get the artistes in time for their performance at the concert. Ms. Malini Bhowmick, one of the producers who handled the arrangements for the musical night, felt bad about the way things were going, even as she was also a part of the protests. She told Dr. Sreedher that she would try to secretly get herself out of the protests from time to time and help coordinate with the artistes.

Dr. Sreedher personally contacted and asked all the special invitees for the show not to appear for the concert but to enjoy it on TV.

Later one more producer who dealt with agriculture broadcasts came forward to help handle the panel for live telecasts. In some more time a few casual announcers and camera persons came out saying that the 'live' telecast should not be disturbed, no matter what.

With their cooperation the DD Music Club event was telecast live through the night and all the eminent artists performed their best.

The next morning the Minister left for Delhi and Dr. Sreedher stayed at his house as it was a Sunday.

That Sunday, Doordarshan Calcutta was supposed to telecast a film that was sponsored. The revenue from the sponsorship was about Rs. 30 lakhs, remembers Dr. Sreedher. The promos for the movie were already on air. But the programming staff, after the defeat of their protests the previous night and no action having been taken against the engineering assistant yet, saw to it that the advertised film was not telecast and some other movie without advertisements was screened. "The staff would go to any extent not minding the loss to the government, to prove their point", says Dr. Sreedher.

The following day, Dr. Sreedher got a call from his Director General. "The DG instructed me to relieve the engineering assistant with immediate effect and put up a notice for the same on the notice board. I tried explaining to the Director General that it would be better if it were dealt with diplomatically. Putting it up on the notice board could get unwanted attention and the engineers could anytime disrupt the transmission. The Director General insisted and I put up the notice on the noticeboard at around 3:30 pm in the afternoon. Within minutes, the engineers had stopped all telecasts, not only in Calcutta but in the entire eastern region," recalls Dr. Sreedher.

Here is what happened next:

"The engineering staff came to my chambers as a large group and asked me to withdraw the notice. Seeing them barge in, the programme staff formed their own group and rushed to my chambers as well. I got all panicky and felt sick in the stomach."

The programme staff called for a doctor and he asked me to get admitted in a hospital. The local police inspector came with intelligence agency officers. I was taken to my quarters with police support. There also I got a call that the engineers were marching towards my house in protest and wanted me to withdraw the notice. The police officers asked me to leave immediately and took me to a less known colony in Calcutta and admitted me in a nursing home.

When I spoke to the Director General, he asked me not to yield to the pressure. Since I was in hospital, he sent the Deputy Director General and a Chief Engineer to negotiate with the engineering faction.

On Wednesday, when I was just walking around the hospital with a policeman, one engineering assistant who had come to the hospital for his wife's treatment saw me and greeted me. The police guessed that things could be worse as now the other engineers would also know my whereabouts and they might come to the hospital to see me there. I decided to apply for leave and go to Madras for a few days. The police asked me to buy a ticket in Damania airlines and told the protestors from office that I would be going by Indian Airlines. While the engineering staff was still preparing to send a delegation to the airport, I had already flown to Madras. I was sick and had diarrhoea. I got admitted in the Devaki Hospital at Mylapore. On Friday, the Director of the Madras

Doordarshan Kendra came and saw me with his engineer. I again felt trouble brewing. The Madras engineers could ask me to get the order revoked for the sake of their union leader.

I thought it better to go home. On Sunday, i.e. after 10 days of the incident, I got a call from Mr. Gopalan, who was to take over as Secretary of I&B ministry on February 28, 1996, as the then secretary was getting superannuated. He wanted me to sort out the issue as soon as possible. I told him that I would go and resolve the issue but let me do it my way and there should not be any intervention from anywhere. On that assurance on 27th February I took a morning flight to Calcutta. I reached office at 11 am and called the warring groups. I had a discussion with them and arrived at an understanding; It was agreed that the engineering assistant would not be relieved immediately but would go once his transfer allowance funds had been arranged for.

The next day, both the factions called off the strike.

Ten days later, again the I&B Minister P.A. Sangma visited Calcutta. At that time transfers to state capitals were done by the Ministry. I told him the whole story and he asked me to give him what I wanted on a piece of paper. He said that the post of Director DDK Madras was to become vacant on 1st July, as the incumbent officer was superannuating. I told him that the general elections were to be announced soon and there would be ban on transfers. We don't know who the new Minister will be, so I couldn't wait till July. So, transfer me as a Chief Producer of DDK Madras and later I will take over as the Director, I told him.

I got relieved and joined Madras Doordarshan Office in March 1996."

When Dr. Sreedher was leaving Calcutta and moving to Madras in March 1996, the same *Aajkal* newspaper that earlier wrote articles criticizing him, came out with a full-page coverage on Dr. Sreedher and his work and achievements in DDK Calcutta. Thus, it all ended on a positive note. It had, nevertheless, been an irksome journey.

5

Turning Academic

The Elusive Post (March 1996)

Just ahead of joining Doordarshan Madras, the Government of India decided to send Dr. Sreedher to Japan for a three day international conference on 'Trans-Border Broadcasting', at the invitation of the Royalty of Japan.

"The Japanese wanted to collect and learn the legalities around television broadcast in different countries of the world to gain a better understanding of the intricacies of trans-national broadcasts through satellite and to assess its potential as a revenue stream. There were two ways they could go about it. One was to send officers to all these countries to get the details and come back. They instead chose a smarter way and invited representatives from these countries to Tokyo and treated them as royal guests. All that they had to do was to send a proforma to the respective countries, get the details of the representatives and ask them to make a presentation. This way they also ensured that a greater number of local delegates were exposed to the knowledge sharing. Also, many of them could interact with the foreign delegates, asking them all the relevant questions pertaining to the theme. Had they gone travelling to these countries collecting information, there is no way they could have have got so much attention, time and information from the local officers. Now that the foreign delegates had travelled for answering their questions, their response was much better," says Dr. Sreedher. He could not help admiring their smart planning and coordination in organizing an event like this. The trip to Japan had been a worthwhile experience.

Meanwhile back in India, the general elections were announced. Dr. Sreedher came back and joined the Doordarshan Kendra at Madras, the city where he belonged. Within a few months of his joining, Madras was officially renamed Chennai. The humid sea breeze, the soaring temperatures, the warmth of staying close to home and being able to work once again in his mother tongue were the privileges that returned to him. He joined as the Chief Producer at DDK Madras, waiting to take over as the new Director when the incumbent Director Mr. A. Natarajan retired in a few months' time. But Mr. Natarajan apparently had other plans.

"In those days the retirement age was 58 and Mr. Natarajan was nearing that. He was a man of influence with the state and central governments and was hoping for an extension of another year," says Dr. Sreedher. "So…he didn't enjoy my presence there, waiting to take over after him and started to find ways to keep me at bay." This was the time when some of the old files in Calcutta were reopened again and issues were created over the projects handled by Dr. Sreedher in the recent past. There was an enquiry on his alleged mishandling of production funds for computerization purposes and the approvals pertaining to it. "Some issues were embarrassing and some more harassing", recalls Dr. Sreedher. The incident when Dr. Sreedher was urgently called back to office for an event, and he had to fly back to Calcutta while he was on leave performing his father's parting rituals in Madras, was dug up again and an issue was created over his expensive flight travel, calling it unnecessary. Later he was made to repay the total cost of his flight. "Left to myself I would have taken a train but took a flight because I was summoned to be back just the next day for the Parliamentary Committee visit. The air ticket cost about Rs. 3,500 in those days, almost equal to my monthly salary," says Dr. Sreedher, who was definitely unhappy with the way things were going for him in Chennai.

Meanwhile, the Director of Pondicherry Doordarshan Kendra was to go on a Haj pilgrimage and Dr. Sreedher was given the responsibility to take additional charge as the Director of Pondicherry Doordarshan Kendra along with his current role. The Pondicherry Doordarshan Kendra operated more like a relay station, with a very small broadcast unit and very few notable programmes. Dr. Sreedher decided to try his best to do some local programmes in whatever ways possible without affecting the existing schedule of programmes. He found a one-minute slot between national and local news broadcast and used that time to do some active coverage of the assembly polls in Pondicherry. Albeit the slot was only a minute long, Dr. Sreedher took the initiative to broadcast some live updates and interviews with political leaders in it, which garnered a positive response from the local audience. The local staff also cooperated exceedingly well and Dr. Sreedher ensured they were compensated well for the additional efforts made.

"When Congress lost the General Elections in India, Mr. Sangma called to inform me that the service of the incumbent Director Mr. Natarajan was to be extended by a year and that he would try to get me a better position with the Government of India in his new capacity. He then went on to become the Speaker of the Lok Sabha," says Dr. Sreedher. Dr. Sreedher, however, decided to stay on and continue as Chief Producer in Chennai for another year at least as there was no point in going on another transfer just within a few months of joining Doordarshan Chennai.

Though the designation of Chief Producer equalled in rank to that of the Director, their distribution of powers was still ambiguous. Dr. Sreedher nevertheless went ahead and took some bold initiatives that made everyone sit up and take notice. For instance, for Diwali celebrations that year, Dr. Sreedher decided to do special programmes and contests using Pager communication, which was quite a sensation at that time. He was also assigned the responsibility to look after the film broadcasts, as there were complaints of corruption and leakage of information to outsiders. There was only one private player in the market who competed with the Doordarshan satellite channel at that time, and somehow, they always played the movies scheduled for broadcast on Doordarshan, a day or two ahead, thus gaining TRP and advertisers. Dr. Sreedher took strict measures to address the issue and ensured that film broadcasts were streamlined.

For the Tamil New Year's Day celebrations, Dr. Sreedher suggested to have a night-long live celebration, as is usually done on the English New Year's Eve. Only this time, it would be celebration of Tamil culture, traditional and folk arts. He wanted to hold the festival in Poompuhar, a city near Thanjavur district of Tamil Nadu and cover it live on the satellite channel, DD 5 which was later renamed as DD Pothigai. When the Director did not approve of the expenses, he suggested doing it in the Island Grounds in Chennai, where people could come and watch the celebrations live. When this too was not approved, a night-long celebration was organized in the Doordarshan studios itself, inviting Tamil traditional and folk artistes to come and perform live. As all infrastructure for covering the event live was already available at the studios, the only expense was of inviting the artistes and their hospitality. A popular brand of stores selling home utilities, came forward and took up the cost of sponsorship for the celebrations. So, a night-long celebration was organized and various performers and artistes performed individually through the night and later rallied together culminating in the huge celebrations. Popular film artistes also marked their presence during the live broadcasts and conveyed their Tamil New Year wishes to the audience. It was a lively and cheerful celebration and the live telecasts garnered a great response from the audience. The next day Dr. Sreedher was surprised to find a poster someone had put up on the Doordarshan campus walls, which hailed the Director of Doordarshan as the saviour of Tamil culture and arts, appreciating him for the previous night's celebration and broadcasts. "So much for almost not letting me do it!" thought Dr. Sreedher.

Dr. Sreedher also fondly recalls the cooperation extended by the entire DDK Chennai staff, particularly of Mr. M.S. Perumal and Mr. U.M. Kanna, in his initiatives.

Visiting NDTV in New Delhi

While he was still working in DDK Chennai, Dr. Sreedher was in Delhi for a visit. He had an invitation from Mr. Prannoy Roy to visit NDTV, which was then functioning from a few floors in Archana Cinema in East of Kailash in New Delhi. He remembers being taken around by Mr. Prannoy Roy and meeting the young and prominent journalists from the team including Barkha Dutt, Rajdeep Sardesai, Arup Ghosh, and Shereen. "Mr. Prannoy Roy was then producing the morning shows on Doordarshan national network. During the visit, I was even offered to join NDTV by Mr. Prannoy Roy. I told him that the government rules prohibit anyone from joining a private organization for a minimum period of two years from resignation or retirement. I thanked him and politely refused the offer," recalls Dr. Sreedher.

Meeting with Thiru M. Karunanidhi Chief Minister of Tamil Nadu (1996)

Once there was a request from the Chief Minister's office to telecast the presentation of the Tamil Nadu budget by the Chief Minister live on Doordarshan. Thiru M. Karunanidhi was the Chief Minister of the Tamil Nadu then. He wanted to telecast the presentation of the Tamil Nadu budget live on Channel DD 1 (now DD National). "Those days Sun TV had already started emerging but they were not allowed to do 'live' programmes. They were broadcasting by sending recorded tapes to Hong Kong, Bangkok or the Philippines. Only DD was in a commanding position to do live telecasts," says Dr. Sreedher. When the request came, the Station Director Mr. Natarajan was away and Dr. Sreedher was acting as the head of programmes. It was agreed that DD1 would relay the Tamil Nadu budget live from 10 am to 11 am and then delink for the telecast of Parliament proceedings at 11 am. This being the first time ever that such an effort was being undertaken, the Chief Minister was happy and there was wide publicity. But when the live telecasts were happening, because of time constraints, DD had to cut off the relay abruptly as the Budget announcement extended beyond 11 am. Dr. Sreedher decided to continue the live relay on DD 5 (now Podhigai). DD 5 being a satellite channel, with cable TV was still in its infant stages, its reach was limited. When the CM was told that DD did not relay his full speech, he was upset. In the meanwhile, Dr. Sreedher took a decision to rebroadcast the entire Tamil Nadu budget speech at 1 pm on the terrestrial channel by replacing the dubbed Hindi serials. He met the Chief Minister in his chambers at around 1 pm the same day and the CM expressed his unhappiness." If this was the case I would have never let DD cover it," he said. Dr. Sreedher did not answer him but just showed him the TV screen in his chambers. DD1 was rebroadcasting the entire TN Budget speech. The Chief Minister saw that, and his anger dissipated, reminisces Dr. Sreedher.

Dr. Sreedher was just getting used to working this way in Doordarshan Chennai, when he was issued an order transferring him to Gulbarga to take over a new upcoming Doordarshan Kendra, a second one in Karnataka. Mr. C.M. Ibrahim was the Minister for Information and Broadcasting then, who belonged to North Karnataka region. But Dr. Sreedher refused to take up the new opportunity not wanting to experiment once again working in an unknown region and an unknown language, having had enough learning experiences in Calcutta. He offered to visit the Gulbarga station as often as required from Chennai and oversee the launch activities, instead of going there on a transfer. "If you don't want me to be in Chennai, you can post me to Mandi House in Delhi and make me the Controller of xxxxxx or something. Or send me back to where I belong...Radio," he remembers telling the officials at Delhi.

He was given a firm 'no' for an answer and the DG insisted he take up charge at Gulbarga. Then without a choice, Dr. Sreedher approached the authorities in the Ministry and explained his situation. They listened to him patiently and decided to send him back to AIR. They wanted to post him in Bhopal as the Director of AIR in Bhopal had died during his term. The DG AIR agreed to take Dr. Sreedher back but told him off for going to Doordarshan and coming back to AIR, 'as per his whims and fancies'. He suggested that Dr. Sreedher should take a posting in Goa, as it was not a Hindi-speaking state and he could work on the English programmes. But the Ministry was firm that Dr. Sreedher was to be posted in Bhopal. He got his appointment order in the next three days and was all set to move to AIR, Bhopal with his family. He remembered to call his DG at Doordarshan to give him an update on his new role.

In Bhopal he joined as the zonal Director and oversaw AIR Bhopal and 19 other AIR stations in the unified Madhya Pradesh which then included the present Chhattisgarh as well.

Election Coverage, Bhopal (1998)

There were 39 constituencies in Madhya Pradesh then. Dr. Sreedher approached BSNL and arranged for 39 temporary telephone lines, one for each constituency and he also arranged for 39 skilled reporters to be sent to each constituency for coverage. 'Matdaan Madhya Pradesh' and 'Matgananaa Madhya Pradesh' were the names of the programmes covering the polling and counting of votes respectively. Things were going as planned and the live coverage was on, when a reporter from Morena reported that a polling booth had been captured in his constituency. Dr. Sreedher immediately called the reporter and got the District Collector on the phone line and recorded a quick interview with him. The Collector confirmed the incident, spoke about the measures being taken to handle the situation and shared the news that six members including a Bahujan Samaj Party MLA had been arrested in connection with the booth capture. Dr. Sreedher played this interview on air, and AIR was the first media to report the news of booth capture in Morena.

Three months later, during the Parliament session, a member raised questions on how AIR could go ahead and announce that one of their MLAs had been arrested during the polls. It affected their image and hence the voter response on the polling day, the member alleged. Based on the allegations, Dr. Sreedher was questioned. Dr. Sreedher explained that, it was not AIR or its staff, but the Collector himself who had shared the information on air and offered the tapes as evidence. The issue was settled with that.

Later, Dr. Sreedher had the opportunity of speaking to the Returning Officers at a workshop organised by the CEC Madhya Pradesh about the importance of the broadcast code or AIR code in addition to the Election Commission's code of conduct. Dr. Sreedher did not forget to mention the Morena Booth capture incident and explained how a possible controversy could have been avoided by simply not mentioning the name of the political party.

During his tenure at Bhopal, once again the opportunity of being appointed as the Director, Doordarshan Chennai came to him and evaded him within 24 hours. In 1998 the Chief Minister of Tamil Nadu, wanted a new Director for Doordarshan Chennai. After considering many names she found Dr. Sreedher to be suitable to head Doordarshan Chennai when finally, Mr. Natarajan was retiring after two years of extension. But when he was approached with the prospect, Dr. Sreedher was unreachable. He was on the train travelling with his mother to Bhopal and his wife had answered the call at his residence. As he was not reachable for another 24 hours, the opportunity was then passed on to someone else. When Dr. Sreedher finally reached Bhopal and rang Mr. Natarajan he was told 'you have lost the race' and that someone had already been appointed.

In spite of making notable achievements in all his postings, there are two things that still make Dr. Sreedher feel discontented about his career. One is the feeling that the right kind of appreciation and merit never came for his work at the right time and from the right people. Secondly, he never got a suitable posting in Tamil Nadu. The more probable it seemed the more it eluded him every time.

But he was never a man to sit back and have regrets. He concentrated on the work at hand and came up with other path-breaking projects. Another notable initiative Dr. Sreedher took while he was at Bhopal was to launch a new song request show at night. 'Raahi Matwale' as the show was called, addressed a major population of truck drivers in the state. It was a live show done over the telephone. AIR reporters would visit the many Dhabas on the national and state highways and engage in conversation with the truck drivers who would halt there for rest and food. They would get them talking about themselves, their favourite song, why they liked it, who they wanted to play it for, their families, love interests, etc. The truck drivers sometimes even opened up about the illicit relationships they had while on their journeys and the makers of the programme used it as an opportunity to spread HIV/AIDS awareness. The show went on to get an appreciation from WHO, which called it a 'Stellar Example of New Communication Initiative'. But when that happened, Dr. Sreedher had already moved on from AIR to join IGNOU and he could not attend the WHO conference, as AIR refused to share the show tapes with him as he was no longer with them when the prize was announced. Dr. Sreedher tried to give the missed opportunity a second try. He approached the station director AIR Jaipur Ms. Aparna Vaish, to replicate a similar show model in Jaipur. The latter obliged and Dr. Sreedher funded the initiative from IGNOU. But when it was sent to the WHO this time, they said that they had adjudged the original programme and would not entertain the second entry. The Jaipur initiative went on to win an Akashwani Award later.

Not all opportunities were missed, though. During his tenure at Bhopal, he landed the opportunity to attend a SAARC conference in Pakistan. It was the SAARC Conference on Science Popularization and Communication held at Islamabad in 1998. (SAARC Conference is different from SAARC Summit.) Even though his stint in the Department of Science and Technology was a short one that lasted only about a year and a half, he continued his association with them. Dr. Narender K. Sehgal was the head of the National Council for Science and Technology Communication (NCSTC) and he intended to send two people to the SAARC conference, one of them being Dr. Sreedher. "In the normal course they should have written to the Ministry of Information and Broadcasting and asked them to suggest a name, after giving the broad parameters about the conference and the eligibility to attend it. In this case it was not done. My selection was approved by the External Affairs Ministry. The I&B Ministry did object to it, but the External Affairs Ministry justified my selection", says Dr. Sreedher.

And just a day before his departure to Islamabad for the conference, he gave an interview for the post of Director, Electronic Media Production Centre at the Indira Gandhi National Open University (IGNOU). He had decided to move back to New Delhi for his children's higher education and started looking for opportunities to move to New Delhi. That is when he came across the opening in IGNOU and decided to apply for it. He had earlier applied for the post in 1992 and attended the interview but was not selected owing to his lack of experience in television. This time he had gained that experience and was more confident. During the interview when the Vice-Chancellor of IGNOU asked him the first questions: "How are you? What do you do?", Dr. Sreedher told him promptly that after the interview he was going to Islamabad for a SAARC Conference. After his interview at IGNOU he went straight to the Pakistan High Commission in Chanakyapuri, New Delhi to collect his official visa.

SAARC Conference (Pakistan 1998)

He landed in Islamabad on a Sunday and was received at the airport by the members of the Pakistan Science Forum. It was then a practice that the Indians visiting Pakistan should first register their visit with the Magistrate at a nearby Court. "Sunday being a holiday, on Monday morning, I was taken to the Court to complete the formalities. The magistrate was running late to office and I was sitting and waiting among other criminals, all the while wondering if I never should have come in the first place. After some time, the Police

Superintendent on duty took kindly to me and offered tea. He introduced himself as being from the Sindh region, closer to India, and as having worked in UN Peacekeeping Missions where he had worked along with Indian army personnel. After learning the purpose of my visit and other details, he helped me finish the formalities of registration, using his powers and discretion. There were similar formalities to be completed before leaving the country as well, and he helped me finish those formalities as well on the same day. I could not be more thankful," recalls Dr. Sreedher. He then remembers visiting the Indian High Commission to give them his attendance and to collect his subsistence allowance. The organizers of the event were giving the allowance in Pakistan rupees and Dr. Sreedher requested for the same to be given in US dollars. They suggested that he could collect his allowance in dollars on return to India from the SAARC headquarters. The second alternative they gave was to collect it from the Indian High Commission in Pakistan. The Indian High Commission agreed to help him and asked him to come and collect his allowance the next day. When Dr. Sreedher went to the Indian High Commission the next day, he was accompanied by the Director General for Science Museum, from the Pakistan government. A Pakistani official visiting the Indian High Commission, aroused suspicion in the intelligence department and the moment they left the Indian High Commission, two men in plain clothes started following their vehicle. They stopped them midway on a highway and Dr. Sreedher's Pakistani friend was quizzed by the two men for about 30 minutes. Dr. Sreedher was losing his patience after waiting for long without a clue of what was going on. He finally asked the men who they were. 'Intelligence', they replied. Still not reading into the situation, Dr. Sreedher asked them rather innocently, 'Indian intelligence? 'ISI' they replied. After the incident he did not fail to notice that till the time he left the country the two men had kept a strict watch on him and his colleague from India, Dr. B.K. Tyagi, from the Department of Science and Technology.

Apart from attending the conference and networking with other science enthusiasts, there was something else that Dr. Sreedher wanted to do in Islamabad. The organizers of the conference planned a two-day sightseeing tour. They wanted the delegates to visit the ancient site of Takshashila or Taxila, in northern Pakistan just about 24 kilometres away from Islamabad. It is a UNESCO heritage site, known to be the home of one of the first universities in the world, where ancient prodigies like Charaka (Ayurveda exponent), Panini (Sanskrit grammarian), Kautilya (the famous author of *Arthashastra* and kingmaker who helped to establish the Mauryan empire) were known to have studied and worked. It is also an important site for Buddhism and Mahayana Buddhism is said to have evolved here. These and many more interesting facts and incidents associated with this historically significant place, made Dr. Sreedher want to pay a visit to this place. "All delegates who attended the conference, except the two members from India, had a restriction-free visa. So they were planning to go and I decided to join them. I did not want to miss the opportunity of visiting Takshashila, having come so close to it. I visited the place and like many other tourists with me, I also bought for myself a Buddha idol as a souvenir," he recounts.

Pakistan's External Affairs Minister, Ms. Abida Hussaini hosted high tea for the guests from SAARC nations and during the conversations, she asked the members where all they had been. When Dr. Sreedher told her that he went to Takshashila and bought a Buddha idol there, she warned him that it might be tough getting it cleared through the customs/security. Dr. Sreedher was next scheduled to travel to Karachi and while the other members who had similar Buddha idols got through the security check, Dr. Sreedher's idol was spotted and he was questioned. After discussing for a while, they let him go considering that he was only going to Karachi and when he would later fly out of Karachi, the Karachi Customs could take a call on the Buddha statue after getting an archaeologist's opinion.

During his flight to Karachi, another local participant of the conference, a journalist with the Pakistan's leading newspaper, *Dawn* suggested to Dr. Sreedher that instead of Dr. Sreedher going through another hassle with the Customs during his next flight, he could instead leave the Buddha idol with him and offered to bring it to India during his next visit. Dr. Sreedher agreed. Later, when Dr. Sreedher was taking a flight from Karachi to Mumbai, the Customs questioned him about the Buddha idol he carried from Islamabad to Karachi and Dr. Sreedher had to explain to them that he left it with the *Dawn* correspondent in Karachi.

Dr. Sreedher was still in Pakistan when he got the news of having been selected to join IGNOU as the Director of the Electronic Media Production Centre. Direct email service between India and Pakistan was not possible at that time. One of the Board members of IGNOU had conveyed the news of his selection to his good friend Mr. Krishnamurthy and he had uploaded the news on a UN website which was accessible from Islamabad. Dr. Sreedher shared the news with the others at the conference and told them that henceforth he was going to be an academic. The organizers of the conference celebrated his selection by offering sweets and tea.

Later, that night the Director General of Pakistan Science Museums took Dr. Sreedher to his home for dinner. He introduced Dr. Sreedher to his school-going daughter as an Indian. Dr. Sreedher remembers how the girl had looked at him with both surprise and fear. Whatever the image the local children seemed to have of Indians, it did not seem friendly, he says.

Dr. Sreedher's visa did not enable a visit to Rawalpindi, even as Islamabad and Rawalpindi are known as twin cities. The foreign office in Pakistan then helped Dr. Sreedher visit and shop at Rawalpindi by sending one of their officials with him.

Overall the visit to Pakistan, had been a memorable trip.

A few years later, the Director General of Pakistan Science Museums visited India. Dr. Sreedher met him at Hotel Ashoka in New Delhi and invited him to IGNOU. He learnt from him that in India, he too had to report at a Police Station and a similar procedure was followed with him in India, as Dr. Sreedher was put through in Pakistan.

When Dr. Sreedher decided to resign his post at AIR, Bhopal and move to New Delhi and join IGNOU, his friends advised him to instead apply for voluntary retirement, as that would ensure him some pension. So he applied for voluntary retirement and waited to be relieved. The officer, who in the capacity of DG Doordarshan insisted that Dr. Sreedher move to Gulbarga on transfer, the same officer had now moved to the Ministry of I&B as the Joint Secretary. And in his new role, it was his prerogative to ensure that the person taking voluntary retirement from AIR was free from all internal enquiries. "He was aware of the enquiry over the computerization of Doordarshan Kolkata which everyone was expecting to blow up into a big scandal. But they found only a minor aberration in administrative and financial procedures and no case was ever filed. So this time again, he wanted to ensure that no vigilance case was pending against me either in AIR or in Doordarshan or in the Prasar Bharati files, before letting me retire... and it was taking time", says Dr. Sreedher.

While Dr. Sreedher was awaiting these clearances, Mr. Muktar Abbas Naqvi, the then Minister of State for Information and Broadcasting was visiting Bhopal. Dr. Sreedher had to take care of the Minister while he was in the city. Normally Doordarshan provided the conveyance for the Minister, whenever he visited Bhopal, but on this occasion, AIR was asked to arrange conveyance due to some crisis that had arisen at Doordarshan. While conversing with the Minister, he shared his plans to join IGNOU. He told the Minister that he was likely to see his retirement file on his table on his return to Delhi. So, when that happened, the Minister cleared it immediately. "Usually before the file went to the Minister it had to be cleared by the Secretary on the recommendations of the Joint Secretary at the Ministry. Mr. O.P. Kejariwal, the then CEO of Prasar Bharati, who also had an academic leaning being a historian, wrote special DO (Demi Official) letters to the Secretary and Joint Secretary stating that he would want me to be relieved at the earliest," recalls Dr. Sreedher.

With a sigh of relief he moved to New Delhi with his family and joined IGNOU.

The IGNOU Experiences (1998-2003)

Dr. Abdul Waheed Khan, who later went on to become the Assistant Director General for Communication and Information with UNESCO, was then the Vice-Chancellor of IGNOU.

"Dr. Abdul Waheed Khan was a man of vision. He had developed a proposal for Kisan Vani—a radio channel for farmers and agriculturists, way back in 1973-75 at the Gobind Ballabh Pant University of Agriculture and Technology. Though Professor Sher Singh, then Minister for Communication, had expressed a favourable opinion on the proposal, formal approval was not granted by the Government of India and hence Kisan Vani was never launched. He later moved to All India Radio in 1975 as the Director of Farm Home Broadcast," recalls Dr. Sreedher.

Dr. Sreedher also remembers how he was in total awe when he first saw the infrastructure at IGNOU. They had a huge television studio, built with a budget of about Rs.100 crore in collaboration with a Japanese organization, JiCA. He was disappointed to learn that the studio had not been put into optimal use and there were plans to lease it out to private productions for shooting purposes. One of the first things he remembers he mentioned to the Vice-Chancellor when he met him was that they could start a new TV channel using all the infrastructure. The Vice-Chancellor asked Dr. Sreedher to just work on producing good educational programmes using the studio infrastructure and not bother about starting a TV channel for now. But the idea of starting a television education channel had already captured Dr. Sreedher's imagination. IGNOU already had a huge back-up of educational video programmes under various topics, for children and adults.

With so much content readily available, it would not cost much to start and run a TV channel, thought Dr. Sreedher.

It was not just Dr. Sreedher who had considered starting an educational television channel using all the infrastructure at IGNOU. Some of the media experts and officials of the central government who visited the campus and saw the infrastructure at IGNOU, also came up with a similar suggestion. In fact the idea to start a television channel had been mooted much earlier by Dr. Abdul Waheed Khan himself.

In his own words, Dr. Abdul Waheed Khan recalls it as follows—"The idea of Gyan Darshan was mooted by me when I was the Director of Communication Division and Professor V.C. Kulandai Swamy was the Vice-Chancellor. IGNOU at that time developed the concept of a Consortium of Educational Media Organizations. IGNOU convened the meeting of the consortium to discuss the idea of pooling the resources of different educational media organizations in the country.

When Mr. M.K. Kaw joined the Ministry of Human Resources Development as the Secretary, he invited me to brief him on the main activities of the University. When he asked me what could be a "star" initiative, I shared my idea of Gyan Bharati with three components: Gyan Darshan (television), Gyan Vani (radio) and Gyan Vahini (internet). Mr Kaw received the idea enthusiastically and assured his full support," he recalls.

Later, a proposal was put together based on Dr. Abdul Waheed Khan's idea and as the proposal was going through various levels of approvals, it landed on the table of the then Additional Secretary at the Ministry of Human Resource Development, and it was someone Dr. Sreedher already knew. Once again it was Mr. K.S. Sarma who had then been transferred from the Ministry of I&B to the Ministry of Human Resource and Development as Additional Secretary. Dr. Sreedher's files always ended up on his table.

But Mr. K.S. Sarma rang up Dr. Sreedher as soon as he saw the proposal on his table. Mr. Sarma talked to the Vice-

Chancellor. The Vice-Chancellor then rang up Dr. Sreedher and asked him to talk to Mr. K.S. Sarma regarding the proposal. The Vice-Chancellor stood guarantee that nothing would go wrong this time and insisted that Dr. Sreedher meet Mr. K.S. Sarma. So, through his Joint Directors Mr. Rama Rao and Mr. Ravikant, Dr. Sreedher arranged for a meeting. Soon, Mr. K.S. Sarma dropped in at the IGNOU campus to discuss the proposal. Like many others who visited the campus, he too was awestruck by its state-of-the-art infrastructure.

This meeting gave both of them an opportunity to develop some understanding of each other, leaving behind the bitter experiences of the past. Both wanted a successful educational channel to be up and running for the country. They went on to build an excellent rapport and together handled the many challenges they faced.

Dr. Sreedher also remembers that Dr. Binod Agarwal (the founder of Taleem Foundation, earlier associated with ISRO) who was an executive committee member with the Development Communicator's Forum had suggested to Dr. Sreedher, that the Forum could talk to Mr. Subhash Chandra, the Chairman of Zee network to get a transponder for broadcasting the channel. Dr. Binod Agarwal did take up the cause seriously but it remained on paper, he recalls.

Gyan Darshan—The Country's First Educational TV Channel

"When we were planning to launch the Gyan Darshan Channel in the second half of 1999, we made a presentation to the Ministry of HRD describing how we could run an educational channel from the content collected by coordinating with all educational institutions in the country which had facilities for video production. They included the 18 Educational Media Research Centres of UGC, the facilities at the six IITs, the State Institutes of Educational Technology, Central Institute for Educational Technology, Indira Gandhi National Open University, National Institute for Open Schooling, Technical Teachers Training Institutes, State Open Universities, Adult Education Department, Department of Health and Family

Welfare, Environment Ministry, UN agencies, etc. Mr. Kaw, a dynamic no nonsense officer, was impressed with the presentation. Now that content could be arranged for, we were then looking for a satellite transponder, to uplink the channel. Indian laws prevented any agency other than Doordarshan from uplinking to satellites. But now that the secretary, MHRD was showing an interest in the project, we were hopeful that something could be worked out. The Vice Chancellor of IGNOU, Dr. Abdul Waheed Khan put all his weight behind the project. Mr. K.S. Sarma, Additional Secretary in MHRD met Mr. Rajiv Rattan Shaw, the CEO of Prasar Bharati and came to an understanding that Doordarshan would place one of its spare transponders at IGNOU for telecast of this channel. They also concluded that the channel would be Doordarshan's educational channel and that all the technical facilities would be provided by IGNOU and MHRD would find the entire project. There was no Secretary level meeting or Minister level meeting. No cabinet notes. No major investment from government. And a channel was to be born", says Dr. Sreedher.

If getting the approvals and arrangements in place was a challenge, it was another challenge to get the existing teams to gear up and work towards launching the channel. "The Electronic Media Production Centre (EMPC) at IGNOU, had quite a large workforce for the work that they were doing. They had state-of-the-art facilities but the staff were very volatile. They wanted to be faculty members of the university and were not willing to work for launching a television channel. Dr. Natarajan Sundaram, the Joint Registrar at IGNOU, was a no nonsense officer and he helped in dealing with the revolting staff and ensured smooth working. He later became the Registrar of Tamil Nadu Open University, Banaras Hindu University and SRM University in Gangtok," recalls Dr. Sreedher.

ISRO and Educational Broadcasts

ISRO, through its Development Education Communication

Unit (DECU), was using their technology and working on projects pertaining to training and development through distance education. They used a mobile earth station called TRACT, which was stationed at IGNOU, for demonstrating the one-way video-two-way audio interactive television technology. Organizations like the Indian Management Association, Teacher Training Centres and Institute of Chartered Accountants were also using the facility for channelling their content. It was called the TDCC—Training and Development Communication Channel.

"While all TV channels in analogue mode were being transmitted using 'C' Band in satellite, ISRO used the 'Extended C band' for its educational projects. In those days downlinking was through very large dish antennas and extended C band required a separate decoder. IGNOU had set up downlink centres at various regional offices and study centres. Each downlink facility cost more than a lakh back then...but today the DTH facility is available for just around Rs. 2,000", says Dr. Sreedher.

"In 1996 IGNOU thought of investing in a permanent earth station in its campus with the help of ISRO and it was given to ISRO as a paid project. But, the establishment of the earth station was getting delayed due to the 'sanctions' issued by developed nations in response to India conducting the second nuclear implosion test in 1998 at Pokhran. They were unable to get a few equipment imported and that was delaying the completion of the setting up of the earth station", he recalls.

Meanwhile, Dr. Sreedher got an idea that when the permanent earth station was ready, it could be used for the uplink of the new educational channel that IGNOU was planning to launch. Dr. Sreedher made efforts to import the equipment required for setting up the earth station, directly from IGNOU and successfully managed to get it done as IGNOU was an educational institution and was exempt from sanctions. Instead of approaching ISRO again, he used his network and staff to get the earth station up and running by buying and borrowing equipment. He loaned an 'upconverter' from AIR for the earth station. He also bought the antenna equipment for the earth station from ECIL—a public sector enterprise from Hyderabad that made smaller antennas that were used during the Kargil war. Fortunately for him, things fell in place and he was able to get the earth station up and running.

When he told the Secretary of the HRD Ministry, Mr. Kaw, that all technology and content was in place to start the channel, the latter willingly agreed to inaugurate the permanent earth station facility. When the Vice Chancellor of IGNOU, Mr. Abdul Waheed Khan learnt about these discussions and developments he summoned Dr. Sreedher and asked him whether he was working for IGNOU or for the Ministry of HRD. "Sir, I work for IGNOU and you are my boss. But the educational channel will be for the country. Hence I am interested in it," he told him. However, DECU-ISRO, was upset at the way the earth station had been put together to be used for the launch of the channel, without their involvement or approvals.

Dr. Sreedher was caught up with all the arrangements and coordination for the launch of the earth station in August 1999, when the news came that his mother was critically ill in Mumbai. He rushed to Mumbai and was at her bedside during her last moments. She having learnt that Dr. Sreedher was working to launch an Education Channel, wished that the country should also have an exclusive channel for children and that it would be nice if Dr. Sreedher could get to start that too. He came back to Delhi after scattering her ashes in the sea and performed the other rituals from his home at Delhi as he had to be back for the inauguration of the earth station at IGNOU. On the tenth day of parting rituals, he remembers waking up at 3 am to finish the rituals and then rushed to the IGNOU campus for the inauguration.

"With the inauguration of the earth station began the test transmissions of the educational channel but when ISRO learnt of the earth station and the satellite uplink being used by IGNOU for running a TV channel without any form of approval from them, they sent a written communication objecting to it, calling it illegal. They also cut off all communication with the satellite from the earth station and with that the whole project came to a standstill," recalls Dr. Sreedher.

He was disappointed as his plan to launch the educational channel for the country was stalled. But at the same time, IGNOU continued to collect tapes of educational content from partner organizations. Time was running out and now he was also worried about losing his job.

On a fine day, he met Mr. Gurumurthy of External Services Division of All India Radio, Delhi at a workshop. He and his wife were earlier trained by Dr. Sreedher in Chennai. Mr. Gurumurthy shared his plan for a special programme that he wanted to do for the New Year—January 1, 2000. He wanted to do an interview in Tamil with Dr. Kasturirangan, the Chairman of ISRO to be broadcast for the listeners in South Asia. He observed that he would like Dr. Sreedher to do the interview for the channel and Dr. Sreedher willingly agreed to do the same.

"When I met Dr. Kasturirangan, at first he was reluctant to talk in Tamil. But he later agreed to do the interview in Tamil," recalls Dr. Sreedher. The recording went on for about two hours and when they were wrapping up, Dr. Sreedher took the opportunity to discuss with him the situation at IGNOU's earth station and how they were unable to link with the satellite. Dr. Kasturirangan agreed to help him and told him that they would need a larger antenna as opposed to the smaller antenna purchased by IGNOU from ECIL. Dr. Kasturirangan then deputed Mr. Rengarajan to help IGNOU in sourcing a large antenna from ECIL and completing the other formalities to be able to uplink the channel. They were also given permission to broadcast for two hours every day using the satellite link.

When Dr. Sreedher wanted to begin transmission, a few of his staff members suggested doing a puja at the studios before the launch. Dr. Sreedher arranged for it and requested the Vice-Chancellor to be present during the puja and launch.

After the puja, the pandit wanted to break a coconut. Gyan Darshan, India's first educational channel, went on air, with the Vice-Chancellor Dr. A.W. Khan sportively breaking the coconut, recalls Dr. Sreedher.

"Once Dr. Murli Manohar Joshi, Minister, HRD, came to know that IGNOU was in a position to broadcast educational programmes, he asked Mr. Khan that a formal launch function be held on January 26, 2000. He suggested this on 16th January, leaving only 10 days to get everything in place. The larger antenna from ECIL arrived only by 20th January. But there were other accessories and approvals that needed to be put in place for that to be usable. It was likely to take a week or so. Later, on 23rd January, Dr. Joshi asked Dr. Khan to contact the Minister for Information and Broadcasting, Mr. Arun Jaitley, to invite him for the launch.

Mr. Jaitley was in Assam and returned to the capital only the next morning. His flight was late because of the fog and he went straight to office owing to his busy schedule that day. IGNOU's Board meeting was underway, when I got Mr. Jaitley on the line and the Vice-Chancellor spoke to him. Mr. Jaitley was too busy to hear through the invitation and thought that IGNOU was inviting him for a programme and confirmed his presence for a few minutes on January 26, 2000," says Dr. Sreedher recalling how he did everything he could to get the larger antenna up and working and be launch ready by 26th of January.

"On the morning of the launch function, the technicians of ECIL found that the length of the special cable was not enough to reach the transmitter from the antenna. Various sources of ready availability were thought of and later we sourced the cable from Doordarshan on loan. The programme was about to start at 5 pm and there were no indications that 'live' telecast would go through. I tried to request DD to loan an OB van with satellite uplink for the event but was told that the entire crew were tired after the 'live' coverage of the Republic Day event. Somehow, exactly at 5 pm the satellite was linked. But we still needed the permission from the Network Operation Coordination Committee to uplink. The NOCC was then headed by Mr. Agarwal who was also a student of IGNOU. Prof. A.W. Khan and Mr. Rama Rao, the engineer had taken Mr. Agarwal into confidence a few days back and he had arranged for special staff to clear the request of DD/IGNOU for uplink from a new location. Thus that was also got. Everything seemed to fall in place at the last minute," recalls Dr. Sreedher.

Recalling the launch function, Dr. Sreedher says "On 26th January, it was around 7 pm in the evening. Dr. Murli Manohar Joshi had already arrived. In fact, everyone came straight from Rashtrapathi Bhavan after attending the reception hosted by the President of India on Republic Day. But when Mr. Arun Jaitley arrived at the inauguration function, he did not have details of the function. Then I explained to him, how the concept of this integrated-cooperative-collaborative-coordinated TV channel for Education came about. Thereafter Mr. Jaitley hugely supported and encouraged the channel, he recalls.

When Dr. Sreedher spoke during the launch of Gyan Darshan, he said that the studio that was a white elephant for IGNOU, had now turned into a golden one, now that it produced valuable educational programmes for the country. Starting with a daily two-hour broadcast, within 6 months of its launch Gyan Darshan started broadcasting up to 18 hours a day, and in a year expanded to round-the-clock transmissions.

Later when another minister took over the Ministry of Information and Broadcasting in a cabinet reshuffle and Dr. Sreedher got to know that the minister had been invited to be the Chief Guest for the launch of a new educational channel by the Zee network.

"In the initial stages, when we were thinking of launching an educational channel, it was considered to make the educational channel a public-private partnership with Zee TV. But the Zee Educational Channel TV CEO only attended a few initial meetings and discussions on content, and they decided to start their own educational channel and education centres later under the name ZED", says Dr. Sreedher.

He recalls another incident pertaining to the launch. "Later when I saw the publicity campaign issued by Zee for the launch of their educational channel...it had said something on the lines of 'For Gyan in small capsules...watch Zee Education'. The usage of the word Gyan irked me and I decided to answer their campaign with an ad from Gyan Darshan. So, on the same day those huge ads appeared in national dailies announcing the launch of the Zee Education channel, Gyan Darshan gave a half page ad in the last page of a national daily which simply read 'For A-to-Zee of Education, watch Gyan Darshan'." Dr. Sreedher remembers having been, soon thereafter, questioned about this by the Vice-Chancellor of IGNOU (who had apparently faced some moments of discomfiture for this perceived tit for tat ad campaign of Gyan Darshan). "The Vice-Chancellor asked me whether it was our work to make educational programmes for the country or to fight advertising battles. But I had only placed the advertisements within the power and budget allocated to me. So, I was safe in my stand," recounts Dr. Sreedher.

"Another problem that eventually came up was that Zee was paying royalty to the content providers for its channel and hence it made monetary sense for various agencies like the UGC or IITs to share their education content with them instead of Gyan Darshan. I discussed this with the officials at the Ministry and finally arrived at a call that, though I could not pay royalty to the content providers as it would be against the norms, I would instead pay the content providers the production costs for the edited and anchored programmes they shared. Now, this worked out to be more than the money ZED was paying for royalty. Thus Gyan Darshan was able to retain their hold on good content," he recalls.

Dr. Sreedher also announced that the content providers could also share their content directly live from the comforts of their own studios and centres, instead of handing the tapes over to IGNOU. He announced they could create a wireless microwave link at the source venue to send the feed to IGNOU for broadcast. And he offered to pay them for setting up the link too. This again ensured that they had access to the good content, while ensuring comfort and rewards for the partner agencies. All this led to a more stable partnership with content sources. Mr. V.S. Pandey IAS, Joint Secretary with the Ministry of HRD, supported Dr. Sreedher in all such initiatives and efforts. Interestingly within a few years, the Zee network had to pull the plug on the ZED channel, due to unviability of operations.

Two years after the launch of Gyan Darshan, when Dr. Sreedher met Dr. Abdul Kalam at a Science Congress in Lucknow, the latter asked Dr. Sreedher how the educational TV channel was doing. Dr. Kalam was then a distinguished professor with Anna University in Chennai. Dr. Sreedher told him that the transponder which they used for the broadcast was an old one from Doordarshan and there were problems of drifting. Dr. Abdul Kalam immediately asked Dr. Kasthurirangan, who was also with them at the Science Congress, "haven't you given them a new transponder?"

"We could give them one soon", said Dr. Kasturirangan. That was all Dr. Sreedher had to hear to set in motion all the formalities required to process the sanctioning of a new transponder. He spoke to the Secretary of the Human Resource Development Ministry who got in touch with Dr. Kasturirangan to initiate and follow up the request for transponder. Dr. Sreedher notes that Dr. Kasturirangan, was avidly interested in projects pertaining to education and he obtained the necessary approvals from the Prime Minister Mr. Atal Bihari Vajpayee to sanction a transponder for the broadcast of the educational channel Gyan Darshan. Dr. Kalam advised Dr. Sreedher to make optimum use of the transponder. Dr. Sreedher intended to use the transponder to simulcast Gyan Darshan on digital as well as analogue modes. But Dr. Kalam insisted that one analogue transponder could be used to telecast six digital channels. These days an even greater number of channels can be broadcast using one transponder. Because of Dr. Kasturirangan's pursuit, the new transponder was sanctioned to be used for six different educational channels. These included a general education channel, a channel for school education, Vyas—the channel for higher education, a channel for agricultural broadcast, Eklavya and a technology-based channel for the IITs. And Mr. K.S. Sarma proactively, in his capacity as the CEO, Prasar Bharati, took the six digital channels under the fold of DD with each having a different coloured logo. He had swiftly moved the Prasar Bharati Board to approve them.

After the successful launch of the six education channels, Dr. Sreedher had proposed an idea to launch a 'Gyan satellite' that could help replicate the model of the Gyan Darshan channel in 18 different languages across the country. The idea was that while the central government provided the satellite and transponders for broadcast, the state governments could use these facilities and take initiatives to produce programmes for school education, higher and technical education, education related to agriculture and so on. Dr. Sreedher remembers making a presentation of his proposed idea to the HRD Ministry in July 2001. "At that time when DECU-ISRO came to know of this proposal, they approached the Vice-Chancellor of IGNOU, and talked to him about improvising on the proposal put forward by me. Later they came out with a modified proposal for EDUSAT, a communication satellite solely for the purpose of education", says Dr. Sreedher.

So, when it was announced that EDUSAT was soon to be launched, Dr. Sreedher never concealed his disappointment and anguish at not being involved and discussed the same with Mr. D.S. Bhatia from ISRO. Though nothing much could be done about it then, Dr. Sreedher ensured he got the best of EDUSAT for his projects at Anna University, where he joined as Director of Audio-Visual Research Centre after IGNOU.

Monsoon Wedding, Mira Nair and IGNOU

Mira Nair's *Monsoon Wedding*, was a film that went on to win several awards globally including the Golden Lion and earned a nomination in the Golden Globe awards. When it was being made, the Director, Mira Nair had approached IGNOU for use of their studios for shooting. The sequence at the beginning of the film, where a television debate is going on in a studio, as the protagonist looks on, was shot in the IGNOU studios.

"We had a very impressive set designed by one of the graphic artists Mr. Anil Tato and Mr. Viswanath. IGNOU is an educational institution and the union is controlled by strong academics. I thought that the film was only depicting Indian culture and IGNOU could get some good revenue by allowing them to shoot. They wanted to shoot only during a weekend, so there was no disturbance to regular work. My media centre staff had to fight hard to convince the establishment to allow that shooting. I got Mr. Ashok Nishesh, a well-known educational TV producer, one who had a strong voice in the establishment, to study the script in advance and he gave me an opinion that I could go ahead. We held a committee meeting to decide on the charges for letting out the studio for shooting, as there was no rate card in place, this being the first time a private shooting was happening in the studios. When I finally gave the go ahead, only a handful of people knew about it.

On a Saturday when tens of cars, vans and vehicles started coming into the campus, the security guards got panicky and called the Registrar. He in turn called me and I told him not to worry and everything was going according to norms. The talk show scene in the opening sequence of the film was shot in the IGNOU studios with its own set as the background and some shots were taken at the make-up room of the studios", recalls Dr. Sreedher.

Dr. Sreedher wanted to film the whole shooting process as it was happening in the studios, to later make a programme on the making of a Hollywood film, but Mira Nair refused permissions for it. "The shooting for the film went on for about 24 hours and on the morning of Sunday the entire crew left without any visible damage to IGNOU or its studios. But it was unfortunate that Mira Nair did not even acknowledge the use of IGNOU studios in the titles of the film", says Dr. Sreedher.

There were other eminent shows and personalities that

made use of the studio infrastructure at IGNOU as well. A health education series was shot at the studios by Mr. Prashant Bhushan. Mr. Karan Thapar used the facilities for his current affairs programme. Mr. T.N. Ninan used the facilities to produce business news magazines for television. Darpan was a first attempt at creating an educational news bulletin that covered campus news for Doordarshan and it was shot at the IGNOU Studios. There was Meri Baat, a daily live programme for school children which was launched by Sushma Swaraj from IGNOU studios, and there were other classical music programmes. Together these generated enough revenue to keep the centre, which was a government initiative to be self-sufficient, recalls Dr. Sreedher.

"When Sushma Swaraj wanted to do a live show for children, every day through the year on DD Bharati channel, the team found it challenging to find a studio available on all days. Doordarshan was unable to offer them a studio. But IGNOU studios were available all through the year and the charges were low and it was to be a government-to-government dealing. She was happy with what IGNOU had to offer. So from Doordarshan alone IGNOU was getting a sizeable revenue running into eight figures", says Dr. Sreedher.

Indian Science Congress

Another milestone during the initial years of the educational TV channel was when it covered a live event of national importance exclusively. In the year 2003, when the 90th Indian Science Congress was held at Bangalore, which saw the participation of both the then President and the Prime Minister of India as special guests, it was covered exclusively by Gyan Darshan channel.

"Dr. Kasturirangan offered ISRO's facilities for uplinking and Doordarshan's OB van was used. All the other media channels that broadcast clippings from the event mentioned 'courtesy- Gyan Darshan' in their coverage. The Indian Science Congress Association headed by Dr. Kasturirangan gave Rs.1 lakh to IGNOU for the coverage", recalls Dr. Sreedher.

An Internal Battle

An industrialist, who was also a board member of IGNOU wanted to produce a serial for Gyan Darshan on a theme pertaining to Indian culture and had given an estimate of around Rs. 2 crore for producing it, which was quite high. He also dropped a few big names in politics trying to prove his influence and there was pressure to commission his serial. Dr. Sreedher and Dr. Khan then had to think of a way to avoid such unreasonable requests and pressures then and in future. They moved the Gyan Darshan Steering Committee and decided that Gyan Darshan (GD) Channel would not commission any programme and would only act as an integrator. The constituent members of the GD could get the programmes produced as per broadcast guidelines and offer it to GD for telecast. "The said board member got upset with the new decision and started expressing it in many ways," recalls Dr. Sreedher.

Once, when Gyan Darshan was facing a technical setback due to failure of one of its electronic devices that was used for uplinking, there was an urgent need to replace it. Dr. Sreedher decided to request a public sector undertaking in India to source it and supply it. He was about to place the order when the board member decided to contest that decision saying that the PSU was charging a higher amount and he had found cheaper deals online. Dr. Sreedher then left it to the statutory committee, which had technical experts from Prasar Bharati and others departments, to take a decision on sourcing the device.

It was around the same time that Dr. Sreedher was aspiring to become the Director General of AIR. There were rumours floating about it already that he was being considered for the post. The late Mr. Atal Bihari Vajpayee was the Prime Minister then and Dr. Sreedher was at the PM's residence to attend an event.

"One of the Prasar Bharati Board members, who earlier worked with the BBC, requested Mr. Atal Bihari Vajpayee to release his book of poetry and the PM agreed to it. He also invited me to the book release function that was held at the PM's residence. So I went to the event, and slowly the guests started arriving. The board member /industrialist who wanted his programme to be commissioned by IGNOU also came to the event. During a casual conversation, one of my well-wishers from AIR, who later became an office bearer at the Delhi Press Club, shared the rumours about me being considered for the DG's post. The board member overheard it and was determined not to allow it to happen. There was a former diplomat who also attended the event and he went and whispered something to him. Then they got talking about a huge scam that was happening in IGNOU and that foreign programmes were being purchased by paying in dollars while they were actually available for free. The Secretary, Ministry of Education who was nearby, was asked to look into the matter. A few days after the event the Secretary, Ministry of Education called the VC of IGNOU and asked him to send the files regarding purchase of foreign programmes. I was in Chennai and the files were in my almirah. When my PA called me I told her that there was nothing to hide and that she could give the files to VC's office. In Shastri Bhawan, the Secretary studied the files himself and photocopied them. He then called me and said that he was visiting London and that he planned to go to Germany to personally understand the issue. He came back from his visits and said that the deal with IGNOU was really economical. He did not find anything wrong with the deal. He even went on to ask me to work out a plan for Indo-German collaboration in educational audio/ video production at IGNOU", says Dr. Sreedher.

Arun Jaitley

"After the inauguration of Gyan Darshan by Dr. Murli Manohar Joshi in the presence of Mr. Arun Jaitley, the latter visited IGNOU studios to participate in Karan Thapar's show. I, as the Director of the Centre used to welcome him. Mr. Jaitley became so passionate about the channel that he even spoke about Gyan Darshan at a meet organized to mark the Silver Jubilee of India's SITE programme in 2001. At a time when leading scientists were in talks with Zee to allot a channel for Education and Science, Mr. Jaitley asked all the scientists present at the event to support Gyan Darshan. When the cable operators refused to provide Gyan Darshan to the viewers, the only choice left was to make it compulsory for them to carry the channel. Mr. Arun Jaitley supported the idea even though some of his cabinet colleagues were not that enthusiastic about it. He used to tell me about the discussions he had with the Prime Minister regarding the same. The channel was ultimately made a 'must carry' channel along with Lok Sabha TV and Rajya Sabha TV channels. But owing to some of the poor decisions made by the later Vice-Chancellors, the channel almost vanished. There was no hue and cry about it and in fact a study conducted by Vibhuti Ramachandran on Gyan Darshan was titled 'The channel that no one sees'," recalls Dr. Sreedher.

World Television Forum

In the year 2000, Dr. Sreedher got an invitation from the United Nations office in India to attend the World Television Forum, a three day event organized by the United Nations to bring together the CEOs of all television channels across the world. He was surprised at how his name was included in the list of invitees that included the heads of the top channels across the world. Shashi Tharoor, the then Under Secretary General Communications at the United Nations was involved in the organization of the event. Indira Mansingh, the Additional Director General Doordarshan along with Sevanthi Ninan, media columnist were among the other invitees. During one of the events, Dr. Sreedher remembers having a conversation with the then head of Discovery Channel, who shared the content policies of the channel with him and told him to never shy away from repeating shows on air, if they had worthwhile content. It was advice he always followed in the years to come while dealing with content. One of the best parts of attending the forum, says Dr. Sreedher, was the range of authentic foods from different nations and cultures that he was able to savour at the UN headquarters.

Gyan Vani, the Educational Radio Channel

In the year 1995, in a landmark ruling, the Supreme Court held that airwaves were public property and rejected the state monopoly on airwaves, thereby opening the doors for private broadcasters to venture into FM broadcast. But it was only five years later, in 2000, that FM frequencies were auctioned to private players for the first time, in 40 cities across the country.

"It was also suggested during the discussions that at least one frequency in every city should be allocated for the social sector, for development-oriented communication. Initially offering licenses to NGOs was considered, but the idea was later dropped due to the circumstances then, considering security issues. Later the idea of allocating the frequency for educational broadcasts garnered much support. The Human Resource Development Ministry could run an educational radio channel, but again it would be state run, so the idea was given up. UGC and NCERT were considered as the next possible alternatives, but no one came forward to take up the project of running an educational FM Channel," recalls Dr. Sreedher.

The Vice-Chancellor of IGNOU was then travelling abroad and Dr. Sreedher was in his place, attending the discussions at the Ministry. During the discussions it occurred to him that IGNOU had 36 Regional Centres in the country and it would not be difficult for them to operate an FM channel each from these centres. Incidentally the cities where the government had proposed to privatize radio, during the first phase of auctions (Phase I), already had an IGNOU Regional Centre. He shared his thoughts with the officials at the meeting and later when the Phase I auctioning was announced, one frequency in each of these cities was reserved for educational broadcasts and IGNOU was announced to be the nodal agency managing the channel.

He called up the Vice-Chancellor of IGNOU who was then in Geneva to keep him informed of the developments. "But all we wanted was permission to run one station," said Mr. Abdul Waheed Khan when he heard that IGNOU was to handle educational broadcasts across all cities. Dr. Sreedher assured him that nothing had been formalized in writing yet and that the government in its wisdom was allowing the 40 channels to be managed by IGNOU. He also explained that IGNOU would get separate funding from the government to operate these channels. The Vice-Chancellor then agreed to the proposal. But he soon left IGNOU to join the Commonwealth of Learning and as an interim arrangement another Vice-Chancellor, Mr. V.S. Prasad took charge. "He too was supportive of Dr. Sreedher initiatives", says Dr. Sreedher.

Meanwhile, Dr. Sreedher met and discussed the idea of IGNOU operating Educational FM channels in the country with Prof. V.C. Kulandaiswamy, who had been a former Vice-Chancellor of IGNOU, Anna University, and Madurai Kamaraj University.

"Why are you getting academics into trouble? Why are you making IGNOU take responsibility to run these stations...? If something goes wrong the Vice-Chancellor is answerable to the Police and Parliament", Prof. Kulandaisamy said. This made Dr. Sreedher reconsider his proposal. Creating the infrastructure to run an FM channel—finding a piece of land, building a studio, erecting a transmission tower—they all required massive investments of time and money. Possibilities of corruption and CBI enquiries also existed. He ruminated on the problems and possibilities and later talked to the then CEO of Prasar Bharati, Mr. Anil Baijal (currently the Lt. Governor of Delhi) and discussed the issue with him. Within the next 48 hours of their meeting, an MOU was signed that AIR and Doordarshan would share their tower infrastructure and offer support in the functioning of the educational FM channel by IGNOU. That took a lot of trouble off IGNOU's shoulders. "That in a way also started the trend of private FM channels hosting their transmitters on AIR or Doordarshan towers", says Dr. Sreedher.

Next he convened a meeting with NGOs interested in community radio, UNICEF and UNESCO and other bodies to come up with regulations and content plan for the educational FM broadcasts in the country. Sixty per cent of the content was to be education-based and the remaining 40 per cent he offered to the NGOs in these cities to broadcast their development-oriented content. But most NGOs insisted that they wanted a channel of their own and not just borrowed airtime.

Meanwhile, Mr. H.P. Dixit took over as the new Vice-Chancellor of IGNOU. He was from Allahabad and suggested that the first 'Gyan Vani' station be launched in Allahabad. Dr. Sreedher agreed and got in touch with AIR Allahabad to implement the same. On November 7, 2001, being Sir C.V. Raman's birth day, was marked as the launch date of the first Gyan Vani FM station in India. Ten anchors were trained for the new channel and the late Mr. Vipin Sharma was posted as the station head. A grand launch event was planned. Cabinet Minister Dr. Murli Manohar Joshi presided over the event. The Minister had organized a havan (a Vedic ritual) ahead of the launch of the station, after which he addressed the listeners live on air in Gyan Vani FM. Dr. Sreedher had a sudden idea that the Minister's address on Gyan Vani, could be broadcast live on TV. But there was no camera crew, or OB vans and other arrangements needed for broadcast were missing. He only had an STD phone line linked to the studio. He called his IGNOU office at Delhi and asked them to relay live the audio of the launch event on Doordarshan channel instead of the regular educational show from Gyan Darshan that was usually broadcast at that time. For visuals, he asked them to use stock shots of Allahabad city and its landmarks and photos of the eminent personalities attending the launch which were available on the Internet. He then informed the minister and the other eminent guests about the live coverage. The late Vipin Sharma conducted studio interviews with the Governor of Jharkhand Mr. Prabhat Kumar, Cabinet Minister Murli Manohar Joshi and Governor of UP Mr. Vishnu Kant Shastri. All these interviews were timed appropriately and broadcast live on Gyan Vani FM radio and nationwide on Doordarshan.

After the studio interaction, a formal launch function was to be held, and a large tent was put in place adjacent to the AIR campus in Allahabad. The function had just begun, when strong winds started blowing and a part of the tent came sliding down. Fortunately, none of the dignitaries were hurt. Everyone was safely hurried to a small hall nearby, where the function resumed in the next ten minutes. As per the earlier plan, the dignitaries on the dais were to participate in a live phone-in programme through Gyan Vani, where they were to answer questions from the callers, live from the dais. All arrangements had been made for the same on the dais and the gadgets were in place. But the sudden shift in the venue made it impossible to continue with the live phone-in as planned. The host for the evening, oblivious of the technical issues, went ahead and announced that a live phone-in show was coming up next and that the dignitaries would be answering the questions from the callers. Amidst all the confusion due to the tent collapse and change in location, there was not enough time for the organizers to tell the anchor not to go ahead with that part of the announcement. Now after the announcements were made, it had to be stage managed some way and Dr. Sreedher who had recorded questions beforehand for the mock drill of the phone in session, decided to use those recorded questions instead of questions from real callers, for the interaction. He played the questions from his pocket tape recorder on to a microphone and the dignitaries on the dais answered them. "Not many knew what exactly was happening, but a few people, including a *Times of India* journalist could make out that the live phone- in was staged. I should probably not have done that," says Dr. Sreedher in retrospect, "but it's difficult to predict how one will react in a crisis...", he adds.

The formal launch function was also covered for television and was aired the next day on Gyan Darshan and Doordarshan channels. But it was recorded on TV camera, edited at IGNOU and broadcast the next day without any flaws.

"After Allahabad, the new Vice-Chancellor of IGNOU wanted to launch the next Gyan Vani station in Bhopal, Madhya Pradesh. Efforts were being made to get the then Chief Minister of Madhya Pradesh from the Congress Party and Central Minister Murli Manohar Joshi of the BJP Party on the same stage. For some reason, the new Vice-Chancellor decided to run the show in Bhopal without my presence. So I went to Coimbatore on leave and monitored the set-up of the Gyan Vani station in Coimbatore. I also followed the launch function that was taking place at Bhopal as it was happening, by keeping in touch with his staff at Bhopal over the phone," recalls Dr. Sreedher. He had a student along with him from Coimbatore who knew Hindi well when he had a mischievous idea. When it was time for the dignitaries to answer live calls during the launch function at Bhopal, Dr. Sreedher made the student with him at Coimbatore call on the studio number and he was connected to Minister Murli Manohar Joshi to ask his question live. The student asked him, when the launch of Gyan Vani was likely to happen in Coimbatore. The Minister gave him a witty reply saying, 'A for Allahabad, B for Bhopal and next was C for Coimbatore'.

But the Chief Minister Digvijaya Singh, an engineer by education, who was also sitting on the dais raised his doubts on how an FM broadcast that could only reach 75-km radius could elicit a response call from as far as Coimbatore?

"The Vice-Chancellor then had to tell him that 'Sreedher is now in Coimbatore and is playing this prank on us'", adds Dr. Sreedher with a chuckle.

It was Republic Day in 2003. Dr. Sreedher was busy organizing an event in the afternoon at the India Habitat Centre, New Delhi. He had timed it such that it did not coincide with the Republic Day Parade. The event was to announce that the IIT's Technology Channel, Gyan Darshan 3—Eklavya, would now broadcast round-the-clock. The event also marked the launch of four Gyan Vani stations across the country—in Lucknow, Visakhapatnam, Mumbai and Coimbatore. They were to be launched at the same time using a video conference-like facility from New Delhi. Central Minister for HRD and Science and Technology Dr. Murli Manohar Joshi and Minister for Information and Broadcasting Ms. Sushma Swaraj were to be the Chief Guests at the event. The live coverage of the event was to be telecast live on Gyan Darshan and DD Bharati channels. The idea was that when Mr. Murali Manohar Joshi pressed a remote button announcing the launching of Gyan Vani Visakhapatnam, the anchor there will go live and inaugurate the station and play the signature tune. The media was supposed to watch the programme from both New Delhi and at the launch venues.

"To get the visuals and sound from the four stations, a television uplink and an OB van were required. The cost per city was coming to about Rs.1 lakh for the equipment. That meant Rs. 4 lakhs for four cities plus the payment for the crew. The Vice-Chancellor bluntly refused to sanction the amount," recalls Dr. Sreedher. He wished to approach Doordarshan for technical support but could not do so as they were all engaged in the Republic Day coverage. He was not even able to arrange for dedicated phone lines for the event and was forced to think of alternative arrangements or as they popularly say in colloquial Hindi, some 'Jugaad'.

He instructed the station managers in all the four stations to pre-shoot the launch sequence in advance and share it with him. So, the visuals of the anchors, along with their announcements and the playing of the signature tune were all dress rehearsed and shot in camera. The footage was received and edited to 50 seconds each, to be used in the launch function at New Delhi. So when the minister pressed the launch button for each station, the control room played the video tapes in appropriate sequence. Meanwhile, in the respective radio stations where the actual launch was happening live, the anchors wore the same clothes and read the same script followed by the signature tune. The local press could watch them through a glass partition. The lip movements of the anchors synched well with the live telecast from New Delhi. "Dr. Daljeet Sachdeva was the producer at the Delhi end. Somehow we were able to create a perception of live launch from New Delhi and no one knew what was up except for my staff at IGNOU. Not even the Ministers who launched it or the Vice-Chancellor knew about it", says Dr. Sreedher."Four stations in four different locations and in four different languages were launched in four minutes. Ms. Sushma Swaraj was so impressed with the launch of Gyan Vani stations and with the variety of content that an educational channel could offer, that she promised to look into and approve immediately the proposals for allotting community radio licences to educational institutions that were on her table," he adds.

Talking about the current state of educational broadcasts in the country, Dr. Sreedher says that though India has a long history of educational broadcasts on radio, starting in 1936 when the first school education programmes were aired with the intent of students even in far-flung areas receiving access to quality education, somewhere down the line we have neglected to evolve these broadcasts creatively and have never actively maintained touch points with schools and teachers to ensure active listenership. "Even after the launch of Gyan Vani, nothing much has changed as I don't think any school child in the listening zone of 37 Gyan Vani stations has heard the name of the station leave alone listening to the programmes," he says. "On the other hand, we hear of thousands of audio books being launched from the developed world. Google, Amazon and other leading companies also provide online audio books. So the medium as such has not lost its relevance, but a significantly new approach is needed to make the education broadcasts relevant to today's audience", he adds.

Radio Vision

Among all media, nothing quite fires one's imagination as the radio medium. But nothing as imaginative has been done with the technology of radio broadcast as the World Space satellite radio network. Taking the lead from an Arthur Clarke fiction where three satellites lead the entire world, it went on to build a communication model that wasn't limited by geographies. The medium that was considered as a local or national broadcast medium suddenly assumed a global dimension.

While working in IGNOU and charting out ways to take quality education to remote areas in the country, Dr. Sreedher realized the potential of a medium like the world space in adding more reach and value to the content and broadcast. He wanted IGNOU's broadcast to be on the world space medium. "As there were no policies in place to allow uplinking from India, he planned to uplink the content for the channel from Nepal and later create an earth station in the IGNOU campus for the same, whenever it became feasible. "But Mr. Khan, who was the Vice-Chancellor of IGNOU, wasn't convinced about the project. Dr. Khan, in his earlier role as an Education Consultant at COL had supported Noah Samora, the brain behind World Space. UNESCO was also supporting him, in his initiatives," he recalls.

Dr. Sreedher, never a man to give up on ideas, pursued the initiative again when Mr. Khan moved on to join the UN and a new VC took over IGNOU. When he discussed his ideas with UNESCO officials from New Delhi they evinced a keen interest in the project.

They wanted Dr. Sreedher to undertake a research project to test the feasibility of doing educational programmes for rural children through a medium like World Space, by playing educative audio programmes and sharing basic power point slides that served as aids in learning. This would save the precious bandwidth and infrastructure that would be required if the same were to be done through television. So, Dr. Sreedher quickly created a few test episodes that were played to different sets of audiences, whose knowledge of the subject was measured before and after taking up the radio programme lesson. And his experiments came out successful and proved that such a model for education was effective and possible soon enough. UNESCO New Delhi published his research in the form of a book, *Radio Vision*. Impressed with his work, they offered him the opportunity to present his work at the Learntec Conference in Karlsruhe, Germany in February 2002, as a keynote speaker.

"There were many test projects being done for WorldSpace in India and many agencies and NGOs were trying to partner with them. But the intellectual lobby at IGNOU viewed IGNOU's involvement with WorldSpace more as a capitalistic invasion and tried spreading gossip and stories around it. One even claimed that I was likely to be the country head of WorldSpace in India. But at the end of all the hype, nothing planned was ever taken forward as the World Space deviated from its original concept of education to entertainment", says Dr. Sreedher. On Republic day in 2002, Dr. Sreedher got to know of a report that was to be published in a national newspaper which said that IGNOU was being sold to multinationals by hiring WorldSpace. Dr. Sreedher intervened and impressed upon the chief editor of the newspaper, through some friends that it was far from the truth and later the report was not carried to print.

World Technology Network

Meanwhile in 2002, Dr. Sreedher was shortlisted by the World Technology Network for an award for his contribution to the field of education. Someone did seem to have taken notice of Dr. Sreedher working on various projects pertaining to educational FM radio, educational TV and satellite radio channels and recommended him to be nominated for the award. Though he still does not know who, but Dr. Sreedher suspects that the then ADG at UNESCO, Dr. Khan could have nominated his name.

Though Dr. Sreedher did not win the award, he became a fellow of the World Technology Network. "One hundred members from across the world were awarded fellowships based on their contributions to technology each year and five for their contribution to education, and that year I was one of them. It was very empowering and elevating to be a part of a forum of which, the best minds from the country like Dr. Abdul Kalam, Dr. M.S. Swaminathan, Bunker Roy, Dr. G. Venkataswamy were a part...," says Dr. Sreedher.

He travelled to New York to attend the convention and on one of those days the programme was conducted at the UN headquarters and Dr. Sreedher remembers meeting the then Secretary General of the UN Kofi Annan and the Under Secretary General Mr. Shashi Tharoor there. His travel to the US was sponsored by the Department of Science and Technology and IGNOU. He approached the Department of Science and Technology to partially sponsor his travel to the US and they agreed. The other half was reimbursed by IGNOU—"the Vice-Chancellor though chose to approve the reimbursements only on my last day at IGNOU with much reluctance", adds Dr. Sreedher.

With time it was getting increasingly difficult for Dr. Sreedher to continue working at IGNOU. Differences and issues with the Vice-Chancellor of IGNOU, Mr. H.P. Dixit and the Pro-Vice-Chancellor Mr. S.C. Garg, made him want to start considering other opportunities. Also, many academics envied Dr. Sreedher for being at the helm of action, despite him being an outsider in the field of education.

He was selected for the post of Director, Consortium of Educational Communication (CEC) in 2002, but the orders were not issued. Meanwhile, Mr. K.S. Sarma, was also looking at the post then, says Dr. Sreedher. "He had been asked to go back to the Andhra Pradesh cadre, but he wished to stay in New Delhi to complete some work pertaining to his earlier roles. So, he asked me to hold back for a while from taking up the new assignment. By that time a new Chairman had taken over UGC, who formed a new committee to look for a Director for CEC. The new committee's chairman Mr. Kiran Karnik too found me to be suitable for the post, but still an order was not issued and went in for another search committee. By then I had joined Anna University in 2003," he recalls.

Dr. Sreedher was in Coimbatore for an official visit when he happened to meet Prof. E. Balagurusamy, the then Vice-Chancellor of Anna University, Chennai. They were introduced to each other by Dr. G.R.D. Padmanabhan of the GRD Group of Institutions and got talking about work and education. Dr. Balagurusamy mentioned that there was an Audio-Visual Research Centre in Anna University and suggested that Dr. Sreedher join as the Director of the same. Dr. Sreedher considered the opportunity and shared his thoughts. "I would love to Sir. But there are issues. Today you might make an appointment, but tomorrow if a new Vice-Chancellor comes, he might not want to retain me. So, it would be appropriate if you selected the Director through the regular procedure of applications and interviews," he told him. Dr. Balagurusamy agreed and soon an advertisement was released, and applications were solicited for the post of Director, AVRC. Through proper procedures and approvals, based on interviews and experience, Dr. Sreedher was chosen as the most suitable candidate for the role. He remembers being interviewed by 11 people including a UGC nominee from Delhi, Pradeep Kaul who was looking after the duties of the Director of Consortium of Educational Communication, the Engineer-in-Chief of Doordarshan Mr. Ramaswamy and Mr. Sashi Kumar Menon, Chairman of the Asian School of Journalism.

When it was time to leave IGNOU, Dr. Sreedher ensured he was cleared of all enquiries or controversies, so there was nothing that would delay or prevent him from getting relieved. The Doordarshan experience made him deal more cautiously with it. With help from the finance officer at IGNOU, Mr. Vikram Chandra who was earlier with the CAG (Comptroller and Auditor General of India), he requested for a special audit of his unit by the CAG, which was considered the most thorough in government audits. Once he answered their queries, he was sure that there would not be any more enquiries or cases against him in IGNOU.

He resigned his role at IGNOU and moved to Chennai.

6

Anna University (2003-05)

The First Campus Community Radio and More

The news of him joining Anna University had spread and a *Times of India* journalist came to meet him. He asked Dr. Sreedher what his plans for the new role were. Dr. Sreedher replied that he wished to start a campus community radio in the university campus and that it could be the first one in the country.

Campus Community Radio

The Union Cabinet, Government of India approved the first community radio policy in late 2002. As per the guidelines, only educational institutions were eligible to apply for a Community Radio license. The first policy strictly banned advertisements or sponsored programmes through the community radio. In fact, the educational institution had to invest in capital expenditure for the hardware and earmark money for the running expenditure.

Dr. Sreedher made his plans and started working on a proposal for community radio. He didn't want Anna University to spend any money on running the radio station and his plan was to generate content with the help of teachers and students of the University. The Vice-Chancellor Prof. E. Balagurusamy approved of his ideas and plans. Mr. Govindaraju, who was then working in the AVRC at Anna University as a Research Officer, helped Dr. Sreedher put together his thoughts and ideas in the form of a proposal for community radio, to be sent to the central and state governments for approval.

Within a week of his joining Anna University, a meeting of all Directors from educational institutions across the country was convened by the UGC. Dr. Sreedher travelled to Delhi to be a part of it. At the meeting, Dr. Sreedher encouraged all the audio-visual and educational media research centres at various universities to apply for a community radio license on behalf of their respective institutions.

As an interesting development around the same time, the then Chief Minister of Tamil Nadu Ms. J. Jayalalitha, had decided to launch Tamil Nadu Open University (TNOU), for distance education in Tamil Nadu. Dr. Sreedher assisted the state government with the requirements and details of starting such an institution in the state. He was a part of the discussions and meetings with the TN government officials regarding the establishment of TNOU. After the Governor approved the proposal for TNOU, there were rumours doing the rounds that Dr. Sreedher was to be nominated as the first Vice-Chancellor of TNOU. But when the actual orders came, someone else had been chosen. Dr. Sreedher was asked to be the Registrar at TNOU, but he politely declined the offer. Later he was posted in the syndicate, the apex decision-making body of the university, by the state government.

Within a few months of having joined Anna University, Dr. Sreedher applied for the post of Director General AIR when he learnt that the post was falling vacant. Dr. Sreedher went ahead and appeared for the interviews. He was interviewed by the Prasar Bharati Board with Mr. K.S. Sarma as the CEO. "Mr. Sarma had told me that though they would select the most suitable candidates for the post, it was up to the government to choose who was appointed. Later with the dissolution of Parliament and impending elections, it was announced that only IAS officers could be made the chief of television and radio in the country. So I had to let the opportunity go," recalls Dr. Sreedher. "When I met Minister Ravi Shankar Prasad during the launch of community radio at Anna University, the Minister told me that he came to know of my interview for the post of DG AIR and offered me the post of Additional Director General at AIR. I politely refused the offer and continued at Anna University," he adds.

Another project that he undertook in his role as Director, AVRC in Anna University was conducting a survey on the response and listenership of private FM channels in Chennai. Students of the media courses in Anna University conducted the survey across the city under the guidance of Mr. Govindaraju. Only two private FM radio channels were operational in the city at that time. Suriyan FM, run by the Sun Group, was found to be the most popular and leading channel, followed by Radio Mirchi and AIR came third. When the findings of the survey were announced, there was quite a flurry around it. People speculated that Dr. Sreedher might even lose his job for announcing the opposition party's channel to be in the lead. But nothing of that sort happened. A team of enthusiastic reporters from the Sun network went straight to Dr. Sreedher's house in the Chennai suburb, to get an interview with him, he remembers.

In spite of the other things at hand, Dr. Sreedher continued to focus on his pet project for Anna University, the community radio. "The first CR policy was limited only to educational institutions and only 100 applications were received in the first year out of which at least 60 of them got the letters of intent. But the policy was strict. No advertisements, no sponsored programmes, no programme in any language other than specified in the application. Every applicant was to get at least 33 clearances including the recommendation from the state government. Getting a frequency was a nightmare. We had to apply with a map supplied by the Geospatial agency in Dehradun. They charged Rs. 10,000 for the map and it took months to get the map. Since ours was the first application, every department was raising doubts and objections", says Dr. Sreedher recollecting the process. But all the clearances were obtained one by one owing to Dr. Sreedher's perseverance, networking, and the enthusiasm shown by some of the TN government officials like the then Education Secretary, Mr. V.K. Subburaj, for the project. Dr. Sreedher was positive about obtaining the license sooner or later and hence began building an audio studio for broadcast and started the process of training students to run the radio station. He even got a grant from the Department of Science and Technology, to produce and air a quiz programme on Water, which he used to construct the audio studio. Anna FM received its LoI or letter of intent on December 28, 2003. Meanwhile, LoI was also readied to launch a community radio at IIT Kanpur.

The central government decided to launch the community radio stations under their 'India Shining' campaign. They were considering starting the first campus community radio at IIT Kanpur, Uttar Pradesh. But the defence approval was getting delayed for that region. Meanwhile the Private Secretary to the Minister for I&B, an IAS officer, happened to visit the studio premises at Anna University and he was impressed with Dr. Sreedher's confidence about the project. He suggested to the Minister that Anna University was ready for launch and the first community radio could be started there. Based on his recommendation, the BECIL (Broadcast Engineering Consultants India Limited), a unit of the Ministry of I&B, sent a team to Anna University to survey their preparedness. When Dr. Sreedher later learnt that the chief engineer from the team had given his opinion that there was still a missing element in the infrastructure at Anna University and some clearances were pending too, Dr. Sreedher decided to act immediately and get things in place for the launch. He quickly worked through his contacts on getting the GoPA (Grant of Permissions Agreement) signed and on securing SACFA (Standing Advisory Committee for Frequency Allocation) clearances. He got in touch with Bharat Electronics, which had showcased a 50-watt transmitter at an exhibition in Kamaraj Arangam in Chennai and requested them to provide the transmitter to Anna University on loan. He fixed a tower on top of the AVRC building and sent the photographs of the latest additions to the Minister the next day itself, to announce that they were all set to go on air.

Meanwhile, Dr. Sreedher went to New Delhi to the launch

event of the UGC channel 'Vyas' on January 26, 2004. He had been a consulting expert to the Ministry of HRD for that channel. He was not very popular with the Consortium of Educational Communication and UGC who ran the channel, as he had vetoed their budget proposal of Rs. 9 crores and suggested to the Ministry to sanction a meagre Rs. 55 lakhs per year to run the channel. He had been invited to the event on behalf of the Ministry and attended it sitting in the last row, he remembers. During tea time, he met Mr. Ravi Shankar Prasad and Dr. Murli Manohar Joshi and exchanged pleasantries. Mr. Ravi Shankar Prasad asked if Anna University would be ready for the launch of community radio within a week's time. Dr. Sreedher replied in the affirmative but also told him that he was still to receive SACFA clearance for the same. The Minister also asked for a suggestion on who should be invited to launch the first community radio in Chennai and Dr. Sreedher suggested that Mr. L.K. Advani inaugurating the community radio would be most appropriate. Mr. Advani, who was then the Deputy PM, was known for his stand on media right from the times of emergency. The Minister agreed to the suggestion and asked Dr. Sreedher to stay back after the event to plan the launch of community radio. The next day the Minister asked his officials to help Anna University in getting all the relevant clearance and licenses for the launch of the community radio. He also got Mr. Advani's approval for attending the launch event. "The minister wanted a formal letter from the University addressed to the Deputy PM. I contacted Dr. Balagurusamy, the Vice-Chancellor of Anna University, and he quickly sent the letter to the Deputy PM and another letter to the Chief Minister of Tamil Nadu requesting her to be present at the launch of the community radio. Chief Minister J. Jayalalitha too readily agreed to preside over the function," recalls Dr. Sreedher.

The launch of the community radio was scheduled on February 1, 2004. On that day, readers across India saw a full-page advertisement regarding the launch of India's first community radio station at Anna University, Chennai as part of the 'India Shining' campaign. Readers in Tamil Nadu saw one more half-page advertisement in the vernacular papers on the same.

Dr. Sreedher had another wish—this being the launch of a community radio, he wanted a part of the listener community to be represented in the launch function. He decided to invite a group of people from the nearby fishing community to be a part of the event. The security arrangements for the event were being discussed at the Secretariat in Chennai when Dr. Sreedher shared his plans to bring a group of people from the fishing community to the event. It was strongly opposed at first, but later when Dr. Sreedher explained and remained persistent, they gave in. The then Vice-Chancellor Prof. E. Balagurusamy paid out of his own reserves and arranged for fresh clothes for all the men from the fishermen community who attended the event, remembers Dr. Sreedher.

Another idea that Dr. Sreedher wanted to implement at the launch event was to bring a radio set on the stage and get the dignitaries to switch it on, to tune in to Anna FM to mark its launch. Again, the security advisors were against bringing a radio set near the dignitaries as it was Z+ category security and said a firm 'no' to Dr. Sreedher. But during the event, without the knowledge of Dr. Sreedher, somehow a radio set was passed on to the hands of Prof. Balagurusamy and he tuned in to 90.4 MHz. He passed it to Mr. L.K. Advani, who later passed it to Chief Minister J. Jayalalithaa to listen to. The photographers also managed to get a photo of Ms. Jayalalitha and Mr. Advani sharing the transistor as they listened to Anna FM. A young and refreshing voice, that of a student presenter Ms. Saisudha enthusiastically announced the launch of the channel, spreading cheer and vigour in the airwaves.

Dr. Sreedher says he still cannot believe how he landed the opportunity to sit on the same stage with the likes of Mr. L.K. Advani and Ms. J. Jayalalitha. He also says he was surprised that he was even allowed to address the gathering in their presence. Cheyon, a popular broadcaster and Deputy Director of AIR Chennai, was in the Anna University studios overseeing the live coverage of the event on Anna FM.

"The fishermen then came and performed before the audience. Among the audience were members of the entire Tamil Nadu Cabinet, Union Ministers, officials of the Ministry of Information and Broadcasting and the CEO of Prasar Bharati. They listened to the voice of the voiceless", says Dr. Sreedher, "and that's what community radio stands for".

"The next day the media did not come out with good coverage of the event at Anna University but mainly highlighted the CM's dinner to Deputy PM and the electoral alliance that both had struck immediately after the function," recalls Dr. Sreedher.

Though the launch of the Community Radio had happened, Dr. Sreedher still had no programmes ready to be broadcast from the station, and simply repeated the coverage of the inauguration function and some instrumental music while introducing the channel to the media. He also went ahead and announced that the channel would broadcast every day for about three hours in the evening from the next day onwards. And the same programmes were to be repeated for three hours the following day in the morning.

"The Chief Minister had instructed all officers, particularly then Police Commissioner of Chennai, Mr. Nataraj, who himself was a son of a Sahitya Academy award winner and former producer of AIR, Mr. Uma Chandran, to make best use of the community radio. Mr. Balamurugan IAS, who was the chairperson of the Tamil Nadu Aadidravidar (SC/ST) Corporation wanted to make use of the channel for the benefit of the underprivileged. Many NGOs like the Ability Foundation, National Institute for Visually Handicapped, NGOs dealing with the differently abled, and the Cancer Institute, Nalamdana, an NGO working on HIV, came forward to make use of the facility" recalls Dr. Sreedher.

In the initial days, putting together a three hour broadcast every day was difficult, but it was managed step-by-step. "I asked the students if any of them played any musical instruments, requesting a few of them to come to the studios and record, on one condition that no Bollywood or Kollywood tunes or songs were to be used. We gathered some 10 students in the studio and gave them a topic to debate on. We got audio tapes from the National Institute for Visually Handicapped, Poonamallee, for free broadcast. The management faculty at Anna University was allotted a weekly slot and Saisudha, an electronic media student, took responsibility for it. Two students Archana Madhubala and Kaushalya Rathnam took the responsibility of creating weekly programmes on the differently abled by collaborating with Vidyasagar, an NGO located close to the University. Other students like Vinay Sekar took care of sports programmes, Joseph Arul Raj did a programme on Career Guidance, Lavanya did a show on travel, Angayarkanni and Divyasri did a show for children. Mohammed Salim took the responsibility of coordinating with the Police Commissioner and organizing a weekly programme. The English department of CEG took care for one weekly slot. The university's hospital took care of the health programmes and invited various specialists visiting the hospital to participate in the programmes. One hundred and four students from the media department recorded one interview each with a BPL family and that gave 104 in-depth interviews with the community. The Anna Gem School near the campus took care of the children's programmes," he says trying to recollect the quick and efficient ways in which they managed to generate content for the radio station.

"Then one day I thought I must go to the community and get their voices on air too. I asked a student, Satish to go to a slum nearby and use CDMA phones to do live phone-in interviews with them. It was a Saturday. He went to Adyar and got two forms one from Reliance and the other from Tata Indicom. I filled up the forms and gave him Rs.2,000. He could get the phones activated by 3 pm. He asked me for the department transport. I agreed. He then said that he wanted to give some small gifts for participation like a few ball point pens. I gave a credit note to the university stores to give him whatever he wanted. He then asked me for some money to buy chocolates and I gave him Rs. 20. He said he would take two of his classmates along. Ms. Mohanapriya and Ms. Lakshmi joined him.

I had already appointed Mr. Balamurugan, to look after the transmission and editing at the station. Satish went to the nearby Kotturpuram slum at around 5 pm and at 5.30 pm called Mr. Balamurugan to patch him 'live' from the venue. He first saw a few children playing in the vicinity and started interacting with them. He asked them their names and made them sing some songs. They had taken a Tata Sumo to the venue. It was the vehicle owned by the EMMRC. As the interaction was happening live on radio, the driver placed the transistor with full volume on top of the Tata Sumo so that the slum dwellers could hear what these children were singing or saying. I was told that initially some women folk from the locality got suspicious of what was happening—that some stranger was interacting with their children and giving them chocolates. They rushed to the site and the programme was stalled for some time and some filler music was broadcast. Then the team for the show explained to the women, cleared their doubts and fears and later they too were interviewed during the programme. This way a one-hour programme was broadcast from a nearby slum giving opportunities to many children and women living in the slums to voice their views through the radio. The radio station also got enough publicity through the initiative. The programme was continued then onwards as a weekly feature.

When we reached the 100th day of the station, we already had 500 hours of original content and had a choice for repeat broadcasts. From Zero content to 500 hours in 100 days was an achievement and the same formula was adopted later by Radioactive CR in Bangalore and the Krishi Radio Dharwad when they launched," recalls Dr. Sreedher.

Sakthi Arivaayadi (Science for Women)—Women's Programme on Health, Nutrition and Hygiene

Having earlier worked at the Department of Science and

Technology, New Delhi, Dr. Sreedher was still actively in touch with the team working there. When he was associated with Anna University, Ms. Ujjwala Tirkey, who had earlier worked with him at DST, approached him, wanting to start a project for women using community radio. He asked Ms. Neeraja Prabhakar, who was pursuing a PhD under his guidance, to draft a project proposal for the same. "Those were the initial days of community radio in the country and commercials were not allowed to be aired. So, this idea was envisaged to create an opportunity for the community radio operators to get some money and partially fund their activities", says Dr. Sreedher. The project named, 'Shakti Arivaayadi', translating loosely as 'know your strength', was launched in Anna FM. It aimed to create science awareness among the women listeners, while giving them information on health, nutrition and hygiene that would help them take better care of themselves and their families. Under the guidance of Ms. Neeraja Prabhakar, the project was conducted meticulously with the student teams scripting and producing the programmes on specific topics, daily, to create scientific awareness among listeners. The programme was packaged entertainingly, so the message was communicated with much less effort and was easier for the women to understand and retain. A feed forward and feedback study was done for each episode to measure the knowledge and awareness levels of these women, before and after they listened to the programme. It was found to be a very successful model and was later decided to be replicated by many other community radio channels across the country. "So far, the DST has supported around 65 radio stations with an annual expenditure of around Rs. 14 lakhs for a daily programme in these stations", says Dr. Sreedher.

Anna FM 90.4 MHz delivered an interesting mix of content put together by a diverse group of students along with the involvement of the community. It defined as well as demonstrated itself as an efficient working model for community radio in the country. In fact, some of those programmes and formats were later adopted by other community radio channels in the country and are still popular.

The late Mrs. Sushila Balaguruswamy, wife of the Vice-Chancellor Dr. E. Balagurusamy, suggested that every student be given an assignment to record an in-depth interview with a person from below the poverty line. Dr. Sreedher specifically remembers two of those interviews, where Saleem, a student did a programme with snake charmers and another student Christy did a recording with the gypsies. Since the outdoor recordings were not always up to the broadcast standards, Christy on a fine Sunday afternoon, brought them to the studios directly. Here is how Dr. Sreedher recalls the incident.

"We had an excellent interview done by a student, Christy, who is now working in the same station after giving up a job at Infosys. I was at home on a Sunday when I got a call from Anna University security that many gypsies were in the radio station and that their children were spoiling the studio floor. In fact, Anna University had a long-time problem with the gypsies who once used to be trespassers at the campus. At the intervention of MGR, former Chief Minister of Tamil Nadu, they were given a piece of land from Anna University for setting up a colony. From that day onwards, Anna University had banned their entry into the campus and high-rise compound walls were built to dissuade trespassers. Christy, who happened to meet a gypsy, decided she wanted to interview one on her show on Anna FM. When she wanted the person to come to the studios for an interview, they insisted that their whole family would come along. Christy's father was running a travel service and he provided a mini-van to bring the gypsies to the studio. Christie recorded an hour-long emotional interview with them. She was a young girl, still innocent of the lives of gypsies, and that lent an unbiased and unassuming interview to unfold. When I played the interview to Mr. Bhaskar Rao, a well-known and an internationally famous media researcher who was then the Chairman for the Centre for Media Studies, New Delhi, he was overwhelmed and said it had all the material for historians, linguists and anthropologists to study. The then Vice-Chancellor of Anna

University, Prof. E. Balagurusamy, did not object to us bringing a gypsy to the studio for the radio programme. But he held the view that if we allowed the students to go to the doorsteps of BPL families and ask them to interact with them, he/she would come to know of the reality of the country. If at least 10 per cent of students realized this and took a vow to do something for the community, through the CR channels, it would be worth the effort...we thought", says Dr. Sreedher.

First Few Years and the Finances

"Meanwhile the Vice-Chancellor, Prof. Balagurusamy asked me how I was planning to run a radio station without any money. He was also kind enough to sanction Rs. 2.1 lakhs for the operations of the community radio for the first three months, using his discretion. Then he went formally to the finance committee and sanctioned Rs. 25 lakhs (Rs. 5 lakhs per year) for five years and asked the station to become self-sufficient within that period. A great humanist, he was committed to the concept of community radio. This helped the station to perform without much difficulty for five years," says Dr. Sreedher.

But there were other hurdles that the station had to face. When the government changed at the Centre, the response and attitude of the I&B Ministry towards the community radio changed as well. First, Dr. Sreedher was sent an infringement notice from the wireless inspector for unauthorized broadcast. "It amounts to a criminal offence and I got the news about it while I was at New Delhi attending a consultation arranged by UNESCO for community radio activists. Luckily, the Wireless Advisor to the Telecomm Department was also chairing a session in the meeting and I drew the matter to his notice. He told me that permanent SACFA for the station had already been cleared and that I could collect it in person the next day itself, thus sorting out the issue for me," recalls Dr. Sreedher.

The station had also received a written memo from the government, disapproving certain programmes that Anna CR was broadcasting. "They objected to the English programme being broadcast on a community radio and asked me why action could not be taken against Anna CR for violating the guidelines. I think that was one of the few memos so far issued by the government to any CR station", says Dr. Sreedher.

"Then there was a question put forward in Parliament about the working of the lone CR in the country. For the first time the UPA government with Mr. Jaipal Reddy as the I&B Minister gave a clean chit to the functioning of this station in Parliament. Many of those who were intending to start community radio stations in the country then started visiting the Anna CR. One prominent person was Amol Goje, the man behind the Vasundhra Vani CR station in Baramati. The Principal of Kongu Engineering College Mr. Natarajan was the first to approach the VC of Anna University for help. Even Vinod Pavarala from the University of Hyderabad visited Anna CR," recalls Dr. Sreedher.

Prof. Gajaraj Dhanarajan, the then President of the Commonwealth of Learning along with the former Chairman of ISRO Dr. Kasturirangan, had visited the Anna FM studios even before the formal launch had happened. "Mr. Dhanarajan had then promised that once it became operational he would assist us in organizing an international meet on Community Radio at Anna University. We wrote to him after the launch and he did offer 30,000 Canadian dollars for organizing the workshop at Anna University in December 2004. We took the opportunity and invited all the 54 applicants for CR license to attend the meet. We had invited officers from the Ministry of I & B, TRAI and other departments of the government. People from 13 countries along with 55 participants from India attended the week-long meet. Mr. David Walker from the Commonwealth of Learning, Vancouver, Mr. M.J.R. David from the BBC who was associated with the Kothmale project in Sri Lanka, the late Mr. Louis Tabing, who is an authority in CR from the Philippines were the experts heading the workshop. At that meet several concrete suggestions were made to improve the guidelines for community radio in India. The documents are available with COL, CEMCA as well as the Ministry of I&B. Most of these suggestions were included in the second community radio policy guidelines issued by the Ministry and some suggestions have been lifted verbatim from our recommendations, though the community radio activists hardly gave any credit to this exercise," says Dr. Sreedher.

The recommendations of the International Workshop on Community Radio held at Anna University, sponsored by the Commonwealth of Learning with support from UNESCO, made the Ministry of I&B think of amending the guidelines. Some of the recommendations were—to drastically reduce the number of steps and clearances involved in getting a CR license, to allow commercials to be aired for 5 minutes per hour, to also allow civil society organizations to apply for a CR license and create a single window clearance mechanism for educational institutions. With a people-friendly thrust from the UPA, Mr. Parsuramen, the Joint Secretary to the Ministry of Information and Broadcasting was instrumental in incorporating all the suggestions that were made at the International Workshop into the new guidelines which tried to enlarge the scope of the licenses to civil society organizations. But in the Cabinet, differences between the Ministers, made the government convene a Group of Ministers to look into the matter. Mr. Sharad Pawar chaired the GoM and its members were Mr. Chidambaram and Mr. Dayanidhi Maran. Finally, in 2006, the revised recommendations, which included the agriculture sector as a separate entity, went to the Cabinet for approval. Mr. Mani Shankar Iyer, the then Minister for Panchayati Raj wanted the Panchayati Raj institutions to be included in the eligible category. The Cabinet again deferred the approvals, convinced the Panchayati Raj Ministry and later approved the revised guidelines in October 2006. It is a different matter that it took more than five years for the first advertisement from DAVP to flow to CR stations", says Dr. Sreedher.

Role of CR in Disaster Management

"The then Secretary to Ministry of I&B Mr. Navin Chawla, who could not make it to the Community Radio Workshop, wanted to visit Anna CR at the earliest opportunity. He asked me if he could visit Anna CR on December 24, 2004. But owing to the poor weather conditions in Delhi, his flight got delayed and he could not make it during the day time, so he visited the station at around 8.30 at night. He interacted with the students, listened to some of their programmes and gave an interview to *The Hindu*. He was then travelling to Madurai and was coming back to Chennai two days later. But on December 26, 2004, a tsunami struck the Chennai coast and the entire southern coastal belt. Anna CR volunteers swung into action and started doing many real time broadcasts—both coverage and relief. Mr. Chawla had a stop over again in Chennai before he went back to Delhi and spent that time at Anna FM studios. He found the students actively going about their work, bringing in stories and recordings from the tsunami affected areas. He was very impressed. The next day, at New Delhi he was appointed as the spokesperson for tsunami relief activities and he issued a statement that was carried by TOI on the front page which spoke about community radio playing in important role during this natural disaster and the role of Anna FM. A project that was perceived as NDA's thus became a UPA initiative thanks to the tsunami coverage by Anna CR and Mr. Navin Chawla's conviction," says Dr. Sreedher.

"The former Chief Election Commissioner and Secretary, Ministry of Information and Broadcasting, Mr. Navin Chawla was convinced that community radio can play a vital role during natural calamities and disasters. Having himself watched the role Anna CR was playing when the tsunami had hit Chennai, he asked Anna University to work on a suitable model for setting up community radio stations in the Andaman and Nicobar Islands. He wrote to the Disaster Management Group in the Government of India and to the Chief Secretary, Andaman and Nicobar Islands to study the proposal given by the Anna University. Anna University in turn consulted Bharat Electronics and the Indian Space Research Organization for advice. BHEL had some expertise in solar powered transmission equipment and Anna University was considering the technology to be ideal for employment in the Andaman and Nicobar Islands. Anna University was also of the opinion that if vital data like the weather information and other warnings obtained from ISRO's remote sensing satellites could be picked up by these community radio stations, then the time lag could be eliminated, and a quicker response could be elicited in times of disaster. Based on its analysis, Anna University put forward the proposal for 'satellite-triggered, solar-powered community radio stations' to be set up in the disaster-prone regions of the Andaman and Nicobar Islands. Meetings were held, and letters exchanged but nothing ever materialized as not even a single application was received from the Andaman and Nicobar Islands for community radio. I happened to go to Andaman and Nicobar at the beginning of 2012. The Administration, and the Disaster Management wing had organized a CR awareness workshop. The Chief Secretary and some bureaucrats evinced a keen interest in CR, but that enthusiasm died within a few months," recalls Dr. Sreedher attributing the lack of response to 'sluggishness, red-tapism and change of guards at various places'.

"I believe that till date we have not given a proper training and education to media on disaster management. I hope that someone will take up the cause of organizing a disaster management orientation programme for the CR stations in the country", he adds.

It is amazing how much exposure one gets with a little media coverage. Mr. Navin Chawla mentioning Dr. Sreedher, Anna CR, and the role of community radio during the tsunami in a press interview was widely covered. A man named Fernando Segarra, representing Global ITI from Japan, came to meet Dr. Sreedher. Having read articles pertaining to community radio and disaster management and especially the role of Anna CR during the tsunami, he wanted to know more details from Dr. Sreedher. He also wanted Dr. Sreedher to help him to conduct a workshop on community radio and disaster management in Chennai, where he wanted to invite representatives from countries like Iran, Thailand and Malaysia to share knowledge and experience. The first meeting happened at Chola Sheraton in Chennai and they tried to come up with a plan that would be applicable globally, to manage disasters effectively using community radio. It was on the lines that whenever a disaster struck a region, a portable community radio transmitter, antenna and radio sets be sent as a part of the relief measures, to the affected area and an effective communication medium should be set up as fast as possible to ensure safety, rehabilitation and prevent rumours and panic. The next workshop for Global ITI was conducted in Phuket, Thailand. This time Dr. Sreedher presented a paper along with Supaporn Phokaew, a professor from Chulalongkorn University in Thailand. During his visit to Thailand he also got an opportunity to see how the illegal community radio in the country operated. "Cellphone tower infrastructure was used and additionally the FM transmitters were put up on them and a small soundproof facility was provided to run these community radio channels", he recalls.

Later another meet on the same lines was also organized in the Philippines, where they invited Louie Tabing, who was considered the father of community radio in the Philippines. "But we don't know what happened that suddenly Mr. Fernando Segarra went out of the radar and the company Global ITI also got out of involvement in the project. It had been a very good discussion forum and learning opportunity", says Dr. Sreedher. Later SEAPA—South East Asian Press Alliance, also invited Dr. Sreedher to give a keynote address on the role of community radio during the tsunami, at a meet that happened in Thailand.

Students of Electronic Media

The launch of Anna FM was remarkable not only in Dr. Sreedher's career but also for many students pursuing electronic media studies at Anna University, who got a hands-on opportunity to run a live radio station. Dr. Sreedher involved these students in production, management and anchoring of programmes in Anna FM, both live and recorded.

Anna University was the first in the country to launch an integrated self-financing five-year course in electronic media. They had also launched a two-year MSc course in electronic media. The only other EMRC to do the same was Devi Ahilya Vidyalaya, Indore, Madhya Pradesh. "The decision to launch the course was taken when Mr. Hari Gautam was the Chairman of UGC. Later when Mr. Arun Nigavekar took over as Chairman UGC, he reversed the decision and no other media centre was thereafter allowed to launch such courses. Anna University then created a new department—the Department of Media Sciences—to continue running the courses," explains Dr. Sreedher.

Though it had been about a year or two since the courses were launched, the students still had a hard time settling down as they did not have a space of their own in the campus and had to share classrooms and labs with the other engineering students. Most of their faculties were visiting or guest faculties. Mr. Ravichandran, who then headed the Department of Media Sciences, suggested that Dr. Sreedher take classes for these students, particularly in subjects of audio production and presentation. Dr. Sreedher also advised his other staff from AVRC like Mr. Surendran, Mr. Kannan and Mr. Raja to handle classes for the students of electronic media. "I did not teach them much but shared my experiences with them. They saw first-hand and participated in the functioning of a live radio, live television, the satellite uplinking of content, the stages of programme production and the roles of various crew members in a studio. I also invited experts from the industry to come and address them on various topics pertaining to media", says Dr. Sreedher.

In a few months' time the Vice-Chancellor Balagurusamy gave the additional responsibility of heading the Department of Media Sciences to Dr. Sreedher. Happy to do all that he could for the students, he first earmarked some classrooms for the students in the campus. Secondly, he along with the Vice-Chancellor recruited permanent staff members for the Department of Media Sciences. Being an honest man, Prof. Balagurusamy never worried about any recommendation or pressure and only hired staff whom he found worthy by following all the relevant procedures, says Dr. Sreedher. About 12 staff members were hired for the Department of Media Sciences. The new staff members were encouraged to pursue PhDs in their area of interest in media, under the guidance of Dr. Sreedher, who was recognized as a PhD supervisor at Anna University. He also formulated the syllabus for the media courses and tried to get it approved first by the Academic Council and Syndicate of Anna University. "But sadly, that work was never completed and the syllabus for the MSc Integrated course in Anna University, that has been running for about 17 years now, did not get its syllabus approved by the statutory bodies for a very long time", says Dr. Sreedher.

Meanwhile he also planned to construct a new building with classrooms, lab and all the other facilities required for the students of media courses. Twice, the previous Head of the Department of Media Sciences had tried to lay a foundation for the new building and rains had played a spoilsport making it impossible to continue with the construction. The third time, Dr. Sreedher tested his luck and laid the building foundation near the AVRC building, so that there was an exchange of talent and gyan from both sides. The funds collected as part of the fees paid by the students was used for the construction of the building.

Dr. Sreedher also remembers launching Gateway, a short film festival that was to give a platform for media and mass communication students nationwide to make a socially relevant short film and get it adjudged by a national jury. The films that were adjudged best were screened at a popular multiplex in Chennai. In the first year the jury consisted of eminent film directors like K. Sankar and Balu Mahendra, Ms. Jai Chandiram former DDG of Doordarshan and the creator of

DD 3, Mr. Abhijit Das Gupta and Dr. Amit Chakraborthy from West Bengal and the Director of Jamia Millia Islamia's A.J.K. Mass Communication Research Centre among many others. I never bothered about sponsorship for these festivals and I believed that the fees paid by these students was to be used for fulfilling their needs, activities and exposure. I even sent the students on study tours and internships to cities across India."

But the best thing he did for these students, Dr. Sreedher says, is paying them for their contribution at Anna FM. "My logic was simple. Had I hired professional talent or full-time staff as anchors and programme executives, it was going to cost me a lot. Meanwhile, if these students were given the same opportunity for a few days a month, I could get a variety of talent to work for the programmes. So, I decided to pay these students half the value of what they would get paid at AIR for their work. And I also kept a cap of Rs. 1,500 for a student per month. It worked well, both for Anna FM and the students. But many people in the University opposed the idea of the university paying students instead of vice versa, but the Vice-Chancellor did not mind and the trend continued even after I left Anna University," observes Dr. Sreedher.

Dr. Sreedher fondly remembers the names and contributions of these students he got to work in close quarters with. Some of those relationships he still maintains avidly through social networking and personal contacts. One student who developed close associations with Dr. Sreedher during his tenure at Anna FM was Satish. He was resourceful, dependable and once helped Dr. Sreedher out in a moment of crisis.

There was a Water Quiz series that was being aired on Anna FM, with support from the Department of Science and Technology. Students from across Tamil Nadu participated in this quiz and it was to be aired as a 26-episode series on Anna FM. Dr. Sreedher wished to use the money raised from this project to build the studio infrastructure at Anna FM. But some of his detractors in the Department were against his new initiatives considering them to be out of the Mandate of EMRC and one of them happened to interfere with the file which had the recording of the semi-finals of the water quiz series. Dr. Sreedher was shocked when he learnt that the file was tampered with and not retractable. Seeing him so worried, one of the student producers, Satish, convinced Dr. Sreedher to lend him the system for a couple of hours so he could work out some way of recovering the lost file. Dr. Sreedher was too disappointed that someone could stoop to the level of tampering with the programme. Without thinking much he gave the young man the opportunity he sought. Satish sat and worked on the system and tried every trick he knew to recover the lost and tampered files. Finally, he succeeded and revived the lost file. Dr. Sreedher could never be more pleased with someone's work and its timing. As a token of appreciation, he offered the student a sum of Rs. 3,000 as an honorarium. It was the beginning of a close association and a fond relationship that he shares with Satish till today.

Another significant development during his tenure at Anna University, was that the name and status of the AVRC that he headed was changed to EMMRC (Educational Multimedia Research Centre). The then UGC Chairman Dr. Arun Nigavekar wanted every media centre to be of a permanent nature and wanted to add a multimedia component to these centres. Hence, he moved a resolution at UGC to rename all such centres in various universities as Educational Multimedia Research Centres.

After successfully launching the community radio at Anna University, Dr. Sreedher next started an educational TV channel from Anna University. The new channel was called AUTDCC (Anna University Training and Development Communication Channel), which broadcast its content on technical education to 65 other institutions in Tamil Nadu. The channel was started without much fuss or publicity. "Prof. Nakkeeran who later became the CEO of the Tamil Virtual University was in charge of Faculty Development and he took a keen interest in creating content for the TV channel", remembers Dr. Sreedher. Dr. Sreedher had asked ISRO to shift the electronic equipment from their TRACT uplink van that was placed in the IGNOU campus in Delhi to Anna University for the uplink of the new channel. But later when he learnt of the plans to launch EDUSAT, the first educational satellite in the country, Dr. Sreedher ensured that Anna University's new channel was the first channel to log on to EDUSAT for broadcast. He also requested ISRO, to help develop an earth station in the Audio-Visual Research Centre in Anna University, just like the one they had in the IGNOU campus. An uplink centre was also developed in the AVRC of Anna University which could broadcast five channels at a time. Later another channel was started for teachers' education across Tamil Nadu, from the Directorate of Collegiate Education, Nungambakkam, Chennai. The content was received at the Anna University uplink centre through fibre and then it was uplinked to satellite.

When the new building constructed for the Department of Media Sciences was almost ready for inauguration, something unexpected and unfortunate happened. Some of Dr. Sreedher's detractors in the department, who did not find support for their cause with him managed to convince the Vice-Chancellor Balagurusamy that Dr. Sreedher was not good enough to continue as the Head of the Department of Media Sciences. Two days ahead of the inauguration of the new building, Dr. Sreedher was served a marching order and was relieved from the additional responsibility of the post of the Head of Department of Media Sciences. It was unfortunate that he could no longer go into the building that he tried to create for the students and share the space with them. Even the plaque that was unveiled on the inauguration day of the new building did not include his name and only mentioned the then Dean and Registrar's names. Dr. Sreedher says, though he has shared a cordial relationship with Balagurusamy through the times he never asked him why he was removed from the post of the Head of Department of Media Sciences.

Dr. Sreedher always thought he was able to do all that he

could at Anna University, mainly because of the support of the Vice-Chancellor E. Balagurusamy. "Prof. Balaguruswamy recognized talent. He was down to earth and caring and never acted egotistically. Whenever he saw some professors waiting for his signature at his office, he would just call them and sign the papers immediately. He was absolutely honest", says Dr. Sreedher describing him. Also, his wife the late Ms. Susheela Balagurusamy took an interest in the workings of the community radio and was a part of a few programmes herself.

When it was time for Prof. Balagurusamy to leave Anna University at the end of his tenure as the Vice-Chancellor, Dr. Sreedher considered resigning as the Director of EMRC. So, when the next Vice-Chancellor Mr. D. Viswanathan, took charge, Dr. Sreedher went to greet him with a flower bouquet and also tendered his resignation. When the new VC inquired what he planned to do next, Dr. Sreedher said he had offers from a few places and was hoping one of them would work out. It was untrue though. He did not have any offers at hand but was sure he would find something worthwhile. In fact, the new Vice-Chancellor Mr. D. Viswanathan, had earlier been an interim Director at the AVRC in Anna University. Later he also appeared for the interviews for the post of Director AVRC at Anna University along with Dr. Sreedher but was not selected. He then had to go back as assistant professor in the Mechanical Engineering Department, before he became the Vice-Chancellor of Anna University.

After tending his resignation, Dr. Sreedher then got in touch with the UGC and Consortium of Educational Communication lead by Prof. G.D. Sharma, former Secretary of UGC, to learn if there were any suitable openings available for him. He was told that similar to his role in Anna University, there was an opening at IIT Roorkee, for the post of Director, EMRC. Though he did not apply for it, he was asked to send the CV which was forwarded. He was later called for the interview. There were about 25 candidates who had come for the interview and Dr. Sreedher remembers feeling somewhat intimidated seeing them, despite his experience and suitability for the role. Most of them appeared sophisticated and confident and Dr. Sreedher suspected they could have powerful recommendations.

But having come as far as Roorkee, Dr. Sreedher decided to stay back for the interview. He made up his mind to leave as soon as it was over, instead of waiting for the results as he was least hopeful. But as he reached the railway station to take a train back, the news of him having been selected as the Director of EMRC also followed him there, much to his surprise.

It was a relief to have found the next opportunity so soon but getting relieved from his role in Anna University was a painful process. "I requested Prof. G.D. Sharma the head of the Consortium for Educational Communication at the UGC to write to the Vice-Chancellor of Anna University requesting him to relieve me, but to that the then Vice-Chancellor Viswanathan replied saying I needed to serve the full notice period and could leave only when he was replaced by someone else. Meanwhile there was a financial audit conducted at the EMRC, Anna University to examine and review the expenses made by me during my tenure. Though nothing came up against me, I was still grilled and questioned through the process. 'Last year you went to the US. You have not got any formal approvals from Delhi. Either you pay up the expense of Rs.1.4 lakh that you had incurred, or it will be deducted from your Provident Fund amount...', they said. I had to formally sign and agree to it, before I could finally be relieved," recalls Dr. Sreedher. He had been to San Francisco in the US in 2004, along with the previous Vice-Chancellor E. Balagurusamy, to attend the annual convention of the World Technology Network, of which he was a fellow. This time Prof. Balagurusamy had been nominated for his contribution to education and Dr. Sreedher was one of the fellows who nominated him.

Dr. Sreedher was glad when he was finally let go from Anna University. Though he had to part with a substantial amount of his PF money, there were other things he had earned that could not be taken away—a few close friends and considerable goodwill—from his students whose lives he was able to touch positively.

7

IIT Roorkee, CEMCA and Other International Projects: October 2005-September 2006

At first, it did concern him that he was paid much less at IIT Roorkee when compared to his roles at Delhi and Chennai, because Roorkee was considered a C class city. The University of Roorkee had been converted into an IIT in 2001. The EMRC there was a UGC-supported unit. It was located behind a centuries-old building, he remembers. Apparently, a fire accident had burnt down the centre earlier and the insurance amount for it arrived when Dr. Sreedher had just taken charge. He used that money in addition to some more investment to refurbish the studios and the centre. He invited his good friend E. Balaguruswamy, who was also an alumnus of the University of Roorkee, to inaugurate the refurbished studios along with then Director of IIT, Roorkee. Later Dr. Sreedher got his staff to use the new studios to produce video programmes for the IIT, for which the IIT started paying the EMRC. "All this happened just within a few months of my joining," recalls Dr. Sreedher.

Having launched the first community radio in the country, there were others who approached Dr. Sreedher for guidance on launching their own community radio channels. Around this time the UNICEF approached him to help them with a framework to work with community radio in the country, to spread messages on women and child welfare. They offered him an opportunity to work for them, eight days a month. He could choose to work on holidays too, so it did not affect his role at IIT, Roorkee. Dr. Sreedher met Prof. G.D. Sharma, the Director of CEC (Consortium of Educational Communication) at Delhi and got the necessary permission to work with UNICEF. He then initiated a UNICEF project with the Aapno Community Radio from Banasthali Vidyapeeth, in Tonk District of Rajasthan, which was the first operational community radio in Rajasthan, on air since 2005. Apart from this, having known that NGOs would also soon be able to hold community radio licenses in the country, Dr. Sreedher travelled across India and identified 12 non-profit entities who could possibly apply for a community radio license and partner with UNICEF in their cause.

Another interesting opportunity came his way when he happened to meet Ms. Usha Reddy, who was then working with the Commonwealth of Learning as Director of CEMCA (Commonwealth Educational Media Centre for Asia). They met at a formal occasion and got talking about their roles and assignments. Dr. Sreedher previously knew Ms. Usha Reddy, as she had been on the panel that interviewed him for his appointment in IGNOU. She had earlier been the Director of EMRC, Osmania University.

"Could you go to Kabul for an assignment Dr. Sreedher?" she asked him during the meeting.

Kabul, Afghanistan, wasn't ever on his list of countries to visit and the question did unsettle him, but he asked for details.

A media centre in Kabul had been destroyed during a Taliban attack and those who had worked there, the regular employees and media personnel had fled to other countries for safety. Now, they had all returned to Kabul and UNESCO had rebuilt their media centre building for them. So, the assignment Dr. Sreedher was offered was to go and meet the staff at this media centre and learn from them and document the kind of training in technology they would require, to restart their work from where they had left.

"But isn't it too risky to undertake something in Afghanistan at this time?" asked Dr. Sreedher.

"I have been there twice myself...You should certainly be able to go", she replied.

Dr. Sreedher considered it and accepted the offer. When the officers from UNESCO who hired him for the project, asked him how much he wanted to be paid, Dr. Sreedher did not know how much to ask for and simply said "a hundred dollars a day would be fine!". Whenever Dr. Sreedher took up a project with international agencies, he never had any idea of how much to charge. So, he always stuck to 'a hundred dollars a day would be fine!' as a response. Later, he was paid around 300 dollars a day for this project considering the risk allowance and other expenses. Having lost a lot of his PF money at Anna University, he thought he could earn something on this project to compensate for it.

The Afghan Trip, May 2006

Dr. Sreedher was very impressed with their creativity and talent when he met the staff at the Kabul media centre for the first time. He personally interacted with them to know what they used to do at the centre before it was demolished, what they intended to do now that they had rejoined and what kind of training and infrastructure would be required for them to do the same. He worked there for about three weeks and returned to India. The locals there spoke in Dari, also known as the Afghan Persian. Dr. Sreedher had a translator, who knew minimal Hindi. Dr. Sreedher's Hindi was very basic too and it was a challenge getting the communication across. Not much casual conversation happened between him and the team there, but from what he could gather, they seemed to connect to India mostly as the home of stars like Shahrukh Khan and Aamir Khan!

He went to Kabul again for the second time to submit his assignment and to have a last round of discussions with the team members before he submitted his recommendations. His second visit to Kabul was much more dramatic and eventful than the first one. "One day while driving down to work, the driver told me, that he could go no further as there were bombings everywhere in the city. A chill ran down my spine and I wondered if I would make it home alive. I was accompanied by Ms. Jackey Sutton, a brave woman and a former BBC journalist working as a consultant with UNESCO, who was in Kabul for the same project. She asked me to leave all the documents and assignments I wished to submit, with her. She promised to submit them later herself, as it would have been too risky for me to go about doing it in such a situation. She asked the driver to take me to the UN office, where I could be safe in a bunker. She came back two hours later and asked another team member David alias Dawood to drop me at the airport safely. In spite of all the constraints, Dawood managed to drop me safely at the airport. The airport was deserted. There were fears that the airport could be bombed too. But there were also rumours that it would not, as the Taliban were expecting their weapons to arrive through flights. I was advised to take the flight at my own risk. But I decided to fly to India as soon as possible, because there was no guarantee of better survival even if I waited for a day or two in Kabul. I somehow reached India and decided to never ever go back to Kabul again. It was later decided by UNESCO, that the trainees from Kabul could come to India and get trained instead of someone travelling from India to Afghanistan for it."he recalls.

Remembering Jackey Sutton for her boldness and commitment to the cause, Dr. Sreedher says she risked her life to save his. "She was posted in Iran and Iraq and I remember telling her as a friend, to get out of the region because of the unsettling situation and threats. But she had different plans for herself", says Dr. Sreedher. It was only unfortunate that many years later in 2015, she was found to have committed suicide at an airport in Turkey.

Back in India, people often questioned him on how he could go to Afghanistan on a project while being the Director of EMRC at Roorkee. Dr. Sreedher had an answer to give. "The central government is supportive of situations where an employee of the government is selected by the United Nations or the organizations under the UN, for a special role or a project. The employee is granted permission to be a part of the exercise as it is considered to be some form of recognition for his skills and accomplishments", he told them.

Prof. G.D. Sharma was strict but a person who achieved many things. He successfully launched and nurtured the Vyas channel along with Dr. Rajender Mishra. He never stood in the way of Sreedher taking assignments from UN organizations. He also allowed Dr. Sreedher international travel for participation in various seminars. Dr. Sreedher remembers that he went to him one night around dinner time and got his permission to go to Bangkok the same night.

Later that year, Dr. Jaya Shreedhar of Internews, who was actively involved in projects pertaining to the cause of HIV/AIDS, got in touch with Dr. Sreedher, asking him to recommend some names, as she was hiring people for an upcoming project. Dr. Sreedher volunteered that he himself was willing to work for it. She requested him for his CV. This was followed by interviews over the phone, with interviewers calling from Internews offices at Bangkok and the US. Dr. Sreedher was finally selected for the project which he promised to deliver in nine months' time.

Meanwhile, Dr. Sreedher had also applied for a role with the Commonwealth of Learning, and he got selected for that too. They gave him three months' time to join duty.

Dr. Sreedher, not wanting to let go of either of the opportunities decided to fast track the Internews assignment and deliver it in four to five months, and requested the Commonwealth of Learning for more time to join. They agreed to extend it up to four months.

Local Voices (October 2006-January 2007)

Dr. Sreedher resigned from the post of Director EMMRC, IIT Roorkee on September 30, 2006 and joined as the Director, Local Voices, an Internews Project. The project was funded by the USAID. It is not out of place to mention here that the amount of PF money that Dr. Sreedher had to part with while leaving Anna University, was equivalent to his one month's salary at Internews. Along with Dr. Sreedher, Dr. Neeraja Prabhakar, who had been his PhD student, joined as a volunteer for the project. Satish Nagaraji, his former student from the Department of Media Sciences joined part-time and Ms. Veena Murugan, another former student from the Department of Media Sciences, also joined. Dr. Sreedher also took his erstwhile PA, Ms. Mangalam to join the project. Dr. Jaya Shreedhar, the youngest daughter of the famous actor Gemini Ganesan, was an excellent communicator and trainer, he remembers. Along with Ms. Mia Malan from Africa, who was an expert with the Internews he organized a major workshop at Kongu Community Radio in Tamil Nadu in January 2007 to train audio broadcasters in communication strategies pertaining to programmes on HIV/AIDS. The team put together a state-of-the-art audio studio in Chennai, for productions pertaining to the project. "The project continued for another year after I left. Later, due to complications with the recognition of foreign NGOs by the Government of India and paucity of funds, the project came to an end," recalls Dr. Sreedher.

CEMCA: Commonwealth Educational Media Centre for Asia (2007-2012)

Dr. E. Balagurusamy and his good friend from the US, Mr. Jeff Rosenberg were the references Dr. Sreedher included in his resume, while applying for a role with CEMCA. "Imagine Dr. Balagurusamy being grilled over the phone by someone from Vancouver on my roles and capabilities for about an hour," says Dr. Sreedher, recollecting the process of his selection. During the interview, Dr. Sreedher made his interests and priorities very clear to the interviewers from the Commonwealth of Learning (COL). "I will offer my services with dedication to this role. But there are other things I am interested in and passionate about, which I would like to pursue", he told them. The two things were his involvement with the community radio in the country and interest in science related programming in various media. His conditions were accepted and after finishing his role in the project for Internews, Dr. Sreedher joined the Commonwealth of Learning as the Director of Commonwealth Educational Media Centre for Asia.

In his new role at CEMCA, he was in charge for planning and developing educational broadcasts in eight different commonwealth nations in Asia: India, Pakistan, Sri Lanka, Bangladesh, Brunei, Malaysia, Singapore, and also Maldives, which is now no longer a member of the Commonwealth. Dr. Sreedher gave the best of his time and efforts to the role.

During the interview, Dr. Sreedher remembers being asked to share his thoughts and ideas for making CEMCA self-sustainable by generating revenue. Dr. Sreedher shared with them the first idea that came to his mind, which was to set up a benchmark or a standardizing institution for educational programmes being produced in various countries.

"A lot of electronic media content is generated in the educational field today in the form of lectures, animations, audio CDs, powerpoint presentations, interactive websites and so on. But there is no standardization or rating of their quality or content. If, like the ISO or the Agmark, there was a certifying agency for such educational content, it would be immensely beneficial for the student and teaching community to choose the best for themselves...", he suggested. "Commonwealth of Learning could take that initiative to define the world standard for educational multimedia programmes that could be updated periodically to keep up with the rapidly evolving technologies. The developers of educational content could follow the basic guidelines put forward by COL and submit their productions to a rating agency appointed by COL in each of these countries to get their content certified by COL. The rating agency would then evaluate the content based on the COL guidelines and issue the certification. COL could collect some royalty for the educational programmes thus certified and charge for the certification process. A part of the collections would have to be shared with the rating agency for their role in it", he explained.

The then President of COL, Sir John Daniel, instantly approved the idea and Dr. Sreedher was asked to work on it as soon as he assumed duty. One of the first things he did was to arrange for a meeting inviting NASSCOM (National Association of Software and Services Companies), NAAC (National Assessment and Accreditation Council that accredits higher education institutions in India) and other private players who were involved in the field of educational content generation like the TCS, WIPRO, Microsoft and Google. Together they were involved in a brainstorming session on the standards to be followed to create educational media content, that would be relevant internationally.

When a presentation was made on the project for the first time before the Advisory Council of CEMCA, the heads and ministers of education from many commonwealth nations were present. The officials from Malaysia, came forward to take up the initiative as an Indo-Malaysian joint venture. "Malaysia not only had good educational institutions but also the Malaysian government promised to take care of 50 per cent of the expenditures till the guidelines were formulated", says Dr. Sreedher. After two years of working with institutions in India and Malaysia, in 2007, they came up with the first version of the guidelines for 'Quality Assurance in Multimedia Material'. "Malaysia went ahead and also implemented the same in its institutions. Whereas India did not do that since the country has too many regulators like the UGC, AICTE, NCTE and so on," adds Dr. Sreedher.

Through this project Dr. Sreedher had a wonderful opportunity to work with the Malaysian Government and institutions. In 2007, he visited the Open University of Malaysia (OUM), that was running an internet radio. Impressed by it, Dr. Sreedher wanted to start something similar in India. "I invited a few experts from OUM to NCERT in New Delhi to train its staff in uploading NCERT's popular Umang and

Tarang programmes on the internet radio. The OUM charged CEMCA a small fee for the training process. Members were also sent for training to Malaysia to get a first-hand experience of the workings of the internet radio. The internet radio from NCERT was launched and functional, but there was a glitch. A very limited bandwidth was allocated by the NIC (National Informatics Centre), for operating the internet radio and that was one of the reasons the project did not last too long", says Dr. Sreedher.

The Maldives

Meanwhile he travelled to the Maldives and the education minister there showed great interest in internet radio, though they did not want to allow community radios to operate in the country. "They have a very good bandwidth and even in mid-sea they have very good internet connectivity", says Dr. Sreedher. With the help of CEMCA, an internet radio was set up in the Maldives. Trainers from Malaysia did the consultation for this station too. New anchors were trained, and they planned to get the internet radio service launched by the then President of Maldives. The President had agreed. But things did not quite go as planned.

"Just a day ahead of the launch, we got information from the Telecom Ministry of Maldives that only 10 people could tune in to the internet radio simultaneously and if any more numbers had to be allowed to tune in, they would have to bear the bandwidth charges amounting to about 4,000 dollars per year. It was too high a cost and being notified at the last minute, we could not agree to it and the launch was put on hold. The matter was then taken to the President of the Maldives. He suggested that the launch of the internet radio should not be stalled, and they be allowed full bandwidth for a few days after the launch and the issues were to be discussed and resolved in the meanwhile. The next day the radio station was inaugurated by the Vice-President of the Maldives who later became the President of the Maldives and is now exiled, says Dr. Sreedher. The internet radio operated well for a few months after the launch but was later shut down owing to some internal political issues in the Maldives, he adds.

Developing Low-Cost Laptops

At the dawn of the new millennium, some time in the year 2005, a non-profit initiative called 'One Laptop Per Child' (OLPC) was launched to promote digital literacy among school children. "Under the initiative it was planned to make $100 computers that would be accessible and affordable to the student community. This required radical innovation as a good computer or a laptop required an investment of about $1,000 and more around that time," recalls Dr. Sreedher. He, along with a long-time colleague, Mr. Krishnamurthy involved himself in the project to come up with cheaper, affordable computers for students. "Mr. Krishnamurthy was a veteran in the field of computers, having worked with them since the time the Bhabha Atomic Research Centre got its first computer in the late 1960s. Though the central government encouraged our initiative to make affordable computers, there was no funding for it," says Dr. Sreedher.

Once, while on a visit to Singapore, Dr. Sreedher and Mr. Krishnamurthy were inspired by a digital photo frame. With a few modifications and improvisations, it could be developed into a low-cost computer, they thought. Mr. Krishnamurthy started experimenting with the idea in his garage, with all the low-cost spare parts he could get, to turn the digital photo frame into a working computer. They were hoping that if the idea succeeded, they would be able to give students a laptop at a price of about $35 each.

When Dr. Sreedher shared the details of the project with Sir John Daniel, the then President and CEO of the Commonwealth of Learning, he showed great interest in it. He even visited the team to assess their progress and encouraged them to pursue it further. He also promised to try and allocate funds for the same. Mr. Krishnamurthy by then took his model to the IIT in Chennai and the Indian Institute of Science, Bangalore to get expert comments and improve his design. He later travelled to China with his friend and had a low-cost computer made for $67, based on his design.

The Commonwealth Heads of Governments' meeting (CHOGM) was to take place in 2009 in Trinidad and Tobago. Sir John Daniel wished to launch the new low-price laptop during the event, as an innovation. Dr. Sreedher was all set to travel to the West Indies for the event, when around the same time, a China-based e-commerce website launched a similar model of laptops, also priced similarly. So, in the wake of it, the plan to launch their laptop at the CHOGM event was called off. Dr. Sreedher and Mr. Krishnamurthy were disappointed as all their efforts seemed to have gone in vain.

The Vice-President of the Commonwealth of Learning, Ms. Asha Kanwar however took an interest in the model developed by Dr. Sreedher and Mr. Krishnamurthy and arranged for funds from Australia to produce 100 such laptops, to be distributed among the school students in one of the islands in the Maldives. Dr. Sreedher and Mr. Krishnamurthy then made efforts to load the local school textbooks onto these laptops.

"A formal function was held, and the laptops were distributed to the students. The response to it was very good and the demand for more such laptops at low cost arose. But the big multinationals in the business, not wanting to lose their customers to a low-cost alternative, tried their best to lure and retain their customer base in the Maldives. Meanwhile, the world over, the price of computers and electronics gadgets began to fall steeply, and the gadgets became naturally more accessible. India tried to market its Akash laptop at a price of $50, but with the eventual slash of prices, the government was able to afford the regular laptops to be given away to school children," recalls Dr. Sreedher.

Though Dr. Sreedher and Mr. Krishnamurthy devoted considerable effort and time in developing a low-cost laptop, the changing times and fast developing technology, rendered it to be not so fruitful.

Dr. Sreedher travelled to many countries during his years at CEMCA. He had the opportunity of visiting Sri Lanka several times. But his first visit to Sri Lanka, was during war time back in 2001, when he was working with IGNOU. The visit was memorable for many reasons.

Sri Lanka (2001)

"Being a Tamilian, I didn't personally want to go and work in Sri Lanka. But my work demanded me to," says Dr. Sreedher. Amidst the tension of the war, he travelled to Colombo, where he worked with the Open University of Sri Lanka and the Colombo Press Club. He was also a part of a team of journalists representing Worldview International Foundation, an NGO, which was initiated by Norwegian politician Arne Fjørtoft. And in that capacity, he accompanied the UN Assistant Secretary General and 100 other people to meet the President of Sri Lanka, to urge her to remove press censorship and guarantee freedom of expression. Along with Dr. Sreedher, among the 100 members, were Mr. Mani Shankar Iyer and Ms. Margaret Alva. "All of us stayed in the same hotel. But Ms. Kumaratunga refused to meet any Indians from the group. She met the representatives from other countries, but never gave an audience to us. But Mr. Mani Shankar Iyer somehow managed to get an appointment with her and met her separately," recalls Dr. Sreedher.

Dr. Arne Fjørtoft, one of the founders of Worldview, took an interest in Dr. Sreedher's work and both of them also seemed to share a common interest in satellites. He wanted Dr. Sreedher to be involved in a new channel that he wished to start for the United Nations, based in Sri Lanka. The famous author of science fiction, Sir Arthur C. Clarke was also involved in the project. Somehow the channel never got launched because of the many hurdles in the way, but Dr. Sreedher still cherishes the memories of working with Mr. Fjortoft and Sir Arthur Clarke.

Meanwhile, Dr. Sreedher also got an opportunity to interview Sir Arthur C. Clarke for Gyan Vani, in which the author shared his ideas to launch the Arthur Clarke satellites and how a leading elevator company had agreed to work on creating a space elevator, just as it was depicted in his fiction.

Dr. Sreedher also visited and worked in Singapore during his years at CEMCA. "Though I never got to visit Bangladesh, I was happy that the community radio policy in Bangladesh is almost the same as that of India. But their transmitters for community radio have double the power of transmitters we have in India, which is good", he says. "The only participation I ever had from Brunei while at CEMCA, was them sending a representative to all the meetings I organized", says Dr. Sreedher adding that "Brunei never encouraged any projects like community radio or internet radio with the COL".

Another interesting experience he had at CEMCA was being a part of the PAN-Commonwealth Forum, where hundreds of delegates from the 53 Commonwealth countries got together to attend workshops and give away the Commonwealth Awards. "I was fortunate to be the chairman of a committee during the PCF5 at London in 2008 and I was a member of the main organizing committee in 2010 when it happened at Kochi. It helped me gain contacts all over the world", says Dr. Sreedher.

Dr. Sreedher has also been a part of the Asian Association of Open Universities. He remembers winning the best paper award while attending the Beijing AAOU Conference in 1999. He was also a member of the jury of AAOU awards held at Penang in 2011. He remembers visiting Vietnam for one of the programmes, but the visit was memorable for entirely different reasons, as his credit card details were stolen from an Indian restaurant he visited and he had to encounter a loss of Rs.6 lakhs.

As a part of his role he visited Canada every year for two to three weeks, to report at the Commonwealth of Learning headquarters in Vancouver.

He was once invited to Berlin to give a keynote address at the Berlin Media Institute, and share his experiences while working in the radio industry in India in the early 1990s.

Amartya Sen 2010

Every fresh experience in life helps us to learn something

new, to grow as a person and to broaden our horizon. An experience that Dr. Sreedher believes truly made him a better person is the opportunity of working with Nobel Laureate Amartya Sen for a Commonwealth project.

In the year 2007, the Commonwealth nations were exploring a comprehensive solution to the problems of extremism, terrorism, conflict and violence that are an immense threat to peace and progress the world over. The Commonwealth Secretary General convened a Commonwealth Commission on 'Respect and Understanding' and asked the Committee to submit a report on the same. Dr. Amartya Sen was involved in the project and they had just come up with their report that was published in the form of a book titled *Civil Paths to Peace*.

The Vice-President of the Commonwealth of Learning Ms. Asha Kanwar, entrusted Dr. Sreedher with the responsibility of getting in touch with Dr. Amartya Sen and arranging for a video interview to be shot with him, to share his views and findings of the report.

"Dr. Amartya Sen used to live in London and visited his home in Shantiniketan, in West Bengal annually. I got in touch with some of Dr. Amartya Sen's relatives in Delhi and was able to get his contact details and time. The shoot was arranged in New Delhi at the India International Centre and Ms. Asha Kanwar was there to interview him. The show was later broadcast on Doordarshan," recalls Dr.Sreedher.

Dr. Sreedher also requested Dr. Amartya Sen for more time and a much-detailed interview later, to which he agreed. This time it was to be shot at Shantiniketan, West Bengal. Dr. Sreedher requested the late Dr. Dileep Padgaonkar, a veteran journalist, who was earlier the chief editor with the *Times of India*, to do the interviews for Doordarshan. He was a member of the National Commission on Minorities and was also a part of the three-member panel of interlocutors for addressing the Kashmir issue. "It was as good as being a Cabinet Minister," says Dr. Sreedher describing the importance of Dr. Padgaonkar's role. But the man was known for his grounded, fuss-free attitude. He readily agreed to do the interviews and gave his time. "Dr. Padgaonkar flew with me in the economy class to Kolkata and we went by road to Shantiniketan where we stayed in a modest accommodation for two nights to complete the shooting with Dr. Amartya Sen", says Dr Sreedher. Mr. Abhijit Das Gupta, who was formerly with Doordarshan Kolkata had made all the necessary arrangements for the shoot and the programme was later aired as a five-part series on Doordarshan.

During the interview, Dr. Amartya Sen gave a message on fostering respect and understanding for people from diverse backgrounds and cultures, and for those with opposing or radically different perspectives. As the truth in it resonated with him, Dr. Sreedher felt a new sense of appreciation and respect for the great men he got to work with, on the project.

Working with Rinalia Abdul Rahim

"Once, during the Commonwealth Education Ministers' Conference in Kuala Lumpur, Prof. Asha Kanwar asked me to get video interviews of various Education Ministers who were attending the event. To contact the Education Ministers from various countries and convince them for a TV interview in a foreign country was not an easy task and it had to be done with the help of stakeholders. So I approached Ms. Rinalia Abdul Rahim, former CEO of Global Knowledge Partnership (GKP) and presently the Vice-President of the Internet Society to help with it. She had agreed... and one cannot appreciate enough the homework, the diligence, the elegance and diplomacy she brings to her work. Thanks to her, we were able to get more than a dozen good recordings pertaining to educational policies across the globe," says Dr. Sreedher, full of admiration. He also recalls another youngster who helped him with the assignment, Sakshi Gulati. "The Open University of Malaysia had good video cameras but not editing facilities. So I had requested them to provide the hardware for the recordings. Sakshi Gulati, now an independent filmmaker, was then a youngster working with a private producer. She volunteered to edit the entire recordings independently and created world class video interviews, and she did not even accept any remuneration for her work. She later became a student leader of FTII Pune and was very active," recalls Dr. Sreedher.

Involvement in the Community Radio Movement in the Country

After having inaugurated the first community radio in the country in 2004, the number of community radio channels in the country was expected to increase to a few hundred in the next few years. But when Dr. Sreedher joined CEMCA in 2007, there were only 13 operational community radio channels in the country. When Dr. Sreedher shared the details of his involvement with the community radio movement in India with his seniors at Vancouver, they encouraged him to pursue it and allowed him to use Commonwealth funds for some of the projects and initiatives.

"Though it was never explicitly mentioned in the guidelines, the Ministry of I&B had initiated a screening process and insisted on a baseline survey to be done before awarding CR licenses to the applicants. The screening committee included representatives from the Community Radio Forum, the Planning Commission, CAPART, Pradhan—an NGO, Ms. Jayalakshmi Chittoor (a community radio enthusiast), UNESCO, UNICEF as special invitees, and myself. The committee was very liberal in recommending applications from the civil society sector and since then the number of community radio channels in the country has been growing," says Dr. Sreedher.

Community Radio Awareness Workshops

When Dr. Sreedher worked for CEMCA, he discussed with the Secretary, Ministry of Information and Broadcasting, Ms. Asha Swaroop about holding community radio awareness workshops for various institutions across the country. The first such workshop was conducted in Lucknow inviting educational institutions and NGOs. They were exposed to the workings of a community radio and their benefits and success stories. The event was organized at City Montessori School, Lucknow, which operated two community radio channels in the city. The Assistant Director General for Communication and Information of UNESCO, Dr. Abdul Waheed Khan, was a special guest to the event. Vice-President of COL, Ms. Asha Kanwar, also attended the event and exhibition. Dr. Sreedher made all the arrangements through CEMCA and later got the expenses reimbursed by the Government of India. Dr. Sreedher and CEMCA were asked to conduct more such workshops in the country by the Government of India.

Dr Sreedher organized more than 50 workshops from 2007-12 for the Government of India which were fully funded by them.

With around 242 community radio stations currently operational in the country, Dr. Sreedher has been directly involved with the teams and launch of almost 160 of these stations. From Kashmir to Kanyakumari, from Gujarat to Arunachal Pradesh, he has personally participated in the setting up and functioning of these stations and most of the first community radios in these Indian states were started with his involvement. He shares his journey and notable moments with some of them here.

Andhra Pradesh

In Andhra Pradesh, a community radio license was given to the Tirupati Devasthanam and they started transmission from the Tirumala Hills in 2007. Sri Venkateshwara was the name of the channel, popularly known as SVFM. But the terrain and the thick vegetation around the area was impeding the transmission of the signal. "They even tried to get a transmitter of a higher power and requested the Minister of I&B for the same. There is a provision in the Community Radio Act to increase the power of the community radio transmitter up to 250 watts, which is five times the power of a regular community radio station. But the Ministry of Telecom did not approve their request and later in 2009 the transmitter was brought down to their educational institution, SV Oriental College campus, through which they had applied for license", says Dr. Sreedher.

Vishnu Engineering College, Bhimavaram, was another institution which Dr. Sreedher was associated with for the start of their community radio, Radio Vishnu.

GMRIT community radio is operated by the GMR Institute of Technology in Rajam, Srikakulam. "I had suggested to the GMR Group, which manages the Delhi Airport, to apply for a radio station to serve the people who have been displaced owing to the expansion of Delhi Airport. But GMR applied for a station in the native village of its proprietor where they have set up a state-of-the-art engineering college." he says.

Assam

The first community radio in Assam was launched in November 2010 called 'Jnan Taranga', operated by the Krishna Kanta Handiqui State Open University in Guwahati. Dr. Sreedher remembers that he shared cordial relations with the Telecom Ministry then and was even able to obtain a temporary permission to run the radio station for three days on a trial basis. In Assam there are three operational community radio channels, the other two being Radio Luit of Guwahati University and Radio Brahmaputra, run by an NGO. Dr. Sreedher remembers that he went to attend the launch of Radio Luit as a guest, and later he was one of the dignitaries inaugurating the Station, as the Chief Minister of Assam who was supposed to do the honours could not show up due to local body elections.

Bihar

In Bihar, he was involved in operationalization of Radio Snehi in the Siwan District. He has also visited Uttam Radio in Patna and Radio Rim Zhim at Gopal Gunj.

Chhattisgarh

Dr. Sreedher was associated with the Community Radio Stations at the Indira Gandhi Krishi Viswavidyalaya, C.V. Raman University, Bilaspur and Neotech CR at Ambikapur.

He also had an occasion to share the dais with Dr. Raman Singh, the Chief Minister of Chhattisgarh.

Delhi

Dr. Sreedher was instrumental in the launch of the DUCR community radio station operating from Delhi University. "It has excellent potential...as they have many students and the signals reach the much-populated locality of Old Delhi. But they have not yet exploited the potential of the CR by ensuring participation from the urban poor", says Dr. Sreedher.

He was invited to give a keynote address when the Jamia CR of the Jamia Millia Islamia University was launched in 2006. He was also associated with Apna CR of the Indian Institute of Mass Communication, which got a frequency from the general pool of spectrum and not one from the frequencies earmarked for community radio. "This was allowed as the Indian Institute of Mass Communication is under the Ministry of I&B and they are making it a deemed university," adds Dr. Sreedher. He had also interacted closely with Radio JIMS at Rohini and another CR of the same name at Vasant Kunj.

Gujarat

In the Ahmedabad District of Gujarat, Dr. Sreedher was involved with SEWA, a self-employed women's association, in helping them get their license and necessary approvals. They launched a radio called Rudi-no-Radio that was run entirely by women. Dr. Sreedher was also involved with another community radio in Gujarat run by the KMVS (Kutch Mahila Vikas Sangathan). He was also consulted for the community radio station operated by EMMRC Gujarat University, Ahmedabad.

MICA Vani at Mudra Institute of Communication also approached Dr. Sreedher for some initial guidance.

Goa, Diu, Daman

St. Xavier's College in Mapusa, Goa was one of the first in the state to get its CR license, but its launch was deferred for a long time. Dr. Sreedher assisted them in applying for a license and later for their operations. More recently he also participated in the CR awareness workshop held there in April 2019 and is likely to be part of an awareness campaign at Daman.

Himachal Pradesh

Dr. Sreedher organized a community radio awareness workshop in Solan in Himachal Pradesh. Later, the M.S. Panwar Institute of Communication and Management, a private educational institution, applied for a CR license and received it. The Chief Secretary of the state was Ms. Asha Swaroop, a former Secretary in the Ministry of Information and Broadcasting. Dr. Sreedher wanted her to inaugurate the community radio station, which was to be the first in the state. Dr. Sreedher had planned the launch event on March 31, 2008 and it was assembly election time in the state. Dr. Sreedher had requested WEBEL (West Bengal Electronics Industry Development Corporation Limited) to supply the transmitter and antenna. They were flown and taken to Solan by road, a day before the launch. But when the inaugural function began, Dr. Sreedher found that there was no sign of a radio station yet as the antennas and transmitters were still to be installed. So, he requested the Chief Guest Ms. Asha Swarup to inaugurate the studios at the end of the session, thinking that the launch of the radio station was in no way possible on that day. But the speed at which things fell into place was nothing short of a miracle, remembers Dr. Sreedher. The engineers from WEBEL with some help from the local people, managed to finish the installations and the radio station started transmission. Within an hour they got feedback that the programmes could be heard well from deep inside the villages on the hillside. So the radio station itself was up and ready for inauguration by the end of the function. The event got ample coverage from the local press. But someone did point out that it was not correct on the part of the dignitaries to have inaugurated the project during the elections. Though no questions were raised about it, Dr. Sreedher had kept his defence ready. The project was planned far ahead and the agreement for the CR was signed long before the announcement of election dates. Dr. Sreedher felt that he could convince the Election Commission, in case any questions were raised. Mr. Gopalaswamy, Mr. Navin Chawla and Mr. S.Y. Qureshi were the Election Commissioners then. And of the three, Dr. Sreedher knew Mr. Chawla and Mr. Qureshi. Mr. Gopalaswamy was from his home state Tamil Nadu, reminisces Dr. Sreedher.

Dr. Sreedher also helped with the launch of Tashi Delek Community Radio, at the Tibetan Children's Village School in Dharamsala, which was inaugurated by the Dalai Lama and Gunjan Radio run by Gunjan, an NGO for community development operating in Dharamsala.

Haryana

Dr. Sreedher was also associated with Radio Mewat, Alfaz-e-Mewat, Manav Rachna, NGF, Hissar Agricultural University Radio, Gurgaon ki Awaaz, Radio Sirsa and Sanjhaa Radio in Yamuna Nagar. "Both the radio stations in Mewat have their own success stories in broadcasting programmes in the poverty-stricken backward areas of Haryana. The Sanjhaa radio is an excellent example of a community radio station which fully exploited its commercial potential," says Dr. Sreedher.

Jammu and Kashmir

Jammu saw more than one CR awareness workshop. The first was organized at Jammu University and they got their clearances after a long wait. Central University near the Indo-Pak border has also obtained its LoI. Dr. Sreedhar is closely associated with Radio Sharda that is run by a society called Pir Panchal, which caters to the displaced Kashmiri Pandits. Recently the government has issued clearances for many institutions located in the Kashmir valley.

Karnataka

The Institute of Agricultural Sciences, Dharwad, was one of

the first institutions to approach Dr. Sreedher for consultancy. He gave the institute all the guidance required for procuring the licenses and the hardware. "A few days before the launch, the engineers of West Bengal Electronics (WEBEL) had installed the transmitter at the venue and given a quick training to some of the staff members and left. Three Ministers from Karnataka participated in the launch function and once it was over, Dr. Devendrappa, who was mandated to run the station, said he was not confident about running the station yet and that the broadcasts could begin after a few months," recalls Dr. Sreedher. But he intervened and told them that they need not wait much longer, and broadcasts could begin as early as the same evening. Dr. Sreedher had taken along with him Dr. Balasubramaniam, a scientist who had worked earlier with Prof. M.S. Swaminathan as a consultant. He also called his student from Anna University, Satish to come and help him with the programmes. "At 6 pm the same evening, transmission began with a volunteer interviewing the Director of Extension Education in the presence of a few farmers. Later some local music content was aired. We were able to manage three hours of transmission on the first day itself, which was repeated on the second day. Slowly, they managed to build content and today the station is doing extremely well and is also organizing training for other agriculture institutions in the country," says Dr. Sreedher.

Dr. Sreedher has done paid consultancy only for three community radio channels out of the 160 that he has worked with. The three being Krishi CR of the Institute of Agricultural Sciences, Dharwad, Radio Active CR of Jain University, Bangalore, and Sivanthi CR of Sivanthi Adithanar College of Arts and Science, Tiruchendur. "The rest were out of goodwill…", he adds.

When he was in Bengaluru to inaugurate the Radio Active CR, he was surprised to find that the IGNOU in Bengaluru was also operating at the same frequency as Radio Active CR, though it was supposed to operate on a different frequency. This was noticed on the day of the launch of the new community radio, an hour before the launch function. Dr. Sreedher felt that this being Bengaluru's first community radio, it was likely to get good media attention and the media might blow up the issue, if they found that the frequency was shared by two channels. "I immediately rang up the Joint Wireless Advisor to the Government of India, Mr. Singaravelu and apprised him on the situation. He said he would advise IGNOU Bangalore to stop broadcast immediately and shift to the frequency allotted to them at the earliest," he recalls. Dr. Sreedher then went ahead with the inauguration and remembers telling the press at the press meet that IGNOU would broadcast at a different frequency from that evening. Thus a possible controversy was averted.

Dr. Sreedher was also involved with the St. Aloysius College in Mangalore in getting their community radio license, and the" Science for Women" project was given to their Radio Sarang by the Department of Science and Technology.

The Department of Journalism at Manipal was known for its proactiveness in campaigning for community radio and Dr. Sreedher even sent some of his staff from IGNOU there to undergo training on community radio, though it was not the norm. "Later the Chancellor of the university contacted the Prasar Bharati chief Dr. Kamath who in turn contacted me through Mr. K.S. Sarma, regarding starting their own community radio," recalls Dr. Sreedher.

Kerala

Dr. Sreedher was also involved in the launch of Radio Mattoli, Kerala's first community radio channel operating in the Wayanad District of Kerala, run by the Wayanad Social Service Society. The channel, he says, is a very good example of a sustainable and successful CR in India. With its transmitter placed on a hilltop, the signals can reach far and wide and get wider listenership beyond the immediate neighbourhood, he adds. He also remembers helping Radio Benziger in Kollam, Radio DC in Thiruvananthapuram and Radio Media Village in Changanassery.

Madhya Pradesh

Dr. Sreedher was instrumental in the starting of Radio Azad Hind in Bhopal. He was also involved with the launching of Vanya community radio channels in different parts of Madhya Pradesh, to work for tribal welfare. In fact, the government took his specific advice regarding the issue of licenses to the Tribal Welfare Department. On his advice, Vanya had applied for licenses for individual schools in various communities. Dr. Sreedher also conducted training and workshops for the weaver community in Chanderi, to run their community radio station, Chanderi ki Awaaz.

"Chanderi ki Awaaz is a standing example of some organizations with funding from multilateral agencies mobilizing the community, training them in broadcasting and then leaving them in the lurch when the funds dried up", says Dr. Sreedher.

Dr. Sreedher also remembers sharing the dais with the Chief Minister Mr. Shivraj Singh Chauhan at the inauguration of a CR station, Radio Azaad Hind at Swaraj Bhawan.

Dr. Sreedher also supported the CR station Awaaz near Bhopal run by an NGO. He had visited the Radio Bundelkhand CR run by Development Alternatives at Taragram near Jhansi. Though the CR was much talked about in various media articles on the internet, Dr. Sreedher found the station to be much less active. Dr. Sreedher had also suggested to UNICEF to set up a community radio station at Shivpuri, which operates by the name of Radio Dhadkan.

Dr. Sreedher had also guided the RKDF group of institutions in Bhopal, in launching Radio Popcorn.

Maharashtra

Dr. Sreedher shares an intersecting experience from his association with community radio Vasundhara Krishi Vahini in Baramati, where the Science for Women project was initiated. "As a part of the project, a doctor's visit was arranged to the villages nearby and during the visit, it suddenly started raining. A local lady, Vandana Kote, invited the 40 members who were at the camp to her place and the check up and recording continued under a thatched roof in her house. Later when we were all leaving after the camp, the lady expressed her interest in participating and producing programmes for the community radio", recalls Dr. Sreedher. The college management then offered her training and inducted her. She also went on to become very popular with the community through her programmes. One year later when Dr. Sreedher visited the community radio station again, he did not find her there. She stopped coming, they told him. When the team travelled to her village and met her at home, she told them that she had become so popular that now she wanted to use the support from community to contest in the Panchayat Board elections. "She also won the elections and went on to become the President of the Panchayat Board", says Dr. Sreedher while explaining that her story is a classic example of how community radio helped a leader to emerge from the grassroots.

Dr. Sreedher was also associated with the community radio stations at Pune University and Pune Film and Television Institute. Yeralavani is one of Dr. Sreedher's favourite CR channels, located in Sangli, bordering the states of Karnataka and Maharashtra. The channel airs programmes in both languages, Marathi and Kannada, and serves the community in the drought-prone region. A radio channel run by Krishi Vigyan Kendra, at Loni, Ahmednagar also deserves special mention. The listening community there loves radio as it was loved 50 years ago, says Dr. Sreedher. Gayatri Mhaske, an RJ from this station, has a fan following equivalent to yesteryear radio announcers. Dr. Sreedher has also helped Vishwas CR in Nashik to evolve and improve their content and connect with the community, by offering suggestions and ideas. Dr. Sreedher also had the opportunity to interact with Snehalaya, an NGO running a CR station at Ahmednagar, Mann Deshi Tarang at Satara, Radio Vishwas in Nashik, Green CR in Sangli and Radio MGRI in Wardha.

Mumbai city at one point had three operating community radio stations. For the launch of the first one at Mumbai University, Dr. Sreedher's views were sought. "Mumbai University had two campuses—one at Churchgate and the other at Kalina near the airport. I suggested to them to host it in the city campus so that it would have maximum listenership. The Gyan Vani of Mumbai was located near the city campus of Mumbai University, hosted by the SNDT Women's University. But Mumbai University wanted to host it in its Kalina campus and since it was too close to the airport, they could not get the clearances, particularly the SACFA. But three years later, when the President of India Pratibha Patil agreed to inaugurate the radio station, the government swung into action and a frequency was earmarked for Mumbai and the clearances obtained," he recalls. The station was then launched and was operational for a while, but is currently dysfunctional.

The second radio station Jago Mumbai located in the city was hosted by Sealine Housing Cooperative Society at Union Park, Khar. This station was known to have been doing well and Dr. Sreedher had a few occasions to interact with them. It even had Bollywood actors endorsing the channel, remembers Dr. Sreedher. The station later had to face some environmental issues regarding their tower and had to close down. Jago Mumbai was roped in by Dr. Sreedher for producing a traffic education programme for auto rickshaw drivers in Mumbai city. The programme titled 'Chalti ka Naam Gadi' was exclusively targeted at the Marathi-speaking auto-drivers.

In 2012 a unique initiative was taken by CEMCA in collaboration with Yashwantrao Chavan Maharashtra Open University. Together they launched a unique graduation programme, Yash Sankalp (BA in Road Transport) for educating drivers in road safety and imparting essential skills like communication and vehicle maintenance. Community radio played an essential role in the initiative as much of the course material was made available in the form of audio programmes on many community radio stations across

Maharashtra. Bollywood actor the late Khader Khan, who had played the character of an auto driver in many of his films endorsed the project. "Mr. Krishankumar who hailed from Tamil Nadu was the Vice-Chancellor of YCMOU then. He was a dynamic person and he made open and distance learning a truly grass root movement. He died prematurely at an early age." says Dr. Sreedher recalling his association with him. He also remembers Dr. Anuradha Deshmukh the Professor from YCMOU who handled the project.

Meghalya

Dr. Sreedher organized a Community Radio awareness workshop in Shillong in 2010. He is happy to note that the city has finally launched its the first CR stations at a school.

Mizoram

In the year 2019, Dr. Sreedher attended a Community Radio awareness workshop held at the Mizoram University. Dr. Ratnabala from MS University in Tirunelveli, Tamil Nadu has joined the University as a faculty. She was earlier associated with Anna CR at the Anna University between 2004-05. "Mizoram University has applied for a CR license and is likely to start its broadcast from its city campus in Aizawl," says Dr. Sreedher.

Odisha (Orissa)

In Odisha, a civil society organization called 'Young India', obtained the license for operating a community radio in Konark. Dr. Sreedher remembers working with RTI activist Shah Ansari, who took the initiative for launching the community radio by the name Namaskar CR. "When the organization lacked funds to set up a transmitter and start operations, UNESCO pitched in and sponsored a transmitter. UNESCO had offered to provide 24 transmitters free of cost to operators of community radio in the country. The same was done by UNICEF for 12 CR stations in the country," notes Dr. Sreedher.

Dr. Sreedher also visited Radio Muskan at Phulbani District in Odisha, which is run by an NGO Disha. "It is situated in a sensitive area where the 'Naxal movement' is strong. But the way, a local girl Muskan runs it is very impressive," says Dr. Sreedher. When he along with another retired senior government official Dr. Brahma visited the place, they saw on TV that there were some killings in the area by militants on that day. Dr. Brahma wanted to meet the District Collector to ask for protection. When they both met the Collector, they enquired about the functioning of the station and the Collector was all praise for it, and when Muskan arrived, he could recognize her. The business model of the station run by a local girl impressed him very much. "With local market people supporting the station with some small money, Muskan is running the station without much difficulty. She has adopted the station name as her own, not wanting to use her original name. It is not uncommon for many female presenters on community radio channels to change their names on air," says Dr. Sreedher.

Dr. Sreedher was also associated with Shiksha Anusandan University in Bhubaneswar which runs a station called SOA with Mrs. Honey Patnaik as the station manager.

Puducherry (Pondicherry)

Dr. Sreedher conducted a community radio workshop in Pondicherry to increase awareness about community radio and ensure more applications. The first community radio channel in Pondicherry, Nila CR from the Manakula Vinayagar Engineering College was already on air. Dr. Sreedher remembers that the listeners in Pondicherry jovially noted the irony in listening to Nila FM (meaning moon in Tamil) during the day and Suryan FM (meaning sun in Tamil), a private radio channel, at night.

Dr. Sreedher also helped to launch the the community radio station at Pondicherry University, called Puduvai Vani in 2008. His name was acknowledged in the foundation stone for the station.

He also offered some help to the radio station run by the Aurobindo Ashram Society.

Punjab

Dr. Sreedher worked closely with the Community Radio stations at Guru Nanak Girls College at Ludhiana, Vivek CR in Chandigarh and Jyotirgamaya at Punjab University, Chandigarh. The first two stations had obtained their licenses in fastest turn around time and Dr. Sreedhar visited these stations in 2006 to suggest details of operations. He has also visited Guru Nanak Girls College in connection with the Punjabi version of Sakthi Arivayadi (science for women) project.

Rajasthan

Dr. Sreedher was also involved with the launch of Tilonia Radio from Ajmer, run by the Barefoot College. Its founder Bunker Roy is an Indian social activist who has won several international awards including the World Technology Network Award for Education. Dr. Sreedher was also associated with Alwar Ki Awaaz—a CR station situated in Alwar. Radio Banasthali, Radio Madhubhan and Radio 7, Kamalvani are a few other stations Dr. Sreedher has been associated with in Rajasthan.

In 2006, Dr. Sreedher had suggested to UNICEF to engage Banasthali Vidyapith to undertake the pilot programme on Women's nutrition and girls' education, as part of the Millennium Development Goals of the UN. "The pilot gave experience to the UNICEF team and they went on to create 12 CR stations in the country and also handheld them for a few years. Then they were handed over to organizations, who possessed a lot of knowledge in theory, and were experts in undertaking international projects. The end result of this is after the UNICEF grant dies out, most of the stations are finding it hard to survive. Of late UNICEF, instead of creating new stations, has begun to support content creation on 60 CR stations through the Sustainable Development Goals of the UN. This kind of transition from providing hardware to creating local content will go a long way in reaching the goals of Community Radio. Ms. Alka Malhotra at UNICEF, has travelled and witnessed the CR movement in the country and it is hoped that she will bring more and more initiatives to strengthen the content and thereby mak the CR stations in the country more sustainable," says Dr. Sreedher.

Sikkim

In the year 2011, Dr. Sreedher organized a Community Radio awareness workshop at Gangtok on behalf of the Ministry of Information and Broadcasting. The Sikkim University hosted the workshop and Dr. Sreedher was glad to meet Mr. T.K. Thomas who worked at the University as a faculty. Mr. T.K. Thomas was earlier associated with Dr. Sreedher during their AIR days, when he used to write scripts for the Radio DATE Project.

Tamil Nadu

When Chennai got its second community radio channel, run by MOP Vaishnav College for Women, Dr. Sreedher was not involved in it. But later when he joined the Commonwealth of Learning, he took the 'Science for Women' project by the Department of Science and Technology to them as well. He remembers that one of his students from Anna University was a faculty with MOP Vaishnav College handling the community radio operations.

Holy Cross College, Trichy

When he had just joined IIT Roorkee, the Principal of the Holy Cross College, Trichy called for his advice. Dr. Sreedher asked him to visit Anna FM to know the workings of the community radio firsthand. In December 2005, when the college got the letter of intent and were ready for broadcast, they called Dr. Sreedher to inaugurate the station. On reaching Trichy, he found that they were still to obtain all the clearances required to go ahead with the broadcast and explained to them that only the letter of intent was not enough to start broadcasting. He suggested that instead of launching the station, they could inaugurate only the studio on the planned date. In the meanwhile, he got in touch with the Joint Wireless Advisor to the Government of India, Mr. Singaravelu and managed to get the SACFA clearance on the same day. Because of his efforts, Holy Cross College was able to begin its test transmissions the very next day along with the studio inauguration. He then guided the team to obtain all clearances and later also conducted workshops at the college.

Dr. Sreedher also helped with the setting up of the community radio at SRM University, Chennai and this time again Divyasri, a student of his from Anna University handled the project. A community radio can truly be called so only when it is accessible to the community it is addressed to. Dr. Sreedher found in SRM that the studio was on the top few floors of a building in their campus and thus not very easily accessible to the members of community outside the campus walls. So, when the Vellore Institute of Technology (VIT) approached him for consultation, for the same reasons, Dr. Sreedher suggested that they create their studio at the fringes of the campus and make it accessible to the community.

A community radio called PARD Vaanoli was started by the People's Association of Rural Development in Tirumangalam, Madurai. "The license was received after facing numerous obstacles and the station finally went on air in 2009. But the station could not garner the necessary community participation and local support", says Dr. Sreedher.

Also, in Madurai, the Subbulakshmi Lakshmipathy College of Science, from the Dinamalar group applied for a community radio license, but they had not begun broadcasting even five years after receiving their license. The Dinamalar group was operating a Tamil radio channel with the WorldSpace and later when WorldSpace declared insolvency, they suffered financial loss. They were apprehensive about trying the medium again and the launch getting deferred. Dr. Sreedher visited the campus a few times and interacted with the faculties and students encouraging them to pursue community radio. Finally, Shyamalavani CR was started in April 2013. Wanting to involve the community, the team got a maid/caretaker from a local school, named Dhanam to be in charge of shows and community interactions. Dhanam then became hugely popular with the audience.

Vayalaga Vanoli is another community radio operating in Kottampatti near Madurai, run by the Madurai District Tank Farmers' Federation. "The radio station is housed in a coconut grove, with a thatched roof for the studio set up and they have kept their antenna as a part of the local BSNL tower. The radio station is popular among the community and they are doing fantastic work", says Dr. Sreedher. One example of their work that Dr. Sreedher particularly remembers is that when they were taught nutrition through radio programmes, they were asked to cook using those principles and they organized a cooking contest locally and the participants enthusiastically brought home cooked healthy foods to share with the community.

Pasumai FM operating from Dindigul in Tamil Nadu is an example of a good community radio station running with the support of local advertisements. Dr. Sreedher also had a role to play in the launch of PGP CR operated by the PGP educational and welfare society in Namakkal District of Tamil Nadu. He not only visited the radio station a number of times for training, but also Mr. M.S. Perumal, former Director of DDK Chennai, who Dr. Sreedher had suggested for managing the community radio at PGP, went on to win two national awards for the station. Another CR channel named Ilanthalir CR is also operating successfully run by the K.S. Rangasamy Group of Institutions in Tiruchengode, Namakkal and once again one of Dr. Sreedher's earlier students had joined there to manage the station.

As a part of the Internews project, that he undertook in 2006, he had already worked with the Kongu Community Radio of the Kongu Engineering College in Perunthurai near Erode on programmes pertaining to HIV/AIDS awareness.

Dr. Sreedher says that since the beginning, the South Indian institutions have shown great interest in operating community radio stations. "There are three community radio stations in Coimbatore, two in Dindigul, one in Konganapuram, one in Kumarapalayam, one in Karur, two in Namakkal and one in Salem. The area is pretty much saturated with community radio stations, but many of them are doing nothing significant. I have visited most of them," says Dr. Sreedher, adding that there is no news about the Mugil CR run by Sengunthar Engineering College in that belt, with no representatives having attended any of his meetings for community radio. Dr. Sreedher had a long association with PSG College of Technology and he says "they were lucky to have obtained a CR license even though the aerial distance between the airport and the college is short, similar to the case of Mumbai University."

Dr. Sreedher notes that Periyar Maniammai University, Thanjavur also has a radio station called PU Radio which is doing well. He has stayed in their campus a number of times and offered his advice to the station. There is no news about the community radio station at the Tamil University, Thanjavur, he notes.

Dr. Sreedher supported the NIIT Trichy to get a community radio license. "The Periyar University in Salem, MS University, Tirunelveli and Alagappa University in Karaikudi, Ayya Nadar Sivami Ammal College, Sivakasi have all received their Letters of Intent and will be launched soon", says an enthused Dr. Sreedher who has guided most of these institutions through the process.

In 2018, Dr. Sreedher was able to help the Sri Sankara College of Arts and Science, Kanchipuram to launch a CR station called 'Shruti'. Its application for license was originally rejected by the Ministry of Information and Broadcasting. They were called again along with others for reconsideration and cleared in 2016. "It took almost six years for them to get all the licenses. But once in place, I saw the same enthusiasm and encouragement that I got at Anna University, in Kanchipuram. The programmes are being prepared entirely with local talent both from inside and outside the college," he adds, with a sense of pride that comes with having successfully served a purpose.

A community radio station was also started in Kalpakkam Township in Tamil Nadu, which houses a nuclear power plant. A CR station in the vicinity of the atomic research centre could play a crucial role during times of disasters or calamities, envisaged Dr. Sreedher and the heads of the Atomic Research Centre. Hence a community radio license was applied for in the name of the Atomic Energy Central School in the vicinity. But the station is run and managed from within the research centre campus, where a space has been allotted to the school to house its community radio studios. A clever arrangement, one must say. "But according to the revised guidelines issued on August 27, 2018, this type of arrangement is permitted and every educational institution can take advantage of the provision," adds Dr. Sreedher.

An NGO named Nalamdhana based in Chennai and Keystone Foundation from Kothagiri also applied for community radio licenses. The two organizations were recommended by Ms. Supriya Sahu, who had become the Joint Secretary, Ministry of Information and Broadcasting. She knew that CEMCA had a special team to follow up with the community radio licenses and set-up, and hence appealed to them to help these NGOs set up their community radio channels. Later the Department of Science and Technology's Science for Women project was given to these two radio stations as well. "Just like UNESCO and UNICEF, BECIL (Broadcast Engineering Consultants India Ltd) also provided free transmitters and broadcast facilities to three CR stations in the country, Keystone's Radio Kotagiri being one of them. The other two were Chanderi ki Awaaz in MP and a community radio channel by Brahma Kumaris in Mount Abu, Rajasthan," he adds.

Tripura

Dr. Sreedher facilitated the creation of a radio station at the Central University Agartala, and its launch is being planned for in 2019.

Uttar Pradesh

NIOS (National Institute of Open Schooling) had been requesting for a community radio license for quite some time. But in certain cities like Delhi, says Dr. Sreedher, there are limitations to the number of community radio stations that can operate and also the distance between those stations needs to be greater than 30 kilometres. So, the license for NIOS was getting delayed for a long time since allotting a frequency to them was a problem as there were other stations operating at a very close range. Finally, NIOS was allotted the frequency of 91.2 MHz, in spite of a private player broadcasting very closely at 91.1 MHz. "I hoped the frequency issues would all get sorted out soon, when India shifts from analog to digital", says Dr. Sreedher. "A handful of countries have already digitized their radio. In the UK it is simulcast; that is, both analogue and digital radio exists. It is time our government decides to digitalize the entire radio sector including commercial and community," he adds.

Dr. Sreedher says that he was proud to be assisting the launch of 'Voice of Azamgarh'—a community radio station in Azamgarh. It is unfortunate that the place is known for crimes and criminals, he adds. Ms. Seema Srivastava, a talent discovered by Dr. Sreedher, and the late Mr. Vipin Sharma at Lucknow headed the station.

Salaam Namaste, a station run by the IMS group of institutions in NOIDA has also seen Dr. Sreedher's helping hand. Dr. Sreedher delivered the keynote address during its launch. He was also honoured with a Lifetime Achievement Award by Radio NOIDA run by the Marwah Institute.

While he was working at CEMCA, Dr. Sreedher helped accelerate the process for the launch of IIT Kanpur's community radio station. Incidentally the first community radio in India was being planned to be launched at IIT Kanpur and later Anna FM became the first as the Defence Clearances at Kanpur were getting delayed. And it took another six years for the station at IIT Kanpur to get finally launched. The Director of EMMRC at IIT Kanpur, Dr. Dhande was known to Dr. Sreedher from his IGNOU days. Dr. Sreedher organized a community radio awareness workshop at IIT Kanpur on behalf of the Ministry of Information Technology. Finally they were able to launch the station on March 31, 2010, recalls Dr. Sreedher.

"The City Montessori School, Lucknow held two CR licenses in the same city. The same thing happened to the JIMS group of institutions in Delhi. JIMS got two licenses, one for its Rohini campus and the other for its Vasant Kunj campus", says Dr. Sreedher, mentioning the special cases. Dr. Sreedher had used the studios of City Montessori School for the broadcast of the Gyan Vani channel in Lucknow. He also guided their community radio station in its initial years.

He was also the advisor for creating the first CR station in Agra at the Agra University. "Agra has got another popular radio station—Aap ki Awaaz. Its founder Mr. Lawani is a resourceful man and the station generates income on par with commercial stations," adds Dr. sreedher.

He has also interacted with Waqt ki Awaaz run by an NGO Shramik Bharti at Kanpur.

Dr. Sreedher had visited Amity CR run by Amity University and Shardha CR operated by Shardha Univeristy. Dr. Sreedher also suggested the setting up of Lalit Lokvani in Lalitpur, UP, by UNICEF.

Uttarakhand

Dr. Sreedher requested the Governor of Uttarakhand, Mrs. Margaret Alva to inaugurate the first community radio in the state, Kumaon Radio for the Energy and Resources Institute. It was set up with the intent that having a community radio channel in a sensitive area, prone to natural disaster would help in effective planning and disaster management. "In the absence of TERI's then Director General Dr. Pachauri at the event, I had to manage the show at 13,000 feet with Dr. Annapurna Vancheswaran who headed the media unit of TERI. The governor graced the occasion and inaugurated the station," recalls Dr. Sreedher.

Dr. Sreedher has also been able to interact with other CR stations in Uttarakhand like the National Institute of Visually Handicapped in Dehradun, Graphic Era University, Dehradun, and Zee University (earlier known as the University of the Sky). He also helped the GB Pant University in Pantnagar and the Uttarakhand Open University at Haldwani with their community radio stations.

West Bengal

In the year 2008, the then Minister of Information and Broadcasting, Mr. Priya Ranjan Dasmunshi showed an interest in community radio and wished to launch one at Kolkata. Dr. Sreedher started working towards it. Kolkata was never easy on Dr. Sreedher and this time too he was prepared to encounter unpleasant surprises. Jadavpur University in Kolkata had already applied for a community radio license. It was then processed, and all the required clearances were obtained. The West Bengal Electronics Industry Development Corporation Limited (WEBEL) helped set up a studio and transmitter in the quickest turnaround time. The Minister of I&B, Mr. Priya Ranjan Dasmunshi was to inaugurate the community radio channel on March 31, 2008. The Minister of Electronics and Information Technology from the West Bengal Government, who had earlier worked at Jadavpur University as a faculty, was also present as a guest.

"There was tension among the student groups with different political leanings pertaining to the event. The hall where the inauguration event was to be held was not cleaned and opened till 9.30 in the morning for the 11 o'clock event," he remembers. However, he ensured that all arrangements were in place by the time of the launch and everything seemed to go well till the hon'ble Minister of I&B rose to give his address, which was to be followed by the launch of the community radio channel. "I learnt that someone had meddled with the wires linked to the transmitter and hence live transmission from the studio would not be possible. I rushed to the Minister and told him in a low voice that he would be only inaugurating the studios and that the launch of the radio would not happen because of the tampering. The Minister agreed. Meanwhile, before the Minister could conclude his speech, another group managed to fix the snag quickly and also brought a radio set to the stage, so the Minister could switch it on and launch the channel. I quickly passed it onto the Minister who then inaugurated the channel. Still in the records of the University, the launch of the community radio channel on March 31, 2008 is not recorded," says Dr. Sreedher.

All politics aside, he also adds that Jadavpur University CR is one of the best community radio stations in the country, with very good programmes designed to match the needs of the community.

Till date, there are only two operational community radio channels in West Bengal. The other one is operated by a private institution, NSHM. A third one that was started in the Satyajit Ray Institute of Film and Television was later closed.

Content Policy on Community Radio

Speaking about the content policy on community radio, Dr. Sreedher says, "The CR regulations clearly state that at least 50 per cent of the content is to be generated by the community to which the station is catering to. But there is no one to guide the rest of the programmes. The CR guidelines also stipulate that the stations should not charge for airing contents. In an ideal situation, the CR stations must invite story ideas and content ideas from the listeners and experts in that area and should provide them their infrastructure including the studio so that the good ideas might become excellent audio programmes. The advantages will be that the station gets good audio content. It identifies new talent. The idea provider gets to realize his dream of making an audio programme. In these cases, the IPR belongs jointly to both, i.e. the station as well as the individual contributing to the programme. This is what a CR station is expected to do. But no one is willing to open their doors to others. In 2008, a senior official from the Ministry of I&B diverted an interested audio producer to approach a CR station in UP to air his contents. The person came back and said that the station was asking for money to air the programme. Unofficial counselling to the station then resulted in reversing the decision. When I requested the community radio stations in Maharashtra to relay the phone-in programme from the internet radio run by the Yashwantrao Chavan Open University, they bluntly refused. The university caters to the need of BPL families, including cobblers, construction workers, barbers, security guards, auto rickshaw drivers, and house maids but they do not have a community radio station of their own. Some stations even demanded money for airing the programme. As long as there is no clarity among the CR stations regarding content, such instances will be unavoidable. I hope someone takes the initiative and brings it to the notice of CR stations that charging for content is illegal and they have an obligation to air programmes produced for the same targeted audience in their locality free of cost. Because they came first, and they got the spectrum depriving others... they need to keep up the spirit of the community radio, taking on board everyone within the listening zone."

Also, many community radio activists have the notion that the campus-based community radio stations work as mere puppets in the hands of the management and that they exist only for the prestige of the institution. This view has constantly been heard in the power corridors of Delhi and featured in the mainstream newspapers in the country. But Dr. Sreedher shares a different experience...

"I am very proud of the kind of community-based programming I was able to achieve at Anna FM. I had an excellent team of 110 students studying electronic media at the Anna University. Each one of them was given hands-on experience in all aspects of broadcast including research, interaction with BPL families, production, presentation and so on. I am glad that at least 15 per cent of them found a place in the radio industry. Each one of them got trained to collect data on the needs of the community. Each one of them was asked to go and interview BPL families, to understand their needs and interests. Every student was given an opportunity to anchor a radio programme. As a result, within 100 days of launch, more than 200 hours of community-based programmes were recorded. "

Community Radio Sammelan

Having conducted a workshop for all the functional community radio stations in India at the Anna University campus in 2008, Dr. Sreedher wanted it to be made a tradition for such an event to be held annually. He discussed the idea with Ms. Supriya Sahu, and the plan to conduct the first community radio sammelan was born. It was first held in 2011 and has been continuing year after year. The same year Dr. Sreedher through CEMCA also instituted 'Community Radio Awards' in various categories to be given away at the community radio sammelans. Another initiative that Dr. Sreedher undertook during the Sammelan, was to garner support from the community radio operators to start a Community Radio Association of India. He ran a signature campaign with the 55 community radio operators in the country during the sammelan, got representatives from seven states across India as the rules demanded, and instituted the Community Radio Association of India. He also ensured that the members were all truly from the community radio industry and no outsiders were allowed. "The association has been functioning in a truly democratic manner and so far four elections have been held," says Dr. Sreedher convinced that he did the right thing by starting the association. A community radio forum existed from as early as 2007, but it did not involve all the operators of community radio in the country and neither did they show any interest in including everyone as members, says Dr. Sreedher.

Community Radio Sammelan 2012

The second community radio sammelan was held in 2012 and this time Dr. Sreedher invited broadcast experts from the

US, Australia and a few other countries to interact with the community radio operators in India. The event in 2012 was much bigger with about 150 community radio operators—those who were operating and others who were awaiting their licenses also participated. Also the first general body meeting of the Community Radio Association of India was held after the sammelan that year in which the community radio think tanks brainstormed about their recommendations for Community Radio Policy 3. The first policy of community radio was implemented in 2002, policy 2 came in 2006 and the third policy is yet to be officially implemented.

Commercials on Community Radio

"The proposal to allow five minutes of local advertisements on community radio stations was first mooted at the international workshop organized by Anna University in December 2004, days before the tsunami. But the government took almost two years to share its new guidelines for community radio, in October 2006. The million-dollar question that came from potential advertisers at that time was: 'What is your listenership?' Unfortunately, till today, I have not come across a single CR station having done a comprehensive survey to ascertain their listenership base, leave alone listenership for a particular programme. It is another question that there is no reliable method of measuring the radio listenership after listenership shifted from fixed licensed radio sets to transistors and mobile phones. So, advertisers were in no mood to give advertisements mainly because there was no formula to calculate the rates," says Dr. Sreedher.

"In 2008, the DAVP, the Union Government's arm for releasing the advertisements for the media was asked to study the question of releasing advertisements to CR stations. They had the same resistance. A committee was formed with Ministry officials headed by Mr. Brahma, Economic Advisor, the Director General of DAVP, and me to come up with a viable formula. We met several people who were running a CR station. After prolonged discussions we came to the conclusion that in the absence of reliable ratings, we could just fix Re. 1 per second as the rate for community radio stations. Supposing a radio station broadcasts 8 hours per day they get 2,400 seconds of advertisement time which will result in a revenue of Rs. 1,44,000 per month. It is a criminal waste to sleep on a frequency by broadcasting for only one or two hours. It is a waste of national natural resources and some highly acclaimed CR stations are just doing that. A minimum of 8 hours of broadcasting is a must to have some sort of acceptable visibility and sustainability. Even if a CR station gets 50 per cent of its ad time marketed, they would have achieved some sort of financial sustainability. But nothing had happened even after the recommendations and the DAVP officials started putting many hurdles like the latest WOL, service tax registration, separate bank account, etc," he adds.

Speaking further about the challenges faced in a CR going comercial, Dr. Sreedher says, "The possessiveness of the organizations holding CR licenses was another great drawback. They mix the aims of the parent organizations with that of the CR station that they are running. It has been made amply clear that they are only custodians of the frequency and the spectrum belongs to the people—the community it is catering to. Their parent organization may be of a non-profit nature, but CR station guidelines still allow five minutes of commercial time. Many auditors of these institutions sometimes advise them against going commercial. Ms. Supriya Sahu, the then Joint Secretary of the Ministry of I&B, the dynamic person that she was, came out with more solutions to break the deadlock and had formed another committee to delve into the matter. Again, it was headed by Mr. Brahma and it gave its recommendation that the rate of Re. 1 per second may be revised to Rs. 4 per second. Imagine if the CR stations were able to do aggressive marketing, quoting this as the basic rate, they would have received Rs. 5 lakhs per month from advertisements alone. Ms. Supriya Sahu also got them exemption from the service tax up to Rs. 9.99 lakhs. The DAVP then started releasing advertisements to CR stations. If the CR stations submitted the documents like GOPA, first WOL and an affidavit with a separate bank account number along with PAN number they would immediately start getting advertisements", says Dr. Sreedher.

Abiding Voices

While working at the Commonwealth of Learning, Dr. Sreedher was jointly involved in publishing a book titled *Abiding Voices—Sustainability of Community Radio in India* along with UNICEF. The idea for the book and the research for it came from the fact that though more and more organizations and institutions were showing an interest in community radio, none of them paid much attention to running it sustainably. Many stations were dependent on external grants and did not have a clue on sustaining the station once the money was spent. So, he took it up as a project and came up with a report on 12 working models of sustainable community radios currently operating in the country. He defined sustainability in four broad parameters—Content, Technology, Finances and Human Resources. On being quizzed why he chose the title Abiding Voices, Dr. Sreedher says that the only other book available on community radios at that time was *Alternate Voices* that started with a discussion on the politics of community radio. He is personally of the opinion that a medium like community radio should be used for development and educational purposes rather than political activism, and he wanted to give it a name that contrasted with the former.

Certificate Course in Community Radio at IGNOU

As the need for proper training in Community Radio operations was increasingly being stressed, in the year 2009 Dr. Sreedher took an initiative. He got all the stakeholders like UNESCO, Community Radio Forum, Development Communication experts, media professionals, and electronic engineers together and created a six month certificate course in community radio through the distance learning mode. CEMCA partnered with IGNOU for the initiative and the course material was put together in record time, recalls Dr. Sreedher. CEMCA offered to pay the full tuition fee (which was nominal) for all those who enrolled in the course and took the final examination. CEMCA also facilitated the process of training by offering the students 'on job' training at a few operational community radio stations. In the year 2010, the course was to be upgraded into a diploma course. "But later, interest in these courses dwindled rapidly as both IGNOU and CEMCA got new leaders."

Community Radio Facilitation Centre

Just before Dr. Sreedher was to retire from his role at CEMCA, he thought of starting a community radio facilitation centre, where applicants could apply for community radio licences and complete the basic formalities. The centre would later follow up with the Ministries and Departments in charge of approvals, thus saving the applicants a lot of time and efforts. It would also serve to ease the confusion and frustration always experienced by community radio applicants. Having helped with the launch of many community radio stations across the country, Dr. Sreedher knew that it was a daunting task for the representatives of institutions to visit the various departments for clearances, wait to meet the personnel in charge and get their files moving through various levels of approvals. Many delegates at the CR sammelans earlier had also shared that they found the process too complicated and tiring. Wanting to address the issue, Dr. Sreedher started a community radio facilitation centre at his CEMCA office. Later Ms. Supriya Sahu offered a space in Shastri Bhawan to run the centre. But CEMCA was asked to refurbish the office space before occupying it. Dr. Sreedher had to fight an internal battle at CEMCA to get permissions approved to refurbish the new office space allotted at Shastri Bhawan. "They didn't see how valuable it was to get an office space in the heart of the city nearer to other government departments. They were worried about spending on an office space that they didn't own...", says Dr. Sreedher. He later had his way and the office space at Shastri Bhawan was refurbished and the centre was moved there. The centre functioned well for about a year with Ms. Roopika Saxena and Ms. Hema Priyadarshini, a former student of his from Anna University handling the applications and processing them. But when the next Director took over CEMCA after Dr. Sreedher retired, he was not much involved with the community radio movement in the country. So, all initiatives and responsibilities with CEMCA pertaining to community radio including the community radio facilitation centre were passed on to an organization named One World.

After assessing the need for proper awareness and training in community radio, Dr. Sreedher felt that it was essential to set up a permanent facility for the purpose in an institution under the Ministry of Information and Broadcasting. He worked with Prof. K.G. Suresh, the Director General of the Indian Institute of Mass Communication (IIMC) in setting up a Community Media Empowerment Centre which was inaugurated on March 31, 2017. But the Centre is still to receive any funding or support from the Ministry, he mentions.

Taking up the Cause for Educational Institutions

When the community radio policy was revised in 2006, it gave an advantageous position to civil society organizations. They could set up their transmitters anywhere within a radius of 15 kilometres from their location. Many have used this loophole to their advantage and set up the transmitters at a nearby hill thus creating 2-3 times the coverage area. Between 2007 and 2014, the government had a more liberal approach in awarding licenses to stations operated by civil society organizations. Educational institutions... though they had the advantage of 'single window clearance', were asked to also appear in front of a titled screening committee. Dr. Sreedher wanted to safeguard the interests of educational institutions applying for a CR license. In May 2018, he took the initiative to meet Mr. Rajyavardhan Singh Rathore, the Union Minister for Information and Broadcasting and gave him a representation to consider single window clearance for government approved educational institutions. He also wanted the Minister to allow the privilege of setting up the transmitter anywhere in 15 kilometres radius, to anyone applying for a CR license and not just civil society organizations. Dr. Sreedher felt elated when on August 27, 2018 the government agreed to these recommendations and issued modifications to the policy.

Apeejay Stya University

Dr. Sreedher was already 65 when he retired from CEMCA. He did not want to continue the regular work routine with an everyday job to report to. A close friend of his, Mr. Ashok Ogra was working with the Apeejay Stya Institute of Mass Communication in Dwarka as the Head of the Department and he inducted Dr. Sreedher into the institute's governing body. He also inducted Dr. Sreedher into the governing body of a new university they were planning to build. Mr. Ogra suggested that Dr. Sreedher join as the Dean for the new Journalism and Mass Communication Institute they were starting under the new university. Dr. Sreedher refused the offer, but later joined as an Emeritus Professor, and agreed to work at the university for 6 days a month.

Personally Dr. Sreedher has great respect for the institution and its values, and if there is one thing he still regrets, that is not having been able to get them a community radio license. "Even after helping to launch 150 community radio stations in the country, I wasn't able to help them, as there was no frequency available to give them in that region", says Dr. Sreedher. But as usual, this time too, he found a way around. He helped them start Satya Vani, an internet radio channel instead.

At Apeejay Stya University, Dr. Sreedher also took initiatives to enrol students of mass communication and media to pursue their PhDs. Though at Anna University, 8 faculty members had enrolled for PhD under his guidance and were almost in the finishing stages of their theses, he could not grant any of them a PhD as he moved out of Anna University and the new VC did not allow him to continue as a guide. Determined to grant PhDs to at least a few students in his lifetime, Dr. Sreedher took the initiative at Apeejay Stya University and six students enrolled under him as a guide. Ms. Jaya Srivatsav, working as Assistant Professor in the APJ Institute of Mass Communication did her PhD on the rural coverage in mainstream newspapers in India, particularly the Delhi editions. Puja Sikka, another of his students was doing a thesis on public relations and brand building. A very senior officer from the DST Ms. Ujjwala Tirkey who was working with various DST projects in community radio, did research based on those projects. Another senior member Mr. B.K. Tyagi, who had worked earlier with Dr. Sreedher in DST and accompanied him on his trip to Islamabad, did his PhD on the role of science clubs in India in propagating science communication. Another young student of his is just submitting her Pre-PhD on Internet radio. Another well-known writer from the *Times of India* Mr. Prabhat Sunglu, is yet to submit his thesis on social media. The university wanted to set high standards in evaluating and approving the theses submitted by the students and hence wanted eminent professionals and experts in the respective fields to evaluate the theses. So, it was not easy for the students to get their PhD and they worked very hard, says Dr. Sreedher.

Having given the community radio movement in the country, the momentum that it needed, Dr. Sreedher still feared that community radio channels might become irrelevant in the years to come, especially when digital radio takes over. With government already considering policies for digital radio, the day is not too far, says Dr. Sreedher. Hence, he started involving himself with projects on internet radio. He was already experimenting with podcasts and audio-on-demand while he was at CEMCA and took initiatives to make the content aired on various community radios in the country be available in the form for podcasts for listening from anywhere in the world at any time.

Dr. Sreedher was also a Board member in a non-profit entity named Media4community, through which he decided to take initiatives to popularize internet radio initiatives in the country. The Secretary of this organization was Mr. Alok Verma, a well-known TV journalist, who was also an expert in digital news at that time (in 2010). Dr. Sreedher worked with him and his son Akshat Verma, who showed great interest in the project and came up with a buffer-less, ad-free internet radio initiative called iradiolive.com. The platform is currently active and 24 radio stations in the country pay a small amount and stream their content on this platform now, says Dr. Sreedher. When MOOC (Mass Open Online Courses) were getting popular in the US, Dr. Sreedher suggested that iradiolive be developed into an Audio MOOC platform, and Mr. Akshat Verma developed the site into the first audio MOOC platform in the country where many eminent universities from India offer their open courses online.

When some applicants for community radio were unable to receive licenses due to non-availability of frequency or any other reason like the NIOS, Noida, Dr. Sreedher encouraged them to use the online platforms. Rashtriya Mukt Vidya Vani was thus started by NIOS. Yashwani was started by the Yashwantrao Chavan Maharashtra Open University, where the then VC of the university Mr. Krishnakumar took innovative measures to increase the reach of the radio station and its impact.

Apart from venturing into internet radio, after retirement, Dr. Sreedher also showed more involvement with his projects at the Department of Science and Technology, by extending the Science for Women projects to a larger number of radio stations and also personally visiting the stations implementing the project. DST also initiated another project called Radio Mathematics to mark the 125th birth anniversary of the mathematical genius Srinivasa Ramanujan. It was initially started in 4 stations in different parts of the country, namely—IIT Kanpur, Jadavpur University in Kolkata, Shyamalavani in Madurai and Mumbai University. The project to teach functional mathematics has been extended now to other radio stations as well.

Later, he got a call again from the Commonwealth of Learning, and they wanted Dr. Sreedher to continue his contribution to educational broadcasts through CEMCA. Dr. Sreedher agreed to allocate 10 days every month to work for them.

Today there are about 242 operational community radio stations in the country, with 34 in Tamil Naidu and four in Chennai. Dr. Sreedher still continues to be involved with them at various levels.

After retirement, he has been invited to be a board member of many universities across the country. He is still an active member of many committees pertaining to broadcast media and education and continues to involve himself with projects and initiatives pertaining to them.

After his retirement from CEMCA, Dr. Sreedher was nominated to be a member of the sub-committee on innovation in film and broadcasting. It was chaired by Ms. Asha Swarup, former Secretary to the Ministry of I & B. The main committee was headed by Sam Pitroda. The member secretary was the renowned Economic Advisor to GOI, Dr. Brahma. Film producers like Mr. Amit Khanna, Vikram Kaushik from Tata Sky and Apoorva Purohit from Radio City were the other members.

Dr. Sreedher was also nominated to be one of the three members of the Technical Advisory Committee for the Prasar Bharati Board in 2012. Prasar Bharati had requested Sam Pitroda to study and suggest the way forward for AIR and DD and formed various sub-committees for the purpose. Dr. Sreedher had the opportunity to be a member of the sub-committee for Digitalization. He remembers interacting often with Sam Pitroda in this capacity.

Dr. Sreedher was the Secretary of Madras Science Association (1990-97), and organized science competitions, workshops and exhibitions independent of his role at AIR after obtaining the required permissions. He was associated with the Institution of Engineers. He was also the founder treasurer of Ariviyal Ilakkiya Kazhagam (Science Literary

Society) and he along with Dr. Kulandaiswamy and Minister Mr. Aranganayagam, organized many activities and events to promote scientific literature in Tamil.

True passion is ageless. And at 72 years of age Dr. Sreedher couldn't be more proactively involved in his professional areas of interest. Whether it is updating oneself on the latest developments in the professional front or about getting accustomed to the latest technological developments and personal gadgets, he does so with immense zeal and acceptance. Complacency is a word that is totally unfamiliar to this man who is constantly brimming with ideas in mind and things to do at hand. He has been fortunate enough to have a long and eventful career that he can look back proudly at, having given his best to all his endeavours uncompromisingly. He has been even luckier to have personally touched and impacted the lives of many people, he has been in touch with. And he has been luckier still for being blessed with a family that has been very supportive through his journey and continues to be so.

8

Gratitude

Though never complacent, Dr. Sreedher is content with all that life has bestowed him with. Looking back, he does realize there is a lot to be thankful for. In this section, he takes the opportunity to thank the people who have inspired, supported and stood by him.

Family First!

Grandfather Gopala Iyer and Grandmother Nagalakshmi—For making him understand the joint family system and simultaneously managing individual households. For making him realize the importance of Tamil literature and Indian values and culture.

Mother Pankajam—He learnt from her how not to express one's own agony and hardships to others and to always volunteer to work for the children and other relations.

Wife Meenakshi—For giving him the freedom to take his professional decisions; for doing an excellent job of raising his two daughters.

Daughters—Sripriya and Gayathri. Both of them studied in government schools, did well for themselves and are well placed in life.

Sons-in-law—Rahul and Santosh. For their affection and care.

Grandsons—Vihaan and Ahaan, and granddaughter Kavya. For the love, joy and playfulness that they add to his life.

Aunt Savithri Venkatachalam—For her sacrifices and helpful attitude towards the entire joint family. She was his role model for making the correct and timely decisions. She showed him the way of networking with the extended family.

Brothers—Chandrasekaran and Rajagopalan. For their cooperation during the difficult days.

Brothers' wives—Uma and Ranjani. For preserving the tradition.

Nephews and Nieces—Gokul, Bhavani, Bhavya and Shreyas. For maintaining the family links and excelling in their own fields.

Sister Uma Jayaraman and Brother-in-law Jayaraman—for their sacrifices in raising their daughters Vidya and Ramya, who are now well placed in life.

He would like to make a special mention of his uncle's daughter Bala Rajkhowa and her husband Akshay Rajkhowa and son Chiranjeev in the family.

Uncle Venkatachalam—"For helping him find opportunities and exposure". For helping him learn the way the government functioned.

His daughters Usha Chandra, Anuradha Hariharan. Sons—Ravi Vish and Venkat Gopalan along with their spouses have a special place in Dr. Sreedher's life.

Uncle Jayaraman—For making him understand how to overcome obstacles—physical and mental. His wife Vasanthi for agreeing to marry a double handicapped person and giving him all the support till his last moments and for relieving the other family members of the responsibility.

Uncle Krishnamurthy and his wife Ms. Jagatheeswari—for undertaking the burden of managing a big family, three sisters and a handicapped brother while working as a scientist at the India Meteorological Department. He was also an inspiration for his love for radio as he used to work on crystal radio sets and repair them at home, thereby setting an atmosphere for listening to radio.

Cousin Raghuraman who was on and off his school mate and his guide.

His wife a fellow chemist Mrs. Kalpagam and brothers Gopalan and Shankar, sister Rama have also contributed to the oneness in the family.

Friends and Mentors

Dr. Abdul Waheed Khan, who retired as Assistant Director General UNESCO and former VC, Indira Gandhi National Open University—For selecting him and initiating him into Educational Media. Dr. Sreedher calls him an example of a truly secular person and he is so grateful to him for the new international opportunities, he received through him.

Mrs. Aparna Vaish who became an Acting Director General of Doordarshan, was a Science Officer from Jaipur who had also worked as an Asst. Director of Programmes (Education) under Dr. Sreedher. He describes her as an honest, loyal, intelligent and hardworking person, who also helped him overcome his difficulties with language. Her creative work was seen in the Science serials like Human Evolution and she gave the most appropriate title 'CHEER' for a Radio Serial on children's enrichment education.

Mr. Alok Verma, who inspired Dr. Sreedher in the way he brought in a combination of business sense and ethical values, to digital broadcasting. Dr. Sreedher describes his son Akshat Verma as a 'role model' of modern day youth. His respect for parents, his behaviour and his diligence, made Dr. Sreedher change his opinion of the present generation.

Prof. Asha Kanwar, the former Pro-Vice-chancellor at IGNOU who later became the President of the Commonwealth of Learning. She gave the toughest assignments to Dr. Sreedher, insisted that he undertake them and monitored him as he worked on them in true letter and spirit of the goals of CEMCA. Dr. Sreedher gained much confidence and international exposure while working with her. "I feel much indebted for all the opportunities. She was officially very strict but personally a true human being," he says. Dr. Sreedher fondly remembers the vegetarian dinners he had with her in Vancouver. He was particularly overwhelmed when he learnt that she had already booked an overcoat for him that was available on 'sale', so he could feel comfortable in the cold and rainy Vancouver weather. "She asked me to do a series on

'Civil Paths to Peace' which changed my thinking altogether. I truly developed respect and understanding of multi-religious, multi-ethnic, multicultural and multilingual people," he says.

Prof. Ashok Ogra—Dr. Sreedher's association with him goes back to about three decades. He says he is forever indebted to him for being very resourceful and often saving his skin.

He was instrumental in making Dr. Sreedher join as Professor (Emeritus) at the reputed School of Journalism and Mass Communication, Apeejay Stya University, Sohna, Gurugram after superannuation from active service. It made Dr. Sreedher academically inclined once again and also enabled him to share his knowledge with young aspiring mass communication students and PhD scholars.

Vice-Chancellor of Anna University Prof. E. Balagurusamy —"For being absolutely honest and professional and being quick with decisions. Prof. Balagurusamy and his wife Sushila Balagurusamy, both were committed to cause and outcomes, insisted on ethics and did not micromanage things. My life would have become dark had not Prof. Balagurusamy spotted me and offered me the job at Anna University," he says.

Ms. Asha Swaroop, former Chief Secretary, Himachal Pradesh and Secretary, Ministry of Information and Broadcasting—For having complete faith in his abilities and allowing him to advise the Ministry in its Community Radio initiatives. She spoke in support of him even to his adversaries and Dr. Sreedher was humbled by the trust she had in him. Incidentally, Ms. Asha Swarup was also the sister of Mr. M.K. Kaw, a Kashmiri intellectual who held several high positions in the Government of India and was also the one who spearheaded Gyan Darshan.

Dr. Brahmananda Brahma, former Chief Economic Advisor to the Government of India—"Without his proactive schemes the Community Radio stations would have had a natural death," says Dr. Sreedher. "I got him interested in the Community Radio Sector. He who was at the helm of affairs, determining the government sponsored advertisement rates to newspapers television and radio, took a bold decision to include community radio for advertising at a rock bottom price of Re. 1 per second and later raised it to Rs. 4 per second. Dr. Brahma is the person behind drafting an excellent proposal to get a funding of Rs. 100 crores for the CR sector from the government," adds Dr. Sreedher.

He is also appreciative of Mrs. Deepa Chandra, who was earlier Science Officer at AIR Bhopal and opted for the Doordarshan cadre. She was in Mumbai when Dr. Sreedher brought her to Delhi to serve in his division as an Assistant Controller of Programmes. "She was the luckiest of DD staff, as she never had to leave Delhi for 25 years, till her retirement," he says. She was also acting Director General of DD and her help in launching and running Gyan Darshan channel as well as the film section of the near monopolist Doordarshan will be unforgettable, says Dr. Sreedher.

Mr. M.S. Gopal, Station Director, AIR Madras—"It was encouraging to hear him praise my work and capabilities."

Jaya Shridhar: The famous health communicator who specialized in AIDS awareness. A doctor by profession and daughter of Gemini Ganesan, the famous South Indian Actor. She recommended Dr. Sreedher for the role of the Director of Local Voices project in Chennai. Her pleasant manners and silent assertiveness were much appreciated by Dr. Sreedher.

Mr. Kandasamy (Thuraivan), Station Director, AIR Madras—"For being a huge support."

Though he occasionally chided Dr. Sreedher at work, he always ensured all due credit for good work did get across to the right person.

Prof. O.P. Kejriwal: Former DG All India Radio, CEO Prasar Bharati, Director, Nehru Memorial Museum & Library, and Member Central Information Commission—Dr. Sreedher recalls his association with him as DG AIR in the late 1990's. "He was responsible for relieving me from AIR when I wanted to join IGNOU. He is a famous historian. Once he called me to get rare recordings of Talat Aziz for use in his research. I got the songs loaded onto a cassette and met him on New Year's day in 1998 and told him it costs Rs. 240. He immediately paid the money from his pocket and everyone was surprised that I asked him to pay such a small amount and at him having paid it. It is very difficult to find such honest officers nowadays," says Dr. Sreedher.

A.R. Krishnamurthy, fondly called ARK—the Programme Officer at AIR Madras who identified the talent and resourcefulness of young Sridharan and led him into the world of broadcasting, being his mentor and "go-to person". For over three decades, ARK stood in support of Dr. Sreedher. He was also the one who advised him to quit broadcasting and become an academic. Every problem that Dr. Sreedher faced in AIR/DD was solved by him.

V. Krishnamoorthy, whom he met first at a software expo in Delhi in 1990, became his fellow traveller for over 28 years. "He kindled my interest in the application of computers to broadcasting. He was one of the oldest scientists to have operated a computer in India. His knowledge in mathematics, physics and computing is amazing. He worked with me in AIR, Doordarshan, IGNOU and CEMCA. Half the credit I got in these places is due to Mr. Krishnamoorthy" he says..

Prof. V.C. Kulandaisamy, former Vice-Chancellor, Anna University—"For his kindness and understanding". Dr. Sreedher had known him through his visits to cover science events at Anna University. An incident that he remembers, where he stood by Dr. Sreedher was when he was the head of the organizing team for the Periyar Centenary celebrations. Dr. Sreedher was covering the event for AIR. When some people raised questions to him on how a Brahmin could be entrusted the responsibility to cover an event on Periyar, the Vice-Chancellor spoke in support of Dr. Sreedher and his calibre. "We are people of scientific perspectives. Don't bring in the Brahmin, non-Brahmin debate here", he retaliated.

Dr. Sreedher shares cordial relations with the publisher of the Tamil daily *Dinamalar*, R. Lakshmipathy for the past 15 years. Dr. Sreedher says he is amazed by his ethical way of working, sticking to his principles, and fearlessness.

Shri P. Murari, former Secretary to the President of India was always kind to Dr. Sreedher. Dr. Sreedher invited him to his programmes at AIR Chennai and Coimbatore, and he always responded positively. He also visited the Ashtasidhivinayak Temple at Selayur twice. He even boldly wrote letters to industrialists Mahalingam and M.A.M. Ramaswamy to help construct the temple. When he was the Secretary to the Ministry of Information and Broadcasting, Dr. Sreedher wished to join Doordarshan. "But even though Secretaries had all the power, Mr. Murari told me that he would do it only if there were any clear vacancies," reminisces Dr. Sreedher. Dr. Sreedher also remembers taking him to the Akashvani Award function at Siri Fort Auditorium through the back stage even though he was the Chief Guest and people were waiting to receive him at the entrance. Mr. Murari was of great help when some electronic goods under Dr. Sreedher's custody were stolen in DST. Even in his capacity at FICCI, he tried to support Dr. Sreedher for getting the DG post at AIR.

Mr. Narender Sehgal, Kalinga Award winner and former Advisor, Department of Science and Technology—"For identifying my interest in science and encouraging me to be a science communicator. For encouraging new ideas and proposals. For teaching me to think bigger and implement Pan India projects. For being a role model in never compromising on rules and ethics." Sehgal is the father of science communication in India.

R. Natraj, who was the Commissioner with the Tamil Nadu Police, has always been supportive of the endeavours of community radio in Chennai. He was also the son of Mr. Uma Chandran, Sahitya Akademi winner and an AIR Producer who was one of those who groomed Dr. Sreedher. In fact many of Natraj's relatives like Poornam Viswanathan and Dharmambal, the famous news reader have served AIR.

Mr. V.S. Pandey who once exposed the scams of top IAS officers in Uttar Pradesh was the Joint Secretary in MHRD when Dr. Sreedher was launching Gyan Darshan and Gyan Vani channels. His proactive decisions helped Dr. Sreedher to launch the channels very fast. "Once during a crisis between a station manager of Gyan Vani and an institution in Allahabad, he sent a letter to IGNOU and the institution stating that nothing should happen without the knowledge of Dr. Sreedher. In another incident when the UGC asked for a separate satellite and a huge budget to launch their Vyas channels, he told them after consulting the HRD Minister, and insisted that the orders of the Ministry be followed. He asked the UGC to follow the plan given by me, even though I was working in a UGC centre in Anna University, at that time," says Dr. Sreedher.

Professor Y.S. Rajan (scientist, who co-authored *Vision 2020* with A.P.J. Abdul Kalam)—Having met for the first time in 1988, they met many times later at different advisory board or committee meetings. Prof. Rajan used to visit the campus community radio Anna FM, to read his pieces of poetry. They are both now on the board of APJ Stya University in Sohna.

Dr. Rajender Mishra, Retired Head of the Research, Consortium of Educational Communication. Dr. Sreedher's association with him goes back to the 1990s when he wanted the UGC to undertake a study of the mega serial 'Human Evolution'. While in most of the cases Dr. Mishra and Dr. Sreedher did not agree with each other, their relationship grew and he is now part of Dr. Sreedher's team in community radio related studies. Mishra later became a family friend, philosopher and guide.

P.S. Rangachar—He guided Dr. Sreedher for his first documentary on Technical Teachers Training Institute in 1974 and later he was his boss at the Central Educational Planning Unit at Directorate General, All India Radio, Delhi. The unit was very lively under his leadership and they were able to simultaneously produce original programmes in 18 different languages to be broadcast by AIR stations across the country. He gave shape and shared his wisdom to many of Dr. Sreedher's projects such as Vigyan Vidhi, Radio DATE, Human Evolution, Project on Radio Education for Adult Literacy (PREAL), Children's Enrichment Education through

Radio (CHEER), computerization of AIR Archives (which is still incomplete). "It was sad that he died just three weeks before his retirement in an accident in New Delhi. One of his daughters is a senior IAS officer from the Tamil Nadu cadre, Mrs. Rangachar Jaya. I had an opportunity to work with the I&B Ministry when Mrs. Jaya was looking after broadcasting," says Dr. Sreedher.

Ratikant Basu—"For believing in me and giving me immense powers and responsibilities at the Doordarshan Headquarters and letting me operate independently without undue interference." He later went on to join STAR TV as its CEO. He ventured into TARA channels and was considering being appointed as the CEO of the Tamil channel. "He was negotiating with JJ TV and told me that the deal could not go through because of suspected money laundering," he adds.

Satish Nagaraji—For being a part of his life, almost like a family member, from the day he was identified in 2003 till date. He has helped Dr. Sreedher in many ways.

P.S. Sundaram, of Technomedia and founder chairman BECIL—Known as the best broadcast engineer in India, he was much interested and immensely supported in launching the Anna FM community radio.

Ms. K.S. Sarma, who once had misgivings about Dr. Sreedher, later became an ardent supporter and facilitator of his initiatives. For over a decade, Dr. Sreedher received his guidance, and made use of his experience and expertise. Dr. Sreedher will never forget the experience of launching Gyan Darshan along with him as he was at the root of the initiative. Dr. Sreedher also has fond memories of Mr. Sarma's term as CEO Prasar Bharati. Mr. Sarma was sincerely hopeful for Dr. Sreedher to be posted as DG, AIR.

N.K. Sinha who retired as Secretary, Ministry of Information and Broadcasting, is regarded as the father of the now acclaimed 'National Mission on Education Through ICT'. While he was the Joint Secretary and Additional Secretary at the Ministry of Human Resource Development, he encouraged Dr. Sreedher to produce the world's first low cost laptop model. "He used to come to Nehru Place market to search for electronic parts along with Mr. Krishnamurthy, the consultant. Even though he was a Joint Secretary he used to come and sit in the Director CEMCA's room to watch demos of the prototypes. An IIT engineer, he excelled in his work and commitment," adds Dr. Sreedher.

Supriya Sahu—She had immense faith in Dr. Sreedher and his abilities. "She called me when I was in a taxi in London and asked me to devise, plan and execute the first CR sammelan in 22 days flat. It was held in Vigyan Bhavan, and CEMCA awards were also instituted and awarded on that occasion apart from an exhibition on CR stations, cultural programmes and release of a compendium of CR stations," recalls Dr. Sreedher. She went out of the way to give space to CEMCA at Shastri Bhawan ("till date no organization could dream of it!") to start a Community Radio Facilitation centre. When Dr. Sreedher was planning with an international agency to start a Community Radio Sustenance fund, Ms. Supriya made a proposal to the Planning Commission and got Rs. 100 crores sanctioned for the CR sector in the Twelfth Five Year Plan, at a time when Dr. Sreedher was thinking of doing it through the private sector.

Administrative heads of CEMCA, the late Mr. Nandagopal, Mr. Dalip Kumar Tetri and Mr. R. Thyagarajan. "They were like the speed breakers—going over them might be irritating, but there is the bigger purpose of avoiding major accidents. They made me understand the importance of alternate routes. Two of them had worked in CAG. Mr. Thyagarajan was thorough in HR rules of the GOI, and had them on his fingertips," he recalls.

Mr. Vikram Chandra, former Finance Officer at IGNOU who worked earlier with the CAG. "He was the one who showed me how to take decisions involving crores of rupees. And if you are clean, he also guided you to stay out of issues by taking the utmost precautions including a voluntary audit by competent authorities," says Dr. Sreedher.

The late Mr. Vipin Sharma—"From the day, i.e. October

20, 2001, when he was first introduced to me till his sudden death in 2018, he acted as a true and most trusted right hand in matters relating to Gyan Vani and community radio."

Shri Venugopal Reddy, who was his first boss and whose encouragement and blessings made life easier at the workplace. Mr. Reddy continued his association with Dr. Sreedher, even as he joined Anna University.

Zora Chatterjee who retired as Secretary to the Government of India—"She was a strict but development-oriented IAS officer in whose period I was able to serve as a member of the Screening Committee for Community Radio Stations. Though she appeared to be strict outside, she was a wonderful human being at heart," says Dr. Sreedher.

He always remembers the help rendered by his Personal/ Professional colleagues Ms. Anuradha Ravi (AIR DD), Dr. Karunanidhi (AIR DD), Ms Neeta Sethi, IGNOU, Mr. Pandian AIR DD Prasar Bharati Delhi, for their cooperation, understanding, hard work, and their presence of mind. He makes a special mention about Ms. Monica Sharma at the Commonwealth Educational Media Centre for Asia and her abilities to manage the unthinkables with dedication and a smile.

Gurumurthy, Lakshmi, Govindaraj, Hema, Indumathy, Sangeetha, Athiyaman, Karunanidhi—"The team that managed my radio programmes when I was on my first trip to the US. They did a commendable job."

Neeta Sethi—former PA at IGNOU.

Amit Chakraborty—former Director AIR, DD and Science Officer AIR Kolkata.

Ravikant—Joint Director, Electronic Media Production Centre, IGNOU.

Suresh Mathur—former Secretary, Ministry of Information and Broadcasting and DG AIR

A.R. Shinde—former Director General, AIR and Chairman, Development Communicators Forum.

Shirley Deepak—Independent consultant and formerly from Holy Cross College, who has turned out to be a confidant in matters relating to baseline surveys for community radio.

Professor G.D. Sharma—former Director of Consortium of Educational Communication, and Secretary, University Grants Commission.

Professor Yashpal—Emeritus Scientist, former Chairman UGC.

Vasant Gowarikar—former Scientific Advisor to Prime Minister and Space Scientist.

Dr. Bal Phondke—former Editor *Science Today* and Director, NISCOM.

Biman Basu—Editor of this book and former Editor, *Science Reporter*.

Kunnakudi Vaidyanathan—Acclaimed violinist and music composer.

T.R. Pappa—Tamil Music Director.

M. Dhanasekaran—Pondicherry MLA and Educationist Professor Venkatachalapathy.

From AIR and DD

M.S. Perumal—who had at Sreedher's insistence headed many CR stations in Tamil Nadu and brought laurels to them.

Mr. Chandramurthy—who competed with Sreedher for Science Reporters' job and later succeeded Sreedher to head the Science Unit at AIR Madras.

Suki Subramaniam, M.P. Somasundaram, Akhilandeswari Ganesan, Nallathambi, Anant Padmanabhan, Latha Raju, Balaramani, Srinivasaragavan.

Madurai Savithra Rajaram

Meiyappan from Dinathanthi,

Frontline senior editor T.S. Subramanian, Pasumai Radio Paul Bhaskar,

Pard Radio—James Rajasekhar.

Professor Shanta, Saleema.

Professor Nagarathnam of Madurai Kamaraj University.

Prof. K.R. Venkatesan, Principal Sri Sankara College of Arts and Sciences, Kanchipuram.

Students of Electronic Media, Anna University who have

worked with him— Jayanth, Alifya, Lavanya, Lakshala, Priya Vanchi, Jayanath Murlidharan, Rakshita, Joseph Arulraj, Mahesh, Vinay Shekhar, Veena, Mohana Priya, Vinod Rajesh, Divyasri, Meera, Angayarkanni, Chitra, Harini Ramji, Vishnu Praveen, Amarnath, Vinod, Sendil, Manivannan, Mirzha, Purushottaman, Vijay, Lakshala, Laya Kuttan, Arun, Premkumar, and Gautham Kumar among many others.

Sai Sudha—The first voice to be heard on the first community radio in India; later worked with BBC India.

Sri Lakshmi—Who was people's RJ and later worked in BBC India.

Kaushalya—The author of this book—brought up in Delhi—won best RJ in Tamil Nadu award and worked in Hello FM.

Archana Madhubala—Had a potential to be a broadcaster but temporarily shifted her attention to IT.

Alifiya—Sai Sudha's school mate and a bold person.

Priya Vanchi—Who did UNESCO projects and now is in the USA.

Hema Priyadarshini—A bold student who later worked with me at CEMCA and stayed in conflict zones of India—presently pursuing a course in Hollywood.

Saleem—The well known face from Thanthi TV who also worked with BBC India; "looks humble but has the potential to be a leading media personality in the country", says Dr. Sreedher.

Christie—Her interview with gypsies is rated one of the most interesting ones.

Narmadha—The women's activist and a development communication writer.

Ponnusamy—The young film director who had close associations with Gnani.

Lakshala—A Sri Lankan Girl who worked very hard while studying at Anna University.

Ms. Radha Bai who assisted him in the Science unit of AIR in the 1980s and later worked as an independent RJ in Anna CR. Mr. Basumani who used to cycle 15 kilometres every morning to Anna CR to begin the morning transmission as a citizen RJ.

Ms. Shanthi Thiruvazhi, Ms. Neeraja Prabhakar, Ms. Venkatalakshmi, Ms. Uma and Ms. Revathi who Dr. Sreedher guided and co-guided in their PhDs.

Dr. Shanta Arunachalam—A Professor in Science Journalism from the Madurai Kamaraj University who with her Media Research Forum supports Dr. Sreedher's projects.

His PhD students from Apeejay Stya University, Ms. Pooja Sikka, Ms. Ujjwala Tirkey, Mr. Brinder Kumar Tyagi and Ms. Priyadarshini Kiran deserve all credits for working with him and earning their doctorate.

Faculties at Anna University—Mr Arul Aram, Mr. C. Velayutham, Ms. Bandita Panda, Ms. Uma, Ms. Sunita Fernando, Ms. Revathi, Ms. Lavanya, Ms. Sunita Kuppuswamy, Mr. Arulselvan, Mr. Subramani.

Entrepreneur Palani G. Periasamy, Educationist G. Viswanathan, Balasubramanian Adithan of the Dinathanthi family, VC of the SRM group of institutions Mr. Sathyanarayana, Head of Kovai Rathinam Group, Mr. Senthil, Kanthi from Lucknow CMS group.

About the Author

Kaushalya Rathnam, is a freelance media professional currently based in Bengaluru. She has worked in the Radio industry for over 9 years, hosting prime time shows on a Private FM Radio Network in Chennai and has won the Best RJ Award from a leading Tamil Weekly in Tamil Nadu. Ms. Rathnam has interviewed a range of eminent personalities like astronaut Sunita Williams, grandmaster Vishwanathan Anand and actor Kamal Hasan. She has worked in the capacity of Assistant Manager Brand Integration, working on campaign ideas to promote top brands on Radio through content, sales and marketing initiatives. She has also been actively involved in various CSR initiatives and is a former student of Dr. Sreedher, from Anna University where she pursued postgraduation in Electronic Media and hosted shows for the first Community Radio in the country, Anna FM.

A retired scientist of the Council of Scientific and Industrial Research (CSIR), Biman Basu is winner of the 1994 *'NCSTC National Award for Science Popularisation'*. He is a recipient of *'Kishore Gyan Vigyan Award'* for Popular Science Writing in Bengali, 1992, and was awarded the *'AWIC Honour 2007'* by the Association of Writers and Illustrators for Children for his contribution to children's literature.

Photo Gallery

Grand Father Prof. Gopala Iyer

Grand Mother Ms. Nagalakshmi

Dr. Sreedher's Parents

With Wife Meenakshi Sreedher

Uncle Jayaraman and Aunt Savithri

Uncle Krishnamoorthy

With Brothers and Sister

Dr. Sreedher's Marriage Reception with his Guide, 1976

Daughters' Family Photo

Faculty Member at Madras Christian College 1975

Interview About FM Radio, 1976

First Science Sammelan, Chennai, 1980

Sky Watching Programme, 1981

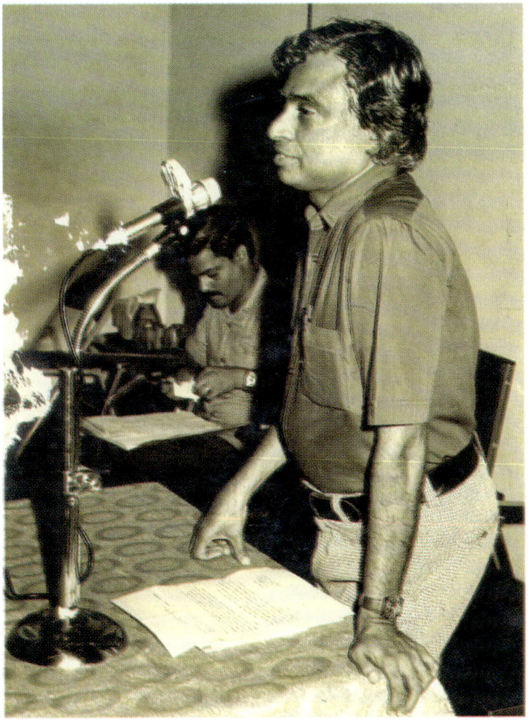

With Dr. A.P.J. Abdul Kalam at AIR Chennai, 1982

ASIAD 1982

With Pratap Reddy at Madras Science Association, 1983

Dr. Sreedher With Nobel Laureate Chandrasekhar, 1985

Receiving National Award for Science Popularization, 1992

At Workshop in Islamabad, Pakistan, 1998

With M.K. Kaw Inaugurating the IGNOU Earth Station, 1999

Gyan Darshan Inauguration, 2000

With Prof. M.S. Swaminathan and John Daniel, 2010

With Dr. Amartya Sen, Dileep Padgaonkar and Abhijit Dasgupta, 2011

At the Community Radio Sammelan, 2012

With Dr. A.P.J. Abdul Kalam, 2014

At PAN Commonwealth Forum, Malaysia, 2016

At Radio Kotagiri, Tamil Nadu, 2017

At Radio Namaskar, Konark, Orissa, 2017